Relating Art
and
Humanities
to the Classroom

TRENDS IN ART EDUCATION

Consulting Editor: **Earl Linderman**
Arizona State University

ART FOR EXCEPTIONAL CHILDREN—DONALD UHLIN,
California State University, Sacramento

ALTERNATIVES FOR ART EDUCATION RESEARCH—KENNETH R. BEITTEL,
The Pennsylvania State University

**CHILDREN'S ART JUDGMENT: A CURRICULUM FOR ELEMENTARY ART
APPRECIATION**—GORDON S. PLUMMER, Associate Dean, Arts and Humanities,
State University College at Buffalo

**ART IN THE ELEMENTARY SCHOOL: DRAWING, PAINTING, AND
CREATING FOR THE CLASSROOM**—MARLENE LINDERMAN,
Arizona State University, Extension Division

EARLY CHILDHOOD ART—BARBARA HERBERHOLZ,
California State University, Sacramento
Extension Division

RELATING ART AND HUMANITIES TO THE CLASSROOM—ROBERT J. SAUNDERS,
Art Consultant
State of Connecticut

**ART AND ETHNICS: BACKGROUND FOR TEACHING YOUTH
IN A PLURALISTIC SOCIETY**—J. EUGENE GRIGSBY,
Arizona State University

Relating Art and Humanities to the Classroom

Robert J. Saunders

Art Consultant
State of Connecticut

wcb

Wm. C. Brown Company Publishers
Dubuque, Iowa

2/17/77 Rel. 5.95

2/17/77 Rel. 5.95

This book was written for elementary classroom teachers. They may be experienced teachers looking for ways to introduce the humanities into their school programs, or confronted with experimental schools and government-funded projects using the arts. They may be future classroom teachers taking teacher preparation courses in art and interdisciplinary education. It was written for those teachers who are responsible for their own arts and humanities programs, or for designing new curriculums.

It will, moreover, have meaning for art specialists in the schools. Special teachers of art, and also art education majors taking elementary art courses, will find this book useful in relating art to the humanities, other subject areas, and arts curriculum design. It will help both art and classroom teachers who are confronted with changes in their school districts, and in education utilizing concepts of the related, unified, or comprehensive arts, or undergoing curriculum revision using behavioral or student performance objectives.

Relating Art and Humanities to the Classroom is planned to provide a philosophical basis and point of view by which arts activities can be related to human needs and values as they are reflected in humanities programs and other subject areas. It suggests techniques for arts and humanities curriculums, identifying goals and objectives, and structuring open-ended lessons. The real problems confronting classroom teachers teaching the arts and humanities occur not so much in finding news ideas for art lessons as in making them relevant to the total school program and therefore ultimately realizing the richer learning potential of children.

The book was planned in a sequence of several parts:

Chapters 1-3 provide background information necessary for identifying the arts and humanities, the nature of goals and objectives, historical orientations, and rationale for justifying the arts in the curriculum. After each chapter, reinforcing activities are provided to help readers clarify their own attitudes about the arts, and relate the chapter's content to themselves.

Chapters 4-6 deal with the interaction between social values, moral education, human needs, and their humanistic application from sociological and psychological sources. Chapter 6 introduces a thematic structure called *Core Monuments* through the use of which social needs and human values can be adapted to the literary, cinematic, and televised narrative themes which interest children.

Chapters 7-9 explain the cognitive, psychomotor, and affective domains of learning in terms of the arts, and illustrate the interaction between them which is necessary for developing creative self-expression.

Chapter 10 briefly outlines stages of development according to Lowenfeld, Erikson, and Piagèt. An autobiographical statement of my own elementary school days is used as an example relating to these stages and the affective domain. The readers are asked to reconsider their own childhoods in helping to formulate their own art abilities and attitudes about the arts.

Chapter 11 integrates the cognitive, affective, and psychomotor domains with areas of aesthetic response, and the six sensory modes (visual, aural, olfactory, gustatory, tactile, and kinesthetic) for a total learning system in Aesthetic Education. It proposes a structure for evaluating aesthetic growth through sensory perception.

Chapter 12 is the only how-to-do-it chapter in the book. It demonstrates how to write behavioral objectives in the arts for each of the cognitive, psychomotor, and affective domains.

Chapters 13-15 provide diverse structures for evaluating child art on an individualized continuous progress basis, define the *creative mental processes* as a basis for art planning, describe a procedure for planning individual and group activities on field trips, deal with teacher readiness for the open-classroom, and provide suggestions for the interaction of art with theater, music, poetry, and environmental education.

Some of the most useful and enjoyable experiences and ideas come from working with children. For this reason, I have drawn from my own teaching experiences because I know and understand them best. Some of my mistakes are also mentioned because they were also learning experiences. The experiences which I draw upon from the past are the ones which I feel offer the greatest potential for teaching for the future—for that ambiguous time beyond the millenium when today's children will determine the future of their children.

Some years ago, I had an unusual dream in which a face turned toward me, an eye was replaced by a pistol which shot point-blank, and a voice said, "Trigger your ideas." It was such a blast that I woke up, got up, and painted it in black india ink on a sheet of white watercolor paper hanging on an easel in my studio. Then I went back to bed. The next day I took the picture to school and hung it in my art room. It has been with me as an inspiration ever since. May this book help you to trigger your own ideas—and so to be more creative teachers through the arts and humanities.

"Trigger Your Ideas"

I am grateful indeed to those teachers under whom I have studied; and have a feeling of indebtedness to those with whom I have worked, for letting me experiment and teach art to their students in my own way. Some are mentioned in the text, others, unnamed, are not forgotten. Nor are the children, who provided the greatest encouragement of all. I recall fondly the support and encouragement of Dr. George I. Thomas and Dr. Thomas Shaheen, my first superintendents, and Douglas Morey, my first elementary school principal, and of course that of Mrs. Lottabell McCord, Director, Junior High School, North Arlington, N. J., who, for several years in succession, advised me not to back away from my first really difficult teaching experiences.

For special help in preparing this book, I am thankful to the following:

My colleagues at the Bureau of Elementary and Secondary Education, Connecticut State Department of Education, who helped me clarify my ideas on the Aesthetic Structure and behavioral objectives, and suggested areas of interaction with their subject matter.

Virgil Thomson, for telling me about the sixth grade production of "Four Saints in Three Acts" and contacting Barth E. M. Suretsky, Jr., who filled in the details.

Bernard B. Shapiro, of Bernard B. Shapiro Associates, then General Manager, Shorewoods Reproductions, Inc., for permission to use the photo reproduction of Edward Lamson Henry's, *Wedding of the Thirties.*

Hank Londoner, photographer, for photographs of the Aesthetic Structure used in chapter 11.

J. Richard McGinnis, photographer, Public Relations, Southern Connecticut State College, New Haven, for photographs of Paul Klee's *Landscape With Yellow Birds,* and the *Cuckoo, Where are you?* drawings (chapter 15), the drawing-to-music examples and the students in a session of Dr. Phyllis Gelineau's summer course (1974), on "Integrating the Arts in the Curriculum."

Edward T. Hall for reading the section adapting his concepts to the public schools, and granting his permission to use them in chapter 15.

Dr. Earl W. Linderman and the staff at Wm. C. Brown Company for their patience with the manuscripts.

My wife, Jean, for her criticism, ideas, encouragement, and typing of the first manuscript.

And to Pamela Engel, who typed the second.

To JEAN
        who typedandtypedandtyped . . .
and RHOM
        who went outdoors to play . . .
                (sometimes)

Identifying goals and objectives in the humanities

Art as currently taught in the public schools is undergoing drastic change. This change reflects the interrelationship that exists between art and other subject areas which often include a humanistic orientation, art teaching strategies and curriculum structure, and accountability as determined through evaluative techniques. As with all forms of cultural change over such an extensive geographically and ethnologically diverse country as the United States, this change is irregular. Some schools, school districts, and art and classroom teacher preparation programs are involved in these changes, while others are not. This book is written to assist elementary classroom and art teachers, both present-day and future, meet the challenge of such change as it affects the **arts and humanities.**

The most dramatic change and that posing the most problems, results from the interdisciplinary potential of the arts. This has various labels: the related arts, unified arts, aesthetic education, synesthetic education, environmental education, and the humanities. The rationale applied to such change may be philosophical or political, but the actual reason is usually based on a matter of economics.

Shifts to the unified arts, related arts, and humanities in the public schools often result from boards of education attempts to lower expenses by cutting the administrative staff and making one director responsible for art, music, industrial arts, and home economics. However, teachers in these subject areas, prepared to think of themselves as unique wheels, frequently do not know how to mesh as cogs with other unique wheels in the newly reassembled educational machinery. More than likely, such teachers have been conditioned by experience and by teacher preparation courses to become isolated within their own fields, and to actually regard any similarities between their own field and those of others as possible threats. They see each teacher of an interrelated subject as the usurper of their own goals and objectives, when really all should be joining hands to strengthen their mutual purposes.

Educational Humanities

This book focuses on relating art and other subject areas to the humanities. It stresses as a basic idea that the approach rather than the subject matter itself decides whether or not that matter is a part of the humanities. This introductory chapter will identify the similarities and differences between the humanistic and nonhumanistic aspects of the same subject area. Implicit in the humanistic aspects of a subject area are their concerns for the human condition, or human enterprise. If they are not the traditional humanities they are the *classroom humanities*—those subjects in the total school curriculum which can deal with some aspect of the human condition and cultural (man-made) belief and value systems.

By using the term "classroom humanities," we distinguish between the approaches to teaching the humanities in the elementary and secondary schools, and those used in the colleges and universities, or by professional scholars. A frequent difficulty in teaching the humanities at the precollege levels results from teachers employing those same methods and techniques by which they themselves were taught humanities at the college level. This becomes most evident in the teaching of art history, where the college-oriented lecture-slide technique, following a chronological sequence from pre-European history to the Impressionists so often penetrates into high school art history courses or study units, or is tried in the elementary schools.

On occasion, when discussing the teaching of art history at the elementary level with college art history teachers, the author finds that they summarily reject the idea, based on the theory that art history should not be taught below the college level. The reasons given often identify student boredom with art history when actually it is the teacher's methods which the students find boring. As shall be demonstrated later, the topical or thematic approach and related art-making activities can make art history more student-interest oriented. Art history has a legitimate place in the social studies, as do art humanities in elementary education. Since the arts of a people, along with music, theater, dance, and literature, are essential part of the cultural history of a nation, the arts should be considered part of the social studies curriculum instead of the arts curriculum.

Both art and classroom teachers need to help children relate what happens to the aesthetic and humanistic purposes of art in the art lesson. Teachers and students in the elementary schools should take time to talk about the arts, their purposes in human existence, and their changing roles amid social, cultural and technological progress in the workaday world, and about art criticism. To neglect this aspect of the arts is to neglect a significant aspect of their contribution to the schools. It goes beyond just the making and doing. It means delving into that aspect of the arts which establishes our attitudes and adult needs for them.

Stated more broadly, similar distinctions can be made between the technical skills and the more humanistic aspects of most school curriculum subject areas, such as mathematics, sciences, social studies, home economics, physical education, and the industrial and language arts. These also have their humanistic aspects, as demonstrated when they are dealt with in terms of their histories, the reasons for their importance to human beings, their changing roles in society, and the principles each discipline uses for evaluating its own quality of performance.

We might ask, "How does this differ from what we have always been teaching?" The differences are in matters of degree, of depth, of priorities, and of the teacher's focus during the act of teaching. Humanism concerns the similarities among peoples, cultures, and periods of time, as well as the differences existing between them. It teaches not only an understanding of other cultures, but empathy and affection as well. Understanding is an intellectual process; empathy and affection are feeling processes. Understanding can grow from cognitive information about superficial cultural differences. Empathy and affection grow from identifying with feelings, attitudes, and opinions of others or groups of others, but first they must result from understanding and accepting ourselves. Knowing *what* other people do does not lead to understanding them nearly as much as knowing *why* they do what they do. The humanities deal with the *why* of human doings rather than just the *what*.

The sense of identity with others results from identifying and empathizing with them; and here we are dealing with the ego-orientation of individuals. Textbooks and nonfiction provide the cognitive data and interpretations about other cultures and periods of time. Novels, plays, music, and the visual arts convey the emotive human element behind the facts found in textbooks. Thus the humanities extend the general objectives of most school subject areas beyond the limitations of the textbook.

Justifying the Humanities in the Classroom

For justification of the humanities in the schools, the goals and objectives set for them must be unique. They must be different than those traditionally enumerated for art, music, physical education, social studies, mathematics, science, and the language arts. When they seem to repeat such aspects as moral development, maintaining the cultural heritage, or understanding others, and the like, then it should be made clear that these are the humanistic goals and objectives common to all such subject areas. Although unique to the humanities, they are applicable to various additional subject areas as well.

When a particular subject area lists specific goals and objectives, then classroom activities should be identifiable as being specifically related to them. This is what accountability is all about. When an art curriculum guide (whether local, state, or borrowed) adopted by the school or school district identifies definite goals and objectives, then it is up to the art and classroom teachers to see to it that the specifications are fulfilled in respect to the types of art activities in which the children become engaged. Goals and objectives in the arts should also be identifiable as related to, or leading to, the fulfillment of specific district-wide goals and objectives adopted by the local boards of education. This includes such commonly listed, but frequently unfulfilled, objectives as the teaching of man's cultural heritage through art history, art in everyday living, and art appreciation (which intrinsically means aesthetic analysis, elements and principles of design, and art criticism).

"In my own art cart-pushing days," the author tells us, "I learned that children liked and responded well to art periods in which we just sat on the floor and looked at and talked about works of art. It took some reconditioning for them to learn that not every art lesson would be spent making something. Usually at the end of the first such lesson, after I took in a painting, art reproduction, sculpture or reduction, art postal cards, or examples of art and architecture for a period of history they may be studying, or looked with them at the art in their history textbooks or classroom encyclopedias, at least one student would ask, 'When are we going to have art?' Then, the class was told, 'Sometimes we will just look at art and talk about it. This, too, is an important art lesson.' Then, if I remembered, I would ask, 'Did you enjoy what we did today?' They usually said, 'Yes,' and I would say, 'Then we will do it again.' Sometimes, if I did not plan to use the pictures for another class, I would leave them behind for the children to look at when they wanted to, and to become more familiar with them.

"As an art consultant, I have on various occasions suggested to elementary art teachers that they schedule time for the students to look at art and talk about it. More than once, from otherwise excellent and creative art teachers who believe in self-expression, the response has been, 'But what do I sacrifice from the *real* art program? How can I take time from the important part to talk about it?' On such occasions I would wonder 'How can you sacrifice the child's knowledge about art for what you call an "art program"?'"

Art appreciation does not result from limiting art activities to art-making exclusively. Nor does it result from only having art reproductions framed and hanging in the corridors or mounted on bulletin boards as if it will just rub off on the children walking by. Children may learn to recognize some famous paintings and their painters, but never really understand why they are considered important. Kenneth Marantz (1965) refers to this bit of aesthetic wishful thinking on the part of art teachers as "indecent exposure." He insists that art appreciation, knowledge about the fine arts (not just school art), does not rub off; it must be taught.

Reading teachers do not expect children to learn to read just by having books in the classroom. Nor do children learn manuscript and cursive writing just because Zaner-Blosser charts are stapled above the front blackboard. Teachers teach children to letter (but call it "printing") and to write by having them imitate the examples and directions in the charts. They teach children to read by helping them transform verbal symbols into spoken sounds and abstracted meanings. Art and classroom teachers must also teach children to interpret the visual symbols and statements in paintings and in their cultural environment if they are to have adequate visual vocabularies to meet the needs of the future.

Legislating the Humanities

Many elementary art programs across the country do include some art history, art criticism, and biographical information about artists, architects, or related professions. There are many innovative, experimental, and visiting artists programs funded during the late 1960s by the Arts and Humanities Act, the Elementary and Secondary Education Act (ESEA), the National Defense Education Act (NDEA), the Arts in General Education program of the John D. Rockefeller III Fund, and Studio Art and Art History and the Humanities in the Advanced Study programs of the College Entrance Boards. From 1970 to 1972, the Interdisciplinary Model Programs in the Arts for Children and Teachers (*Arts Impact* 1973), funded by the U.S. Office of Education, as part of the Teacher Retraining Authorization of the Education Professions Development Act, placed the arts (visual, music, dance, theater, etc.) as the center of the curriculum, and essential to the retraining of elementary classroom teachers. It was, in general, a visiting artist and artist-in-residence program which proved its objectives in Columbus, Ohio; Eugene, Oregon; Glendale, California; Philadelphia; and Troy, Alabama; in inner-city, suburban, and rural schools (*Arts Impact,* 1973).

When the congressmen and leaders in the field designed the National Foundation on the Arts and Humanities Act (1965) they decided to recognize each area as a separate entity. In so doing they separated art from the humanities in a terminological sense, but included them both in the funding. (For a historical background on the differences between the arts and the humanities, see chapter 2.) The designers of the act apparently feared that the law would be interpreted to mean only the academic and verbal approaches to the humanities, to the neglect of the making and performing aspects of producing and reproducing the arts.

The National Foundation on the Arts and Humanities Act (1965) officially defines the arts as, but does not limit them to,

music (instrumental and vocal), dance, drama, folk art, creative writing, architecture and allied fields, painting, sculpture, photography, graphic and crafts arts, industrial design, costume and fashion design, motion pictures, television, radio, tape and sound recording, the arts related to the presentation, performance, execution, and exhibition of such major art forms, and the study and application of the arts to the human environment (Arts and Humanities Act 1965, p. 2).

The legislators designing the Arts and Humanities Act defined the humanities as including, but not being restricted to the study of

language, both modern and classical; linguistics; literature; history; jurisprudence; philosophy; archeology; the history, criticism, theory, and practice of the arts; those aspects of the social sciences which have humanistic content and employ humanistic methods; and the study and application of the human environment with particular attention to the relevance of the humanities to the current condition of national life (Arts and Humanities Act 1965, p. 2).

Just what "humanistic methods" are may still be in need of interpretation. The methods may include scholarship, library research, experimental inquiry, use of the imagination, making and performing arts activities, or humanistic encounter groups.

Although such areas of study cannot be included as specific courses at the elementary level, they do lend themselves to the interdisciplinary-related arts, or comprehensive arts aspects of the total school curriculum. A sizable proportion of areas may be reserved for the secondary and college levels, but the foundations begin in the elementary schools by developing within the growing children predilections toward the humanistic and aesthetic aspects of their work.

Official Goals

With the Arts and Humanities Act, and its subsequent funding, the U.S.O.E. established an arts and humanities division and prepared a set of Instructional Objectives, quoted by Harold Taylor (1968). Although called objectives, they are quite long-range and global in scope. For this reason they read more like goals than "instructional objectives" as they will be treated in chapter 12. They do provide, however, an *official* basis for further curriculum development.

1. To introduce all students (including the vocationally minded who will not go beyond high school) to the study of man—his nature, the full development of his faculties, the realization of his aspirations, and the securing of his well being.

2. To help the student come to know himself, to understand what has shaped his beliefs, attitudes, and fortunes, and to develop a critical sense which will allow him as an individual to select and preserve the best in human societies.

3. To develop in the student an attitude toward life which centers on the inherent dignity of each individual human being.

4. To help the student reconcile individual freedom with social control.

5. To cultivate his understanding of the unresolved conflicts and struggles that have persisted throughout human history.

6. To develop his understanding of how social relations between segments of society condition the form and the content of literature and the arts.

7. To develop in the student an understanding of how language shapes ideas within a culture and is at the same time an expression of that culture.

8. To give the student the experience of personal involvement with ideas that have moved and shaped human societies. (Taylor 1968, pp. 30-31 [numeral sequence by the author].)

By funding the arts and humanities in education the federal government is actually saying that the average American home is not artistically and humanistically oriented enough to be able to supply the above-stated objectives to the children who will comprise the next adult population. Until now, conservative or arch-conservative parents have identified these areas as "frills," and have left the responsibility for supplying them up to those parents who wanted them, through special instruction, for their own children. Similar questions of public school or parental responsibility are raised about the teaching of morality, ethics, sex, and drug education. Our current generation of adults is not capable of either supplementing their children's education in the arts and humanities or supporting school budgets that could. This inability reflects the continuation of the cultural and social values of previous generations—status quo.

By taking a leadership role to improve the state of the arts and humanities in culture, the federal government indicated officially that our previous attitudes and responses have not been enough. The ugliness of our cities, the antihuman technologies of our computerized efficiency, the poverty of quality in existence, the common disregard for human needs—all a direct legacy derived from the absence of a humanistic and aesthetic emphasis in our culture and educational systems.

The Humanities and Humanistic Education

In this introductory chapter the author has to this point used the words "humanities" and "humanistic" somewhat interchangeably. However, "humanistic" is not to be used here in the same context as in the term "humanistic education." Both deal with developing personal values, but "humanistic education" does not, as a rule, use the arts as the source of exploring personal values and human needs. The major thrust of the humanities is in the study of the human condition or enterprise; that is, the process of being human. This involves dealing with aesthetic, moral, and ethical values as revealed through the various subject matters and art forms of the humanities.

Those classroom activities using human behavior and ourselves as sources for value inquiry, rather than employing art and literature, are often referred to as humanistic Education, or Humanistic Awareness. They are oriented to the here and now and ourselves, rather than the long history of conflicting human values and human needs as revealed in the arts and humanities.

Their approaches are exemplified by Raths, Harmin, and Simon in *Values and Teaching* (1966), and Kirshenbaum, Howe, and Simon in *Values Clarification* (1972), and Weinstein and Fantini in *Toward Humanistic Education: A Curriculum of Affect* (1970). They all use classroom discussion and role-playing techniques. Although not dealing specifically with classroom methods and curriculum theory, the works on transactional analysis by Eric M. Berne (1961) and Thomas A. Harris (1969) have been used by teachers exploring humanistic awareness techniques with their students. Approaches used at the Esalen Institute and popularized through Roberto Assagioli's works (1965, 1973), and to Gestalt therapy described by Fritz Perls (1973) have also been used by teachers.

Some of their suggestions for making value judgments will be used in the related reinforcing activities at the end of each chapter, but this book will emphasize human values and human needs as explored through the arts and humanities.

Structuralism and the Humanities

I have previously suggested that one of the unique aspects of the humanities is the study of similarities, rather than differences, among peoples, cultures, and periods of time. This is somewhat related to the concepts of *structuralism*, wherein the similarities of cultures are studied for what they reveal about growth and development in the wider range of mankind. In chapter 4 we will deal briefly with the studies of Lawrence Kohlberg, who is extending Jean Piaget's concepts of *Structuralism* (1971) by defining specific stages of moral development.

There is also some early evidence of structuralism in the universality of children's stages of development as identified in the Child Study movements of the 1890s in England, Germany, and the United States. They were continued through the work of Viktor Lowenfeld (1947) and Rhoda Kellogg (1969), but this does not imply that either of them were or are structuralists. However, the stages of development in child art are applicable to the concepts of structuralism.

In chapter 6, on Core Monuments concluding Part I of this book, I shall relate various myths, legends, folklore, and fairy tales to basic human needs and values. They are far removed from the deeply wrought studies of Claude Lévi-Strauss in his theories of *Structural Anthropology* (1967), and discussed by Howard Gardner in *The Quest for Mind* (1973). They may provide a basis for relating the studies of the humanities to the concepts of structuralism. Lévi-Strauss's use of myths in primitive societies in his *Introduction to a Science of Mythology* series (1969, 1973), suggests a close linkage between this aspect of the humanities and anthropology.

It seems almost impossible to fail to disclose some linkage between any subject area and the arts or humanities. The remainder of the first part of this book will attempt to make the above claim more realizable.

Reinforcing Activities

1. Review the instructional objectives in the humanities of the U.S.O.E. listed above and write an example of each relating it to an elementary school program.

2. Share and discuss your example with others in your class.
3. Review any art or elementary curriculum guides available to you and determine:
   a) which goals or objectives already fit those defined as humanistic by the U.S.O.E.;
   b) which goals and objectives are not really humanistic in concept; and
   c) with rewording can they be adapted to the U.S.O.E. goals for the arts and humanities?
4. If you are a student teacher, or one already in the field, locate the goals and/or objectives of your local board of education, and:
   a) select those goals which apply to the arts and humanities,
   b) write an example for each one selected, applying it to the humanities as a justification to the board for your program, and
   c) discuss in class.

References

ARTS IMPACT EVALUATION TEAM. *Arts Impact: Curriculum for Change.* Presented by the U.S. Office of Education, University Park, Pa.: Pennsylvania State University, March 1973.

ASSAGIOLI, ROBERTO, M.D. *The Art of Will.* New York: Viking Press, 1973.

———. *Psychosynthesis.* New York: Viking Press, 1965.

BERNE, ERIC, M.D. *Transactional Analysis in Psycho-Therapy.* New York: Grove Press, 1961.

89TH CONGRESS OF THE UNITED STATES. *National Foundation on the Arts and Humanities Act of 1965.* Washington, D. C.: U.S. Government Printing Office, 1971.

EISNER, ELLIOT W. "American Education and the Future of Art Education." In *Art Education,* edited by W. Reid Hastie, pp. 311-13. Chicago: National Society for the Study of Education, 1965.

GARDNER, HOWARD. *The Quest for Mind: Piaget, Levi-Strauss and the Structuralist Movement.* New York: Alfred A. Knopf, 1973.

HARRIS, NEIL. *The Artist in American Society: The Formative Years 1790-1860.* New York: George Braziller, 1966.

HARRIS, THOMAS A. *I'm O.K., You're O.K.: A Practical Guide to Transactional Analysis.* New York: Harper and Row, Publishers, 1969.

KELLOGG, RHODA. *Analyzing Children's Art.* Palo Alto, Calif.: National Press Books, 1969.

KIRSCHENBAUM, HOWARD; SIMON, SIDNEY B.; and HOWE, LELAND W. *Values Clarification.* New York: Hart Publishing Company, 1972.

LÉVI-STRAUSS, CLAUDE. *Structural Anthropology.* New York: Doubleday Publishing Company, Anchor Books, 1967.

———. *The Raw and the Cooked,* vol. 1. *Honey and Ashes,* vol. 2. Introduction to a Science of Mythology. Translated from the French by John and Doreen Weightman. New York: Harper and Row, Publishers, 1969 and 1973.

LOWENFELD, VIKTOR, and BRITTAIN, WM. LAMBERT. *Creative and Mental Growth.* 5th rev. ed. New York: Macmillan Co., 1970.

MARANTZ, KENNETH. "Indecent Exposure." In *Studies in Art Education* 6, no. 1 (1964):20-24.

PERLS, FRITZ. *The Gestalt Approach and Eyewitness to Gestalt Therapy.* Ben Lomond, Calif.: Science and Behavior Books, 1973.

PIAGET, JEAN. *Structuralism.* New York: Harper and Row, Publishers, Torch Books, 1971.

RATHS, LOUIS E.; HARMIN, MERRILL; and SIMON, SIDNEY B. *Values and Teaching, Working with Values in the Classroom.* Columbus, Ohio: Charles E. Merrill Co., 1966.

TAYLOR, HAROLD, ed. *Humanities in the Schools.* New York: Citation Press, a division of Scholastic Magazines, Inc., 1968.

WEINSTEIN, GERALD, and FANTINI, MARIO D., eds. *Toward Humanistic Education: A Curriculum of Affect.* New York: The Ford Foundation, Praeger Publishers, Inc., 1970.

2

Historical background:
good-bye, Hegel; hello, Star Child

Arts education requires a deeper involvement on the part of children, teachers, parents, and public in the aesthetic experience—for a period of time sufficient for all of those involved to feel enriched because of it. It takes a prolonged personal involvement capable of being sustained, to want more, and from that the participant comes away more perceptively aware of the richness of life, of the senses, and of what mankind has to offer the human spirit. Even with full public support, no school budget can by itself offer this. These experiences need outside funding.

The Arts and Humanities Act (1965) resulted from President Kennedy's awareness of the fact that the arts were both important and neglected. He appointed August Heckscher as his special Consultant in the Arts. Between March 1962 and May 1963 Heckscher examined the governmental scene, including the United States Office of Education, in relation to the arts. He found a wide variety of policies, standards, and activities which affected the arts, sometimes supportively, other times negatively, principally through neglect. As a consequence, he recommended that the U.S.O.E. provide support for the arts and humanities the same as it had for mathematics, science, and modern languages—support which included materials, equipment, and teacher preparation. He found that the U.S.O.E. panel on Educational Research and Development had neglected the arts and humanities. As a result, CEMREL, Inc., a research and development center, was expanded to include aesthetic education experiments in teaching and curriculum development through an interdisciplinary approach.

When the legislators, artists, aestheticians, and cultural leaders gathered to set up the Arts and Humanities Act, they decided to use both of the words in the title. Their dilemma in trying to decide whether to include the skills and techniques of making the arts among the humanities was not unlike that confronting scholars about what to include, and how to interpret the humanities since their origin. The contents and purposes of the humanities have changed throughout history, as the culture and human need for them has also changed. The current confusions over their content and meaning is part of that history of transition and adaptability.

Time Capsule: Artes Liberales and Serviles

Throughout the history of education in the western European culture, and the United States in particular

there has been a conflict between the liberal arts (of which the humanities and fine arts are now considered a part) and practical or basic education. For the origins of this conflict we turn to the Dorian Greeks.

Greek and Roman

In the times of ancient Greece, the first age of humanism, the arts were identified as either *artes liberales* (liberal arts) or *artes serviles* (manual or servile arts).

The liberal arts were identified as intellectual pursuits for exploitation during leisure time. They included the language arts, literature, philosophy, science, mathematics, history, and the fine arts. However, the fine arts of that age consisted of music, poetry, and dance, but did not include painting and sculpture as they do now.

The manual, or practical, arts were those requiring the use of the hands rather than pure intellect. From these arts one earned a living. They were part of the world of work, rather than of recreation and leisure time, and included shipbuilding, toolmaking, engineering, architecture, and crafts such as painting, pottery making, sculpting or carving, jewelry making, and working in leather, wood, and metals. Workers in these arts were called artisans.

The painters painted murals in wet plaster directly on the walls, and polychromed buildings and sculptured pieces. They worked side by side with the architects and the sculptors. Painters and sculptors continued to work in this capacity until the Renaissance (Pieper 1963, pp. 20-34).

Humanistic inquiry belonged to the philosophers and teachers who established rules and values for human conduct, government, and learning. Education was a visual-aural process. Learning took place through the senses and intellect. Playwrights and poets told of great events through epic poetry, and of noble human responses to disaster through tragedies; they pointed to human foibles through satires, and amused through comedies. History was taught through memorized narrative, plays, and song. Mathematics was a part of musical rhythms and dance. Thought was developed through aural discourse.

The early Greeks enjoyed taking part in plays, festivals, and religious rituals—in playing games, arguing, and talking—very much as people do today. However, as Jarrett suggests, they did "all these human things with a flair and a style that made them somehow worthy of recording and remembering" (1973, p. 1).

During the Hellenic and Hellenistic Ages the liberal and manual arts grew further apart. A liberal arts education in philosophy, law, poetry, and mathematics was given the growing freeman (gentleman), while a practical education in crafts and trades was given the worker and slave. Drawing provided practical knowledge in learning lengths and measures, but Aristotle argued on behalf of its liberal values—that it helped the well-educated man refine his perception of his environment. The freeman still learned the lyre—to sing and to dance—but preferred being a spectator, and made a distinction between himself and professional performers. The manual arts, rooted more deeply within the working class, were identified with artisan trades and menial labor.

At the time of the Roman Republic, the educated Roman followed the liberal arts tradition, adding to it foreign languages since it entailed his learning Greek. In literature he also kept up with the more recent writers, while rules for rhetoric became more dogmatic. Together, they became identified as the seven liberal arts: grammar, rhetoric, logic, arithmetic, astronomy, music, and Greek. Since then, periods of major cultural change have instituted their own reidentification, reclassification, and shifting priorities to the content of the liberal arts. However, neither the Greeks nor the Romans called them the humanities.

Middle Ages and Renaissance

Medieval Scholasticism stressed logic, while scientists turned to mathematics, geometry, astronomy, natural history, and natural philosophy. It was an age of conflicts between heaven and hell, of deep-seated religious beliefs and superstitions. The so-called "black arts," using science and philosophy for alchemical purposes, received an enthusiastic reception from those employing alternate avenues of inquiry into human existence, while mathematics made its way into astrology and the occult.

The Renaissance saw the making of the first major thrust towards humanism in the modern world. It enveloped the liberal arts in the study of man; henceforth the humanities. Its advocates were called humanists. They sought to bring harmony and unity to the education of the whole man. It was more a time of arts and letters than philosophy. They turned against the logic of Scholasticism, pursued literary activities, learned Latin and Greek. While emphasizing rhetoric and style, they overlooked the distinctions separating religions, philosophies, and the sciences. Through their rediscovery of the classical style of the ancient Greeks brought up in discoveries of ancient Rome, Renaissance man at first maintained the distinctions between the liberal and manual arts through the humanities (Butts 1955, pp. 177-93).

The first humanists were more interested in literature and poetry than in the visual arts. The invention of the printing press increased the verbal orientation of the humanists to almost all spoken and written enter-

prises, adding art and music criticism, but rejecting the logic and dialectic of Scholasticism. As the Renaissance progressed, painting and sculpture were included in the study of man, a result in part of the psychological insight of painters such as Leonardo da Vinci or Michelangelo. Leonardo in his treatise *The Art of Painting* and Leon Battista Alberti in *On Painting* established proportions for drawing the human figure, methods for rendering light and shade, rules of optics and for drawing linear perspective. These rules, through tradition, are still given priority today in those art programs which are now called "academic."

In spite of their genius, Leonardo, Michelangelo, and Raphael were nonetheless identified with the artisan class, a classification which they protested against because of the high degree of technical skill, imagination, and intellect with which they approached their work. They had the ears of influential friends—writers, poets, and art critics—who argued on their behalf. Within their lifetimes they were raised in status to the rank of artist, on a par with the poets.

The Renaissance also brought a change in their working conditions. Since the time of the ancient Egyptians and Greeks, artisan painters worked on wet plaster (a fresco technique), applied directly on the wall of the structure. Sculptors carved directly from the wall of the structure in space provided for that purpose (bas-relief), or from stones already in place. The Renaissance painter began working on wooden panels in his studio and either delivering them to his patron, the donor, or installing them in the building site. The sculptor also worked in his studio, and upon completion transported the sculpted piece to the place it would stand. Thus the painter and sculptor was freed of the tyranny of the building site. They were no longer like the stonemason and other laborers who, like today's hard-hat construction crews, represented the artisan, the uneducated, conservative aspect of society; that is, uneducated in the sense of the Greek and Roman "freeman," the Renaissance "whole man," or the English and American "gentleman."

Courtly Art and the Middle Class

The patron of the artists in Italy, and the royal sponsorship of court painters in France and Spain sustained the raised status of the painter and sculptor. Status, as such, was not so clear-cut as regards the middle class, which was itself rising out of the working and peasant class; after all, the fine arts still reflected the leisure class. Court painters, such as Jean Antoine Watteau, François Boucher, Jean-Honore Fragonard, and Diego Velazquez recorded life at the court, its pleasures, games, masques, and its personnages, in their paintings. Bourgeois painters, such as Jean-Baptiste Greuze, and Jean-Baptiste-Siméon-Chardin recorded the activities of French merchants and the rising middle class. Such painters had a middle-class status. They sold their work through dealers who supported them by contract, to merchants, bankers, and sometimes on the open market.

This was particularly true in Holland and the Netherlands during the sixteenth and seventeenth centuries, the "Golden Age" of Dutch painting. Artists painted landscapes, still lifes, biblical scenes, figure studies, portraits, and historical events, of their own free will. They became less dependent upon commissions or assignments, and painted for an open competitive market. Paintings decorated the walls of the houses of the wealthier members of the upper middle class who could afford their luxury, and desired to exhibit their wealth.

For the Protestants, Jean Calvin had established the proper middle-class attitude toward the arts. In his *Institutes of the Christian Religion* (1536), he recognized painting and sculpture to be "the gifts of the Gods" but warned against using them to represent spiritual images and heavenly beings. Art, when used to depict historical events, should be limited to recording only those events contemporary with the artist rather than the spiritual events of heaven (Calvin 1936, vol. 1, pp. 114-31). Paintings and sculpture had been used in the Roman Catholic churches to inform the illiterate masses of religious and Christian events. Calvin, in his iconoclasm, insisted that the true form for the message of God was in written and spoken word, not in the visual image. Calvin's doctrine influenced the taste of the middle class for representational subject matter of the world around them. Works of the imagination were discredited. His doctrine also reinforced the spoken and written word as the basis for education and religious instruction. He established even more pronouncedly the verbal directions for learning during the Renaissance, following the invention of the printing press. The visual-aural and sensory approaches to learning found in the ancient Greek liberal arts became more remote and neglected. As the working class rose to middle-class status, it brought along with it that orientation to practical education originally accorded artisans and slave labor.

Age of Enlightenment

Sweeping advances in science, technology, and mathematics gave the enlightenment of the seventeenth century a strong shove towards rationalism and the search for an order to the universe and to all natural phenomena, including the human being. It was still an age of literary, artistic, and musical achievements, but such philosophers as René Descartes, Francis Bacon, and John Locke were prescribing "reason, clarity, method, regularity and order—in short, the whole array of virtues that the new scientific writing strove to embody" (Jarrett 1973, p. 31). As the essence of knowledge, art criticism followed a similar intent. Artists shifted from representing the ideal as found in nature to representing an imitation of the ideal, and to depicting the form and character within the subject matter as found in the work of Sir Joshua Reynolds.

In counteraction to scientific rationalism, David Hume, Adam Smith, and John Stuart Mill, among others, were moralists who placed human feelings at the center of the moral life. The study of man was the proper avenue to "all other studies, from mathematics to natural (i.e., nonrevealed) religion." Hume identified four moral sciences as the basis of study: logic, morals, criticism, and politics.

But the sensory learning processes were not entirely neglected. Within the decade 1750-60, Alexander Baumgarten published his book, *Aesthetiks*, the title of which was derived from the ancient Greeks, and which meant learning through the senses—through perceptions rather than through the intellect. He brought down the ire of Immanuel Kant, who criticized the book in his own, *The Critique of Pure Reason* (1781), but who nevertheless provided a stronger philosophical base for aesthetic judgment than Baumgarten was able to do. He suggested that aesthetic judgment, unlike scientific and moral judgment used feelings rather than concepts.

Georg Wilhelm Friedrich Hegel, in his *Encyclopedia of Philosophical Sciences*, contributed to the artists' achievement of status. Hegel's system of human consciousness classified art with religion and philosophy as an example of *absolute spirit*, leading the mind or intellect to an awareness of truth, and raising the content of art to the sublime. Paintings portrayed the ideal of beauty, as well as the spiritual and moral in their subject matter. Aesthetic values under Hegel become spiritual, and contribute to the rising of the human being beyond its human self.

Eighteenth-century humanities continued the older tradition of the liberal arts, which preceded the subsidence of philosophy during the Renaissance, and also continued the emphasis on mathematics and natural sciences which had gained in favor during the seventeenth century. The eighteenth-century gentleman, a product of the upper middle class who hobnobbed with the aristocracy, was the humanistic descendant of the freeman of ancient Greece and Rome. He was probably more adept at conversation than at discourse. Jarrett suggests that the eighteenth century was "the last age in which the humanities was widely respected as an obviously valuable, indeed indispensible, part of education" (1973, p. 35).

The American Tradition in Art Education and the Humanities

In the five hundred years since the Italian Renaissance the artist-artisan status conflict shifted one way or the other according to the role of the artist in the prevailing culture, and the position of ascent or descent of the upper economic leisure class in the prevailing culture. (A similar conflict exists today in American colleges between studio art teachers who identify with the artists, but who associate the art education student or future art teacher with a status related to the artisan class. However, art and classroom teachers identify with the professional, rather than the working class.) The humanities were taught in the colleges and universities of Britain, the North American colonies, and the new United States as symbols of the educated gentleman, more from snob appeal than from any really serious belief in their essential importance to the heritage of their testament.

The liberal arts, as taught in the elementary and secondary schools of the colonies, continued in the classical tradition with the study of Greek, Latin, and Hebrew. For the Calvinists, Anglicans, and Roman Catholics the goals were to train leaders to serve the church or state. In the eighteenth century there was a gradual trend towards making education more practical for economic reasons, as well as towards developing political ideals and scientific interests.

With the American Revolution and the new nation, vocational and professional education came in the forms of natural sciences for merchants and mechanics; Latin and Greek for ministers; Latin, Greek, and French for medical students; and French, German, and Spanish for merchants. Rather than being taught for a better understanding of world literature or for humanistic purposes, foreign languages were taught in order to fulfill professional needs, and for reasons of profit. The theory was that to be successful educational and cultural enterprises in the United States had to be practical. During the colonial and post-revolutionary periods, reading was taught, not to enable the reader to experience great literature, but to be able to read and interpret the Bible—to read newspapers and voting ballots. Writing was taught for communicative purposes rather than for developing the aesthetic qualities of verbal expression—as style, for example. Arithmetic, rather than mathematics, was taught, not for scientific inquiry, but as ciphering for accounting and bookkeeping. Thus, we have the three R's, each limited to the practical education of the manual arts, rather than the humanistic education of the liberal arts.

Common (Public) and Private Schools

Drawing was not taught in the common or public schools until about four decades (1820s) after the American Revolution. Prior to that time, such artisans were painters, stainers, sign painters, or limners painting "likenesses." They learned through an apprenticeship method. Even then, art was taught as a means of geometric delineation and measurement, rather than as a means for expression of visual concepts or of the imagination. Indeed, during the nineteenth century, any attempt to draw landscapes, flowers, or solely from the imagination was discouraged as the work of the devil. Even Horace Mann told of having his fingers rapped with a stick when his teacher caught him drawing a sunset (Mary Peabody Mann 1865, 1937, pp. 11-12).

Geometric and manual drawing was taught for the purpose of preparing young people to obtain jobs as draftsmen, machinists, tool and die makers, cabinetmakers, and to draw house plans. The drawing materials were the clay stylus for slate, pencils, and pen and ink

for paper. Color and color theory was not taught because watercolors were expensive, and even by the end of the century it was reserved for advanced secondary level work. Wax crayons were not invented until the late 1880s. Color also suggested "picture making," which was associated with the fine arts, and thus derived from the imagination—the work of the devil.

As a result, the common man was conditioned to think of linear perspective as the ultimate in the representational drawing of space, and of art as a "frill" if it had no practical value. He knew nothing of the Hegelian dialectic or the spiritual value of art. He thought of the artist as a ne' er-do-well, starving in a garrett, incapable of earning a practical living. This attitude has continued to the present day, despite the growth of commercial art, advertising, photography, filmmaking and film animation, interior and textile design, and other design occupations operating at the practical professional level. If the common man thought of the arts and humanities at all, he relegated them to the upper middle class. Private schools were sponsored by the upper and upper middle class to provide more of a liberal education than a trade school education for their children. They were taught in the homes of sponsoring parents, in rooms rented in boarding houses, or in other appropriate places. Although Bronson Alcott's Temple School (1834-36) was not completely typical it does demonstrate the differences that existed between private schools and the common (or public) schools described above. Alcott explored the world of thought with his students, putting questions to them about their observations on God, love, will, conscience, obedience, appetites (physical and spiritual), nature, and their own individual growth. He encouraged them to keep journals. Alcott taught drawing, by having the little children copy from prints and steel engravings of natural and man-made objects and alphabetical letters. He asked them questions about their observations. Elizabeth Peabody, who taught there part-time, while conducting her own schools, wrote a book, *Record of a School* (1835), on Alcott's methods.

Francis Graeter, who taught drawing in several of Elizabeth's schools and at Temple School on Tuesdays, also had the children copying from prints and engravings. But they also observed nature, and were asked questions about the geometric order of what they saw. The engraved prints depicted the patterns and designs found in trees, leaves, flowers, petals, seashells, and other objects of nature. Graeter related their structures to the divine order of the universe, the design of a supreme spiritual being. He felt that the correct observation of nature was more a matter of aesthetic sensibility than of intellect.

In her own schools, Elizabeth taught Latin, history (Greek, Roman, and Hebrew), moral development, and reading and writing. She also taught music, dance, rhythms, and gymnastics, which she related to natural order and harmonies. Drawing was taught to develop visual perceptions and a sense of divine order. She took the children on walking tours of Boston Common, which she called "natural object lessons." They found and discussed more evidence of the divine design.

Mary Peabody Mann, Elizabeth's sister and Horace Mann's wife, helped conduct their schools but preferred teaching arithmetic, languages (French and probably German), and some drawing. Sophia, their sister who married Nathaniel Hawthorne, was considered the artist of the family and frequently taught the drawing lessons. Both Elizabeth and Mary had strong convictions about the first purpose of education being to develop character, and the second—to teach knowledge. Theirs was a philosophy which they called "moral culture."

In an essay, "The Dorian Measure: A Modern Application" (1848), Elizabeth extolled early Greek classicism as the ideal educational approach for young children. Music, dance, songs, games (including fencing), gymnastics, and playing musical instruments were all taught as aspects of harmonious organization in man and nature. Drawing educated the eye to order, and modeling in clay educated the eye to form. Both, along with music and the dance, were taught before reading and writing—saved for ages six and seven. Music and dance began with Mother Goose, but continued to the higher forms of ballet and opera, which Elizabeth related to physical culture. Grammar and logic she suggested be taught as forms of thought, and reading be taught through philology rather than through meaningless memorization of words and spelling. Elizabeth was, in 1848, calling for a humanistic renaissance after the medievalism of the puritan doctrines. She wanted education to develop the "whole man," which meant all of the senses and aesthetic sensibilities.

Together Alcott, Graeter, and the Peabody sisters reflected the moral rationalism of the seventeenth century in their educational philosophy. Not entirely original with them, aspects of it were found in the teachings of Johann Heinrich Pestalozzi and Friedrich Froebel. Elizabeth introduced the theories of the latter into the first English-speaking kindergarten in the United States (1862).

Art Appreciation and the Democratization of Art

Following the Civil War there was a great opening of public museums and libraries, theaters, world's fairs, expositions, and cultural events. The Industrial Age and growth of great fortunes established a wealthy leisure class essential for the flourishing of the arts. The philanthropic gestures of Carnegie, the Vanderbilts, Astors, and Mellons provided the means for building and supporting museums, and for supplying the art collections to put into them. The paintings and sculpture from palaces and the country homes of Europe were brought to the museums of the United States. The arts were democratized. They had been made available to the middle and working classes.

The first courses in art appreciation at the college level were begun at Harvard in 1874. Taught by Charles Eliot Norton, they were entitled "The Rise and Fall of the Arts in Venice" and "The Italian Renaissance." Their purposes were practical, rather than classical, humanistic, or spiritual. They emphasized art recognition, the identification of artists by the techniques and quality of their work, and their place in art history. The objectives of the courses were essentially the preparation of the young gentlemen of the upper classes for purchasing and collecting art wisely when traveling in Europe. "Art appreciation" meant "to appreciate in monetary value" more than to enjoy art for its own sake.

In 1870 the Massachusetts State legislature passed the Industrial Drawing Act, requiring that manual drawing be taught in every town of 20,000 population or over. This put an official seal on the direction of art in the schools: artisan training over fine arts and humanistic education. Manual drawing became identified as industrial arts, and the remainder as the fine arts. But the die was cast, and about the 1880s the phrase "art is a frill" was popularly voiced. At that time, artists worked in garrets, and did only paintings. There were no commercial arts, filmmaking, advertising, interior and tapestry designers, and the like. Unfortunately, as new art careers opened up and became available, the attitude "art is a frill" failed to change.

In 1898 *picture study units* were introduced into the public schools by Henry Turner Bailey and the *School Arts Book*. Picture study units consisted of appropriate art reproductions for each grade level, and were used for classroom instruction and school decoration. The subjects were chosen to appeal to children, and convey a moral or spiritual concept or show family unity and hard work. As a result, Jean François Millet's *The Angelus, The Gleaners,* and *Feeding the Birds;* Sir Lawrence Alma-Tedema's *Reading of Homer;* and Raphael's *Sistine Madonna* were established as standards of popular taste.

They hung in flat oak frames, beautifying school buildings' walls along with plaster bas-reliefs of Greek sculpture. In order to obtain funds to buy more of these, schools sponsored tableaux for which the children dressed up as people in the paintings, and posed against backgrounds made in school, to represent famous paintings. The public paid to attend these presentations when they were given in the schools.

Guides for picture study units consisted of descriptions of each picture, biographical information on the artist, and questions dealing with the moral or other lessons to be learned from it. Primary children were given the moral lessons, while the upper elementary children were supposed to get lessons on aesthetic aspects of the pictures. However, the guides do not seem to have penetrated that far, with the result that children grew into adulthood having learned only the narrative and moral aspects of art, but little of the aesthetic analysis and art criticism.

Aesthetic analysis and art criticism are based on abstract criteria or principles of design. Henry Turner Bailey defined them as the "Elements of Beauty" (*School*

Arts Book, 1911-12), and listed: unity, color, form, suggestiveness (now called balance), and rhyme (now called repetition). Arthur Dow, in *Composition* (1899), provided a set of principles of design which continued in use through thirteen editions until 1929. He identified "Elements of Harmony" as: line, notan (light and dark balance, now called negative-positive space), and color. Among the "Principles of Composition" he listed: opposition, transition, subordination, repetition, and symmetry.

As close as our educational programs came to a humanistic curriculum was the progressive education movement, which ultimately responded to the demands of industry for hireable and trainable future employees from the schools, with the result that the aesthetic aspects of sociocultural need were then relegated to the fine arts or frill areas. Even the industrial arts had their causes attacked, but they responded by pointing to the practicality and major social value of industrial art: profitable occupational employment, which the fine arts did not. Until the current interest by the government in career education, the fine arts continued to identify mainly with leisure-time activities.

Progressive Education and Education-Through-Art

John Dewey published *School and Society* in 1898, which gave impetus to the progressive education movement, and "Deweyism" became synonymous with the movement. However, "progressive" did not mean progress in the sense of futuristic or way-out, but in the sense of progression from one stage or level of learning to the one above it. We now call it, "sequential learning." Its direction toward a pragmatic or practical education, being asked for by the industrialists, led to the early adaptation of manual arts and crafts for the making of leather-work objects, flat wood carving, and stencilled pillows. By the 1920s, the fine arts also became involved through integrating or correlating with social studies, English, mathematics, and other academic subject areas. Children built models of Greek temples, made samples of folk art, peasant costumes for plays and dances, dug clay from the ground for making primitive pottery, wove baskets, pressed berries, and dyed cloth. It was a movement which continued into the 1930s and the depression years, spurred on by student projects reported on and photographed by teachers in *School Arts* and *The Instructor* magazines. They reflected the practical education of the artisan.

Dewey's *Art as Experience,* which identified him as an aesthetician and more solidly as an influence on art education, was not published until 1934. It introduced an intellectual and highly complex rationale for making the act of doing a learning experience. The final phase of the experience was a recapitulation or discussion of the activity, so that the child would become conscious of what had been done, why, and what was learned. The child was encouraged to make his own choices, decide his own learning activities, but all too often the final stage of articulating, evaluating, and discussing what was learned by the activity was neglected, thus nullifying much of the learning process. Art became a fun time, somewhat laissez-faire, and re-established itself as a happy time, but still a frill.

The humanistic and child growth aspects of progressive art education continued to be promoted through the Progressive Education Association's *The Visual Arts in General Education* (1940), edited by Victor D'Amico. It was directed mainly towards integrating the arts at the secondary level, and developing the expressive in art. It brought in the work of modern artists, which had been neglected in the schools still using picture study units. His later book, *Creative Teaching in Art,* identified children as artists, sculptors, potters, and so on, and reflected the children's classes at the Museum of Modern Art in New York City, where he was director of the Education Department. The children were encouraged to express their own ideas and their environment in murals, model city plans, paintings, ceramics, and use of scrap materials for mobiles, stabiles, and collages.

Herbert Read, in *Education Through Art* (1945), gave a title to the movement. An art critic and art philosopher, he analyzed the intellectual and emotive visual-haptic aspects of child art, using it to develop social and moral consciousness. Read placed art and aesthetic learning activities at the center of the curriculum rather than at the periphery. He related the creative-expressive aspects of child art to their psychological development, and provided a basis for analyzing children's paintings according to Jung's psychological types (Thinking, Feeling, Sensation, and Intuitive) and the unconscious. He preceded the "British Primary" concepts by almost three decades.

In 1947, Viktor Lowenfeld (whose book, the *Nature of Creative Activity* Herbert Read had helped get published in 1939) published *Creative and Mental Growth.* It had a profound effect on art education in this country. He synthesized German Gestalt psychology with the stages of development in child art, which had been defined by the Child Study movements of England, Italy, Germany, and the United States during the 1890s. He expanded the stages from manipulative, cataloging (symbolic), narrative, and ideational, to Scribbling (2-4 years) Preschematic (4-7 years), Schematic (7-9 years), Dawning Realism (9-11 years), Pseudo-naturalistic (11-13 years), and the Period of Decision (adolescence). He developed practical teaching methods for leading the child from stage to stage, developing the visual-haptic (intellectual and sensory) potentials of the child through motivations of acting out an activity before making a drawing, painting, or modeling it. Lowenfeld related aesthetic concepts to child art as an essentially humanistic, child-oriented point of view, and provided charts and criteria for evaluating children's aesthetic, intellectual, social, and physical growth through their art work. He interpreted art history and the aesthetic experience in the light of the ability to visualize, or the hapticity of the culture which produced it. Art was a means for extending the total growth of the individual.

Art in Everyday Living

There has always been some aspect of art devoted to a more aesthetic and beautiful life, or environment, but it shows up more as an art objective on curriculum guides than it actually shows up in the elementary art lesson. The content of units on art in daily living focused more on the aesthetic quality of practical design in the home: furniture, interior decoration, pictures on the wall, landscaping, and styles of domestic architecture. It was more closely allied to home economics than to the fine arts; taught more at the secondary than elementary levels. But elementary classrooms began to get "art corners," consisting of art reproductions, or a pretty picture on a bulletin board or screen; with a table, vase of flowers, a few books, and a chair.

During the depression, when school budgets were cut, the attitude "art is a frill" was generated. At that time, the Carnegie Foundation for the Advancement of Teaching sponsored the Owatonna Art Education Project—planned to show in a typical American middle western community that art was an important part of community life and daily living. Between 1934 and 1938 a group of resident artists lived in Owatonna, Minnesota. Melvin Haggerty, Dean of Education, University of Minnesota, initiated and directed the project, while Ernest Ziegfeld, a landscape architect, was the resident director. The staff taught art in the cafeteria of the school, before and after lunch, put up window displays, store exhibits, small parks and landscaping in the town and yards, taught evening adult art classes, and talked to social and business clubs. Additional art books, reproductions, and exhibits were added to the library. It was a total community arts project at the applied arts level. The fine arts and art history were kept a minor part of the program. A complete art curriculum was also planned for publication afterwards, but was delayed until 1944. By that time Ziegfeld, with Gerald Hill and Ray Faulkner (two other project members), had already published *Art Today* (1941), and the United States was in World War II. The Owatonna Project was restricted to the applied arts, and the artisan traditions. Accordingly it fell short of dealing with the "higher" Hegelian values of art and humanistic affectiveness. Even after the project, art was still being taught in the cafeteria, with no room of its own. It remains historically important, but the curriculum guidelines were published too late to have the major influence on art education that it might have had if published before World War II.

The Humanities, Aesthetic Education, and "2001"

The real legacy of the very brief Kennedy administration was the resurgence of the Camelot concept, of an American renaissance demonstrating as never before how essential a rich involvement in the arts and humanities are to the human condition. They can only be effective when involvement begins at an early age. Discovery of the arts at the college and adult level is initially remedial.

Group singing of little songs in school, the applied music of marching school bands, the making of small arts and crafts projects in thirty or forty minutes once a week will not achieve the involvement in the arts necessary to prove their worth. In three-quarters of a century such school art activities have not done it. If they had, then most of today's adults, parents and voters, who think the arts are frills would not think so.

The Arts and Humanities Act and Title III of the Elementary Secondary Education Act (ESEA-1965) focused on the fine arts, not on the applied or servile arts. The National Endowment for the Arts and the states arts councils and committees have shown that the government can subsidize the arts without controlling artists or using them for propaganda for the state as in a dictatorship. The John F. Kennedy Center for the Performing Arts and the affiliated Alliance for Arts Education is weaving a network for communication between the states with the idea of recognizing and sharing the best they have to offer in community and educational arts programs and activities. *Impact*, a program of the U.S.O.E. exploring the use of visiting and residence artists, sculptors, poets, filmmakers, composers, etc., has demonstrated that the fine arts and professionals can have a dynamic positive impact on the education of children.

Private enterprise and philanthropy have also turned to support the arts through the Businessmen's Committee on the Arts. The John D. Rockefeller III Fund sponsors the "Arts in General Education" program which has specific projects in midwestern, inner-city, and suburban locations. Kathryn Bloom, who taught art in Owatonna after the project left, and was the first director of the Arts and Humanities Office of the U.S.O.E., has directed the program's projects experimenting in arts curriculum, aesthetic education, and subsidized visiting and resident artists; also in school performances of orchestral, dance, ballet, theater, and opera programs; to establish that the fine arts instead of being peripheral can be the center of the curriculum and are essential to the welfare of the people. They deal not with the tradesmen-artisan view of the practical arts, but with the freeman's view of aesthetic involvement in the fine arts.

But what of the future? The year 2001 is only a short time span away. Today's kindergarten children will be only a little more than twenty-five years old. How are they being prepared to live in the twenty-first century? Will values in the humanistic traditions and needs for the arts be fulfilled in their lives? Will technology and science reinforce humanistic values, or avoid them? Edmund Feldman suggests in *Becoming Human Through Art,*

When the humanists examine technology, languages, social and political institutions, science, art and religion, it is for the purpose of finding out what light they can shed on man and the problem of being a man. It is time for art education to reconstitute itself as the study of man through art (1970, p. 174).

Can we predict from past action and current change what the year 2001 will be like? It may come too soon to be a real space odyssey. A great deal of it will probably be like it is now. Many of our houses, apartments, condominiums, skyscrapers, cathedrals, New England churches, Spanish missions, and the pyramids will still be standing. Museums will still house art collections of the past and the changing present. Beethoven and Bach will still be played in concert halls and on probably more facile sound equipment. We will continue to get new art forms and styles which we cannot as yet anticipate, nor can we as yet determine the aesthetic criteria used to evaluate it. For myself, all I know for certain about the year 2001 is that I will be seventy-five years old (if I am alive).

If, as some predict, we or our children will blow up the world, what kind of age will the last age of mankind be? Will our children have realized what has been blasted away? Will they have known the joy of having been part of the greatness of the human race, or will they wonder, "What was life all about anyway?"

If, as many ecologists fear, we will continue to destroy and pollute the earth, and we go out, not with a "bang but a whimper," what kind of world will our children live in? Will it be a barren earth, or preserved under domes by chic technology? Is is possible that all they will know of nature will be coloring-book pigeons on the plastic grass? Alas!

If as *Star Trek*, and the concepts of ancient astronauts suggest, we will travel through space, will we be able to build pyramids in a jungle to equal those of the Mayans and Aztecs in Mexico as Erich von Däniken suggests? What kind of star children will be our space heirs?

Figure 2.1 "The Star Child," a still from **2001: A Space Odyssey.** (Copyright © 1968 Metro-Goldwyn-Mayer, Inc.)

Reinforcing Activities

1. Ask yourself, and express in written words for discussion in class, what you want for the twenty-first-century adult. You will be teaching the child while he or she is growing up.
2. Define in a journal what is meant by the "whole man" in terms of today.
3. In your journal, analyze your own strengths and weaknesses in the areas of art and aesthetic awareness. Which areas are missing to make you feel less *whole* than you may wish to be. To what extent are these missing areas a result of the school programs in which you grew up?
4. If you are presently teaching or practice-teaching, assess your current priorities in the classroom. Do they reflect your strengths adequately? To what extent do your lowest priorities in your program reflect your weaknesses?
5. If your special subject (art, music, physical education, dance) teachers were cut from the school budget, how much of their responsibilities for humanistic and aesthetic education could you assume with confidence?

References

ARBERG, HAROLD. "Preface." In *Arts and Humanities, Report on Research Projects*, Diana Vogelson, Research Assistant. Washington, D. C.: U.S. Office of Education, 1971, pp. iii-iv.

BUTTS, R. FREEMAN. *A Cultural History of Western Education*. New York: McGraw-Hill Book Co., 1955.

BUTTS, R. FREEMAN and CREMIN, LAWRENCE A. *A History of Education in American Culture*. New York: Henry Holt and Co., 1954.

CALVIN, JEAN. *Institutes of the Christian Religion*. Philadelphia: Presbyterian Board of Education, 1936, vol. 1.

CREMIN, LAWRENCE A. *A History of Education in American Culture*. New York: Henry Holt and Co., 1954.

CREMIN, LAWRENCE A. *The Transformation of the School: Progressivism in American Education, 1876-1957*. New York: Alfred A. Knopf, Vintage Books, 1961.

D'AMICO, VICTOR. *Creative Teaching in Art*. Scranton, Pa.: International Textbook Co., 1942.

DEWEY, JOHN. *Art as Experience*. New York: Minton Balch and Co., 1934.

DOW, ARTHUR WESLEY. *Composition*. 1898. 12th ed. rev. Garden City, N. Y.: Doubleday and Company, 1924.

FELDMAN, EDMUND BURKE. *Becoming Human Through Art*. Englewood Cliffs, N. J.: Prentice-Hall, 1970.

HARRIS, NEIL. *The Artist in American Society—The Formative Years 1790-1860*. New York: George Braziller, 1966.

HAUSER, ARNOLD. A Social History of Art, vol. 2. *Renaissance Mannerism Baroque*. New York: Alfred A. Knopf, Vintage Press, 1957.

JARRETT, JAMES L. *The Humanities and Humanistic Education*. Reading, Mass.: Addison-Wesley Publishing Company, Inc., 1973.

KEEL, JOHN S. "Sir Herbert Read and the Discipline of Art." *Art Education* 19 (1966):1.

LOWENFELD, VIKTOR. *The Nature of Creative Activity*. Translated by O. A. Oeser. London: Routledge and Kegan Paul, 1939.

———. *Creative and Mental Growth*. New York: Macmillan Company, 1947.

OWATONNA ART EDUCATION PROJECT. "Fifth Annual Report." New York: Carnegie Corporation [files], c. 1942.

MANN, MARY PEABODY. *Life of Horace Mann, by his Wife*. (1865). Washington, D. C.: National Education Association, 1937.

PEABODY, ELIZABETH P. "The Dorian Measure: A Modern Application" (1848). In *Last Evening with Allston and Other Papers*. Boston: D. Lothrop and Co., 1886.

———. *Record of a School*. 3d ed. rev. Roberts Brothers, 1874.

———. *Reminiscences of William Ellery Channing, D.D*. Boston: Roberts Brothers, 1880.

PIEPER, JOSEF. *Leisure: The Basis of Culture*. Translated by Alexander Dru. New York: New American Library, Mentor-Omega paperback, 1963.

PROGRESSIVE EDUCATION ASSOCIATION. *The Visual Arts in General Education*: A report of the committee on the Function of Art in General Education for the commission on secondary school curriculum. New York: Appleton-Century-Crofts, 1940.

READ, SIR HERBERT. *Education Through Art*. 2d. ed. New York: Pantheon Books, 1945.

SAUNDERS, ROBERT J. "Contributions of Horace Mann, Mary Peabody Mann and Elizabeth Peabody to Art Education in the United States." Ed. D. dissertation. Pennsylvania State University, 1961.

———. "A History of Teaching Art Appreciation in the Public Schools." In *Improving the Teaching of Art Appreciation*. Edited by David W. Ecker. U.S. Department of Health, Education, and Welfare. *Cooperative Research Project No. V-006*. Contract No. OE-5-10-308. Columbus, Ohio: The Ohio State University.

———. "Art Education History." In *Acad-Cana*. vol. 1. The Encyclopedia of Education. New York: Macmillan Company, and The Free Press, 1971.

STACE, W. T. *The Philosophy of Hegel*. New York: Dover Publications, 1955.

TAYLOR, HAROLD, ed. *The Humanities in the School*. New York: Citation Press, a division of Scholastic Magazines, 1968.

3

Justifying the arts in the schools

At the 1972 Eastern Regional conference (Eastern Arts Association) of the National Art Education Association (NAEA) in New York City, Ernest Goldstein, then Director of Innovative Programs for the American Book Company, commented in the coffee shop one morning about "art in the extremities." When asked what he meant, he went on to say that "in education we turn to art to help straighten things out, to bring order to the chaos we created by neglecting it. We turn to art in the extremities." Indeed, this seems to be the case in the schools and in our culture.

"Art in the Extremities"

Elementary classroom teachers have traditionally preferred scheduling art in the afternoons after their students have completed the "really important" academic studies in the morning, when their minds are fresh. More realistically, art is scheduled in the afternoon when the children are restless from a morning of book learning and paperwork—when even the teacher needs a break. One first-grade teacher mentioned to the author that her class always behaved better on the afternoons following art.

There are some historical precedents for this. In an issue of the *Common School Journal* for 1840, an anonymous author suggested that children who finish their lessons in reading, writing, and ciphering before the others could be given slates for drawing geometrical shapes, human figures, houses, and outlines of animals. The author felt this would be "better than drawing in spittle on the shoes" and relieve "one-third of the tedium and mischief in the class."

More recently, in elementary schools, a child who misbehaves might be told, "If you don't behave, you can't have art today." Paradoxically, in the high schools, nonreaders with more study halls than their amount of academic studies need are frequently scheduled in art.

In many of today's open- and nongraded classrooms, restless tension does not accumulate to any great extent simply because the children have choices of activities and ways of learning academic subjects other than by sitting at their desks reading and listening to the teacher ask convergent questions. The use of teacher aides, and the grouping of students between teachers in a single unit, provide breaks for the teacher.

One major thesis of this book is that teachers of the arts and classroom teachers should mesh—work together as a team. But in order to meet those situations in which there are no art, music, or physical education teachers, classroom teachers should be well enough prepared in the arts and humanities to be able to conduct meaningful programs of their own without resorting to the use of quickie art projects as substitutes for quality art-learning experiences.

What then are the goals, objectives, and purposes for teaching the arts in the public schools? Art curriculum guides for local school districts usually list some variation of goals and objectives dealing with creativity, developing aesthetic values, and cultural heritage. Very often such goals and objectives are based on previous curriculum guides and those that are reviewed from other school districts, and/or the state art curriculum guide (if there is one). Within recent years the National Assessment Program has focused on establishing nationwide goals for reading, writing, mathematics, humanism, science, music, and art.

National Assessment in Art

In 1971 a committee of art teachers and art educators, under the chairmanship of Brent Wilson, developed a set of art objectives for the National Assessment Program. They designed a sequence of five basic areas under which most of the cognitive, affective, psychomotor, expressive, art historical, and aesthetic objectives of art education can be subcategorized. Consistent with the National Assessment Program, the committee identified terminal objectives in each major subject area for children at the ages of 9, 13, and 17, or grades 3-4, 7-8, and 11-12. The following objectives were suggested in Art Objective for the National Assessment Program for Art (Wilson 1971).

I. *Perceive and Respond to the Aspects of Art.*
   A. Recognize and describe the subject.
   B. Go beyond the recognition of subject matter to the perception and description of formal qualities and expressive content (the combined effect of the subject matter and the specific visual form that characterizes a particular work of art).
II. *Value Art as an Important Realization of Human Experience.*
   A. Be affectively oriented toward art.
   B. Participate in activities related to art.
   C. Express reasonably sophisticated conceptions about and positive attitudes toward art and artists.

D. Demonstrate an open-mindedness toward different forms and styles of art.
III. *Produce Works of Art.*
   A. Produce original and imaginative works of art.
   B. Express visual ideas fluently.
   C. Produce works of art with a particular composition, subject matter, expressive character, or expressive content.
   D. Produce works of art that contain various visual conceptions.
   E. Demonstrate knowledge and application of media, tools, techniques, and forming processes.
IV. *Know about Art.*
   A. Recognize major figures and works in the history of art and understand their significance. (Significance as it is used here refers to such things as works of art that began new styles, markedly influenced subsequent works, changed the directions of art, contained visual and technical discoveries, expressed particularly well the spirit of their age, and those considered to be the major works of major artists.)
   B. Recognize styles of art, understand the concept of style, and analyse works of art on the basis of style.
   C. Know the history of man's art activity and understand the relation of one style or period to other styles and periods.
   D. Distinguish between factors of works of art that relate principally to the personal style of the artist and factors that relate to the stylistic period or the entire age.
   E. Know and recognize the relationships that existed between art and the other disciplines of the humanities (literature, music, and particularly the history of ideas and philosophy) during a given period.
V. *Make and Justify Judgments about Aesthetic Merit.*
   A. Make and justify judgments about aesthetic merit.
   B. Make and justify judgments about aesthetic quality.
   C. Apply specific criteria in judging works of art.
   D. Know and understand criteria for making aesthetic judgments.

Only the major objectives and subobjectives have been listed above. The *National Assessment Art Objectives* report provided examples of specific further subobjectives for each of the 9-, 13- and 17-year-old age levels, except for objectives III-E, IV-D, and IV-E which had no recommendations for age 9. To achieve the additional objectives for age 13, instruction should not be withheld until age 12, but begin at least at age 10, because learning in art, like other subject areas, is an accumulative and sequential process.

Most art objectives for local school districts and state guidelines can be grouped under these five national art objectives. However, objective III (Produce Works of Art) is only one of five objectives, but pertains to ninety-nine percent of the art lessons currently taught at the elementary level by both art and classroom teachers.

Identifying Art Purposes

It is simple enough to identify goals and objectives for art, music, and physical education, but when we consider the roles they play in the public schools, identification is more complex. To identify and justify the specific purposes of a subject matter, they must be isolated by their uniqueness. We must be able to say that without this or that subject, such and such will not take place in the school program. This at least was the criteria used by the National Education Association's Educational Policies Commission when they studied the "Roles of the Arts in Education (*E.P.C. Report* 1971)."

In pursuing their objective, the Educational Policies Commission members sought the arguments provided in art, music, and related curriculum guides, in arts education literature, in statements of arts education and humanities conferences, and various reports of other committees on the arts.

They found a certain pattern to exist, not only in the arts and humanities but in the sequence of purposes for art, music, physical education, social studies, history, and other subjects. First, each area listed "good citizenship," "ethical behavior," "insight into values of mankind," and "patriotism." Every field claimed the same highly moral, spiritual, ethical, patriotic values to such extent that they all seemed to say the same. James Russell, Chairman of the commission at a curriculum development conference held by state art directors in 1966, stated that after reading enough of the literature, "you learn a technique for reading it." The real issues and purposes are never the first three; these are usually something like, "God, home, mother, country." Around number four or five, the guides relate or confess to purposes relating to the subject matter (Russell 1967).

Actually, what Russell found in those first four or five moral, ethical, and patriotic principles were humanistic values and purposes. They were found in each because they were common to each. Each subject area achieved them through the knowledge and affect of its own discipline. It was the specific skills and techniques of each subject matter which Russell found, beginning with items four and five.

The commission's next problems were (1) to identify the unique contributions of the regular arts subject matter areas in the schools, and then (2) to determine how they could be applied to that aspect of the school program called the arts. The Educational Policies Commission read through a good deal of literature, philosophy, and vague and astute concepts about the arts to identify six underlying reasons for teaching them in the schools. They used as their criteria: can any other subject matter make this statement? If another subject area could or did make the same statement, then it was not considered unique to the arts. This did not invalidate its use in an arts lesson or guide, but it did invalidate it as unique to the arts.

For example, one rationale for art used in art guides is "to learn to get along with others." Producing puppet shows, making murals, or other group art activities help children learn to share, exchange ideas, and get along with each other. But games, parties, group research projects, plays, and so on all provide the social interaction which help children get along with others. Because this rationale was common to many nonarts subjects, it was not considered unique to the arts, so it was not included in the final commission report.

The commission was also "concerned that forms of education which have served the nation well in the past may not be equally well suited to the needs of the future" (*E.P.C. Report* 1967, p. 1). They addressed themselves to the fine arts in educating all the people rather than on the formation of the practicing artist. Under the heading "fine arts," in addition to painting and music, they included literature, poetry, drama, dance, architecture, photography, and cinema. But, since the public schools have two distinct functions, first to teach quality general education to all children, and second, to provide the basis for career orientation necessary to all adults, then developing talents leading toward professional occupations in the fine arts should have been considered a valid rationale.

In 1968, the National Education Association published the report of the Educational Policies Commission under the title, "The Role of the Fine Arts in Education." The commission had previously studied the role of science in education. Investigating the role of the arts was their last activity before disbanding.

Eight Justifications for the Fine Arts in Education

The commission defined six justifications in their final report. The author has added two more. Their first four have traditionally been applied to the arts: (1) historical, (2) art-for-arts-sake, (3) therapy, and (4) creativity. The commission felt their next two were not usually considered: (5) acceptance of subjectivity, and (6) art for the end of work. Actually, their sixth seems the most traditional of all. Art instruction is more often justified as a leisure time pursuit for everybody than as a career orientation for the artistically gifted and talented. This is quite in opposition to the Protestant Ethic and has relegated art to the "frill" areas. All aspects should be recognized, not just one to the neglect of the other.

To these six have been added (7) art for the world of work, and reinstated one mentioned by James Russell at the conference in 1966, (8) enrichment of the nonart curriculum. The order of their presentation does not constitute a sequence of priorities, which changes as the specific purpose of the arts program changes to meet the needs of the growing children and the community.

Before examining each rationale, it should be pointed out that each of the arts represent a specific sensory mode (visual, aural, tactile, kinesthetic, gustatory, and olfactory). The one unique factor of the visual arts is that they deal with a visual product. Art is the only subject in the curriculum which deals with visual symbology, or the aesthetic visual quality of a product whether it be a written report, a painting, or a piece of architecture.

Let us now examine each rationale.

1. The *Historical rationale* is based on the importance of the arts as transmitters of the cultural heritage and the responsibility of schools to impart that heritage to the children. As a consequence, "an education which does not teach art is deficient because it does not teach the culture" (*E.P.C. Report* 1967, p. 2). The history of art also provides a visual basis for observing and identifying cultural differences, architectural changes, studying the changing role of art in society, or understanding a primitive, prehistoric, or specific culture.

2. The *Art-for-Art's-Sake rationale* results from occasional disdainful attitudes taken by artists and arts educators against having the arts put to use for purposes other than the purely aesthetic and artistic. As a rationale it focuses on the quality of living, joy, aesthetic responses and experiences which have recently been found deficient in our culture as it now exists. In art and architecture it concerns the visual environment, eye pollution, and sensorial chaos of our communities and cities. It also includes aesthetic analysis and criticism of works and productions in the arts.

3. The *Therapy rationale* employs the arts to release emotional tensions, remediate growth problems, to provide means for self-expression, to individual personal achievement, and to strengthen weak self-images. Recent trends include the arts in special education to help children with learning disabilities, mental retardation, and physical handicaps by concentrating on sensory modes of learning rather than on verbal techniques. The arts therapy rationale is getting increased application in situations pertaining to the inner city, prisons, hospitals, homes for the aged, institutions, and clinics.

4. The *Creativity rationale* or some aspect of it, such as "developing the imagination," has been a constant objective in art curriculum guides for most of the twentieth century. The thrust in creativity of the 1950s and 60s made it even more vital to the arts education field, although many arts teachers resisted "getting on the bandwagon." They felt that the spiritual and divine endowment of creative genius was threatened, and so, paradoxically, insisted that creativity cannot be taught. Subsequent research has indicated the factors of creativity can be isolated, therefore teaching methods in the arts can either stifle or encourage creative growth. This will be discussed further in chapter 14.

5. The *Acceptance-of-Subjectivity rationale* is felt by the commission to be newly discovered. Through it, people recognize and accept their own subjectivity and irrational actions. It is closely aligned with existential and humanistic psychology, and opposes the objectivity stressed in the behavioral sciences. The report indicates that many theorists in these fields "now feel

strongly a need to begin stressing the valuable contributions to creative thinking and insight which come from relaxing and making friends with the nonobjective aspects of one's mind." The arts have a unique place in education because "they deal directly with emotional, intuitive, and subjective responses." (*E.P.C. Report* 1967, p. 6). This is perhaps the most humanistic of the rationales provided, since it focuses on the human as both a rational and an irrational being.

6. The *End-of-Work rationale* is the most future oriented of the commission's justifications. It goes beyond the leisure-time concept mentioned before, to that time in the remote future when machines may replace all activities by which people now earn their livelihoods. It predicts a time when "usefulness," now attributed to work and deeply rooted in the Puritan Ethic, will be redirected toward those intellectual and creative enterprises producing a society of individuals who are concerned "with each other, with themselves, and with whatever expressive endeavors might meet their taste" (*E.P.C. Report* 1967, p. 9). The commission was not concerned with art for leisure, which is terminal, but with the actual end of a major value orientation based on work.

In the meantime, we still have the arts as creative recreational and leisure-time pursuits. They counteract destructive activities which seem to result from long hot summers, prisons, and unemployment—situations in which people find excessive time on their hands, with an itch for something to do. Given a frustrated society or a hostile environment, the combination makes for explosive situations which can result in such destructive expressions as riots and gang wars. In a healthy society, or an open environment, this element of excess time and the itch to do can be diverted into creative expressions through various forms of the arts, community theater, dance, and parallel activities.

7. The *Art-for-the-World-of-Work rationale* will still be maintained as an arts justification until we reach the commission's end-of-work prophecy. Young people must still find their role in society through job orientation. For healthy maturing growth, this should take place in late puberty or early adolescence. The elementary arts and classroom teachers have a responsibility to let children with a particular talent or interest in the arts know that art careers are of as much importance as those of the postman, the policeman, and other community helpers and are available to them too.

The scope of the fine arts practitioner has moved far and away beyond the last century's painter-starving-in-a-garret stereotype. Included in the arts today are commercial and industrial design, graphics, advertising, package design, television and filmmaking, textile design, book illustration, and such areas of environmental design as architecture, landscape architecture, and community planning. Moreover art museums need historians, conservators, and curators. Besides, we will still want painters and crafts persons to give us those individual and exclusive works of art which cannot be mass-produced or computerized.

8. *Enriching the Nonart Curriculum* is closely related to the education-through-arts approaches discussed in the previous chapter. The arts help textbook subject matter come alive. As novels provide an empathy for people and events of the past which history books do not, so paintings and other illustrations provide visual statements of the past which communicate details and feelings which pages of unbroken text cannot do. They also open up lively discussion among, and communicate to children with reading problems. Working in an art medium or technique, or recreating subject matter through making a movie or mural, both reinforces and enriches the learning process, which general textbook programs cannot do.

Each of these eight rationales are roles the arts play in public school education. Although briefly described, they do include most of the priorities essential to an elementary art and humanities program. A well-planned arts program, whether in the single classroom for a year, or throughout the entire school from kindergarten to grade six, is balanced between aspects of these eight rationales and the National Assessment objectives. Art projects do not constitute a total arts program by themselves. They need some relatedness to each other, the children, and the broader aspects of the arts and humanities to be considered as part of an art *program*.

Reinforcing Activities

1. Review the National Assessment in Art Objectives. Categorize your own art education activities and approaches according to the related objective.
2. Discuss in class the eight rationales for the arts and determine classroom activities which might make them realizable in your classroom or at a specific grade level.
3. Compare the National Assessment in Art Objectives and the eight rationales for the arts with local or state art curriculum guides to determine similarities and differences.
4. If you are currently teaching or practice-teaching in a school district, obtain a copy of the board of education's statement of philosophy and objectives for the district. What aspects of the objectives and rationales discussed in this chapter can help the district philosophy and objectives become realizable in your classroom?

References

EDUCATIONAL POLICIES COMMISSION REPORT. "The Role of the Fine Arts in Education." Washington, D.C.: National Education Association, 1968. Reprinted in *Art Education* 21, no. 7 (1968):3-7.

RUSSELL, JAMES E. "The Role of the Arts in Education." In *Conference on Curriculum and Instruction Development in*

Art Education: A Project Report. Project No. 6-1772, ED017-045. Alice H. D. Baumgarner, Director. Washington, D. C.: National Art Education Association, 1967.

WILSON, BRENT. *Art Objectives.* Denver: National Assessment Office, 1971.

4

Values development:
aesthetic, moralistic, and ethical

When reading chapters 2 and 3 about the differences between vocational training and fine arts education did you find yourself identifying with one point of view more than the other?

Think back.

How have your own art experiences, or lack of them, in school and at home, given you your present arts- and humanities-related value system? Does it reflect your parents' attitude towards art? Does it reflect the socio-economic system in which you grew up? If it differs from the attitude of your parents, to what extent? What value do you place on the arts in your life? Do you place the same value on the arts in education?

Only you can answer these questions. This chapter will deal with types of humanistic values, how we develop value systems, and traditional American values effecting the teaching of the arts in the schools.

Types of Humanistic Value Systems

A value system is generally a set of values related to a specific aspect of society. They may be monetary, religious, moral, ethical, cultural, aesthetic, and the like. There are two sets of values to which humanistic studies are applied in the schools, (1) aesthetic values and (2) moral and ethical values.

Aesthetic values are concerned with the quality of works of art, musical composition, writing, cinema, and of performances within the arts, including reading aloud. Although famous artists, monetary values, and historical factors are generally considered nonaesthetic aspects of art, they have been included here under aesthetic values because they deal directly with the work of art rather than applying the work of art to an extra-art or nonart purpose.

Moral and ethical values, as extracted from works of art might be called applied humanities. Such works as paintings, sculpture, music, dances, plays, novels, poems, and films are studied for what they reveal of the human enterprise, attitudes about love, pleasure, war and peace, right and wrong, and so forth.

Throughout history artists, novelists, composers, choreographers, dramatists, poets, and filmmakers have used their art forms to express moral conflict. The arts have been a seedbed for planting and growing human values in successive generations of human beings. They also provide the seedlings of change in social and cultural values, and reflect the disintegration of values.

In his mural, *Guernica*, Pablo Picasso depicted the horrors of war following the first saturation bombing of the entire town of Guernica, Spain, by German planes under the order of General Francisco Franco on April 26, 1937. The effect of war on human beings has been a popular theme in literature from Euripides' *The Trojan Women*, through Leo Tolstoy's *War and Peace*, to Stephen Crane's *Red Badge of Courage* and Margaret Mitchell's *Gone With the Wind*.

The conflict with evil, as depicted through the temptations of St. Anthony, is a frequent theme in western European art. Both Pieter Brueghel the Elder and Max Ernst depicted St. Anthony's temptations as evil, ugly, repulsive; lizards, salamanders, and demons picking at his old anguished body. More reasonably, Sassetta depicted one temptation as a beautiful young girl, though, not too noticeable to St. Anthony, with small devil's wings on her back. Each artist made moral judgments about temptations. However, temptations in themselves are not ugly. They are attractive and seductive; otherwise, how can they tempt?

Contemporary American values are depicted through the giant Campbell's soup cans and Brillo boxes of Andy Warhol, the comic strip paintings of Roy Lichtenstein, and the various Pop art and anti-art movements. The visual arts reflect the values of a society and culture through its activities and images. They reflect the breakdown of value systems through what Erich Kahler calls "the disintegration of form" (1968).

Conflicts between individuals with opposing value orientations provide the basis of much of our literature. They are fought in the living room of Edith Wharton, on the high seas of Henry Melville and Joseph Conrad, in the New England settings of Nathaniel Hawthorne and Eugene O'Neill, and on the various European hillsides and towns of Ernest Hemingway. The constancy of conflict between two generations within the same family are exemplified in William Shakespeare's *Romeo and Juliet* and John Steinbeck's *East of Eden*.

Values Formations and Conflicts

How do these value conflicts arise, if as the ancient Greeks believed, there are three eternal or universal truths (eternal verities), *truth, beauty,* and *goodness*? The conflicts arise because of the diverse nature of human needs, which are not the same as human values. They are, none the less intricately interrelated. Milton

Rokeach, in *The Nature of Human Values,* suggests that values are the representation of human (individual), societal, and institutional needs. They result from both sociological and psychological forces acting upon the individual.[1]

There is little doubt that we are living through a period of dynamic change and confusion about our values and value systems. As long as children and adults continue to grow, meet different life experiences, change their peer orientations, and recognize new personal human needs they will be confronted by differing sets of values. The source of these values is a complex maze of social, economic, and educational factors which might be called the "cultural environment." It consists of (1) *cultural institutions,* such as the home (family and relatives), churches, schools, prisons, and museums, (2) *community factors,* such as neighbors, peers, public opinion, and the physical surroundings, and (3) *influencing media,* such as television, radio, movies, literature, periodicals, art, and theater. People motivate these various forces of the cultural environment, and sustain and perpetuate the values related to them. Conflicts in a value system can only be the result of a viable culture. And our culture, it would seem, has never been more alive than at the present time.

Gordon W. Allport, a humanistic psychologist, defines an individual value system as a "personal schemata of values" directly related to the individual's self-image. He describes its development through three stages leading from the external sanctions of "must consciousness" (integrating personal values) to the "ought consciousness," giving direction to personal conduct (Allport 1955, pp. 73-78).

Another humanistic psychologist, Abraham Maslow extends the "must-ought" structure to an is-ought reality system, wherein a fusion of facts and values lead to an individual forming a self-image. Maslow defines facts as the "is" reality recognitions (tell it the way it is), which are different than "ought" recognitions (the verbal tradition of value systems). They may fuse for an individual through peak experiences of self-discovery or through introspective activities. Therapeutic processes may require an arduous route for the individual personalities of the "is" and the "ought to be," and the projective self-image to change sufficiently to become compatible with each other. At that time, a realistic self-image leads to a healthy self-actualizing life. "Getting rid of arbitrary 'oughts' and 'shoulds' makes possible an embracing and enjoying of what is."[2]

Well-selected examples in the arts and humanities can provide the basis for classroom discussion and lead to the personal resolution of value conflicts before they threaten the growing individual's self-image. They provide a basis on which to resolve confusions about value decisions and valuactions. These confusions result from conflicts between *is realities* and *ought recognitions,* or between two or more differing ought recognitions. The following diagram may help illustrate this point (see fig. 4.1).

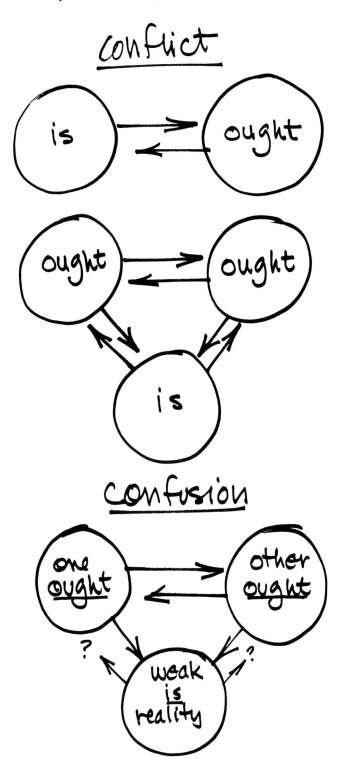

Figure 4.1 Conflicts and confusions.

1. Milton Rokeach, *The Nature of Human Values,* Copyright © 1973 by The Free Press, a division of Macmillan Publishing Co., Inc., pp. 19-21.
2. From *The Farther Reaches of Human Nature* by Abraham Maslow. Copyright © 1971 by Bertha G. Maslow. Reprinted by permission of The Viking Press, Inc., p. 114.

The diagram above (fig. 4.1) might be applied to children in the two following situations. The ought recognitions (fig. 4.2) can be either adult authority or peer authority, that is, another child or a friend. The example of the art and classroom teachers (fig. 4.3) represents a frequent conflict of values, not just between the art teacher and classroom teachers, but between the art teacher, principal, and custodian. The example is not farfetched. An elementary art teacher told the author of an actual incident which was very similar. There was no place left in the art room for the children to lay out their watercolor paintings to dry, so she had them hold their pictures flat in front of them while lined up at the door for the classroom teacher to arrive. On arrival, the classroom teacher reacted, when the children showed her their paintings by pointing to the trash barrel at the door and saying, "Throw those messy things out right here. I don't want them dripping on my floor." The children as they marched from the *is* reality of the art room into the *is* reality of the classroom threw their paintings into the trash barrel. The art teacher was so dumbfounded and so angry that she could not rescue the situation with an alternative action.

As they grow up, children develop moral and ethical value systems of their own. Altercations between adults, or inconsistencies between the ought recognition and *is* reality behavior of an adult authority figure (teacher or parent) can only add confusion to the child's own development of a value system which helps decide action.

Stages of Moral Growth

Jean Piaget, and seven assistants, studied the way children at different ages played the game of marbles. They analyzed and synthesized the results, and in *The Moral Judgment of the Child* (1962) published what at the time was a unique theory. Through the game of marbles they observed that children make their own rules, make variations on existing rules, and accept those handed down from older children. They then extrapolated what they observed by applying it to a wider range of moral development and ethical procedure discovered through dialogue with children.

Piaget with his assistants in the Department of Child Psychology, University of Geneva, identified three stages of moral development in children: (1) the *motor rule*, (2) the *coercive rule*, and (3) the *rational rule*.

The *motor rule* (about ten months to two or three years) covers a period of preverbal motor intelligence relatively independent of any social contract of a ritualistic nature developing out of a repetition of activity. Children do not distinguish between their own rules and those from the outside (eating, sleeping, eliminating body waste) until the age of two years. As they play more with other children, they begin to recognize other game rules.

The *coercive rule* (two or three to seven years) is a period of *unilateral respect*, reflecting the egocentrism usually identified with this age. Although these children know certain outside rules exist, they still prefer to use their own. It is both a presocial and parasocial stage in which children must still learn to separate their egos from the outside (sociocentric) suggestions and learn to cooperate one with the other. According to Piaget, egocentric rationale interprets all outside rules as universal and are thereby transcendental. He further relates egocentrism with the belief in the divine origins of institutions.[3]

The stage of *rational rules* (seven to twelve years) begins the period leading to mutual respect which should begin about twelve or thirteen years of age. Here children begin to select those rules they will follow and those they will not, those individuals they will follow and those they will not. Their decisions are based on a rationale of mutual respect between themselves and the rule giver. It is a period of reciprocity and agreement. Rules may be changed by common consent. Piaget makes a distinction here between mutual respect and mutual consent as felt by two personalities, and which is specifically related to the child's concept of morality. The rational rule is defined as either a *constitutive rule* which is practical or theoretical, and the *constituted rule* which results from mutual consent and can be altered by general opinion.

The interrelationship between one stage and the other, and the factors which continue from one to the other is much more complex than that discussed here. Lawrence Kohlberg, in building on the work of Piaget provides the three main stages with a different nomenclature and provides a series of six substages. Kohlberg and his colleagues studied a group of seventy-five boys for twelve years, into young adulthood. They compared their results with those of children in Taiwan, Mexico, Turkey, and Yucatan to determine the potential universal structuralism of their findings.

Kohlberg (1968) identified three major levels of moral development: (1) the preconventional, (2) conventional, and (3) postconventional. Each has two substages, making a total of six stages.

Preconventional level (generally four to ten years):
Stage 1—oriented toward punishment. Children accept superior power. The physical consequences of an action determines its goodness or badness regardless of its human meaning or value.
Stage 2—oriented toward satisfying one's needs and occasionally the needs of others. Elements of fairness and reciprocity, and of equal sharing, are interpreted in a physical (material), practical way.

Conventional level (about ten to thirteen years):
Stage 3—oriented towards being good boys and girls. They try to please or help others for approval, and con-

3. Jean Piaget, *The Moral Judgment of the Child.* Translated by Marjorie Gabin. Copyright © 1962. Crowell-Collier Publ. Co., p. 93. By permission of Macmillan Publishing Co., Inc.

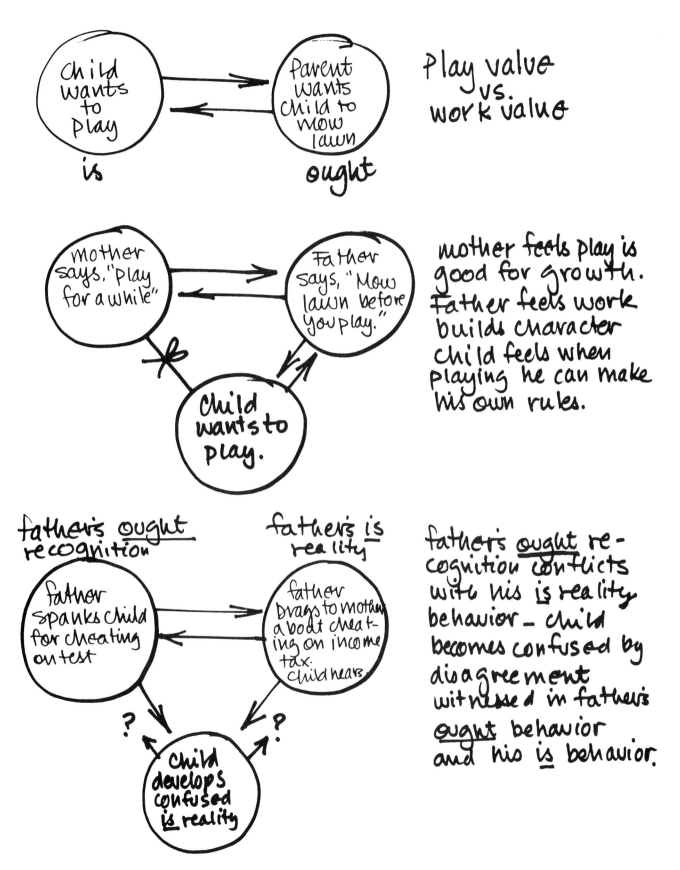

Figure 4.2 Value conflicts and confusions.

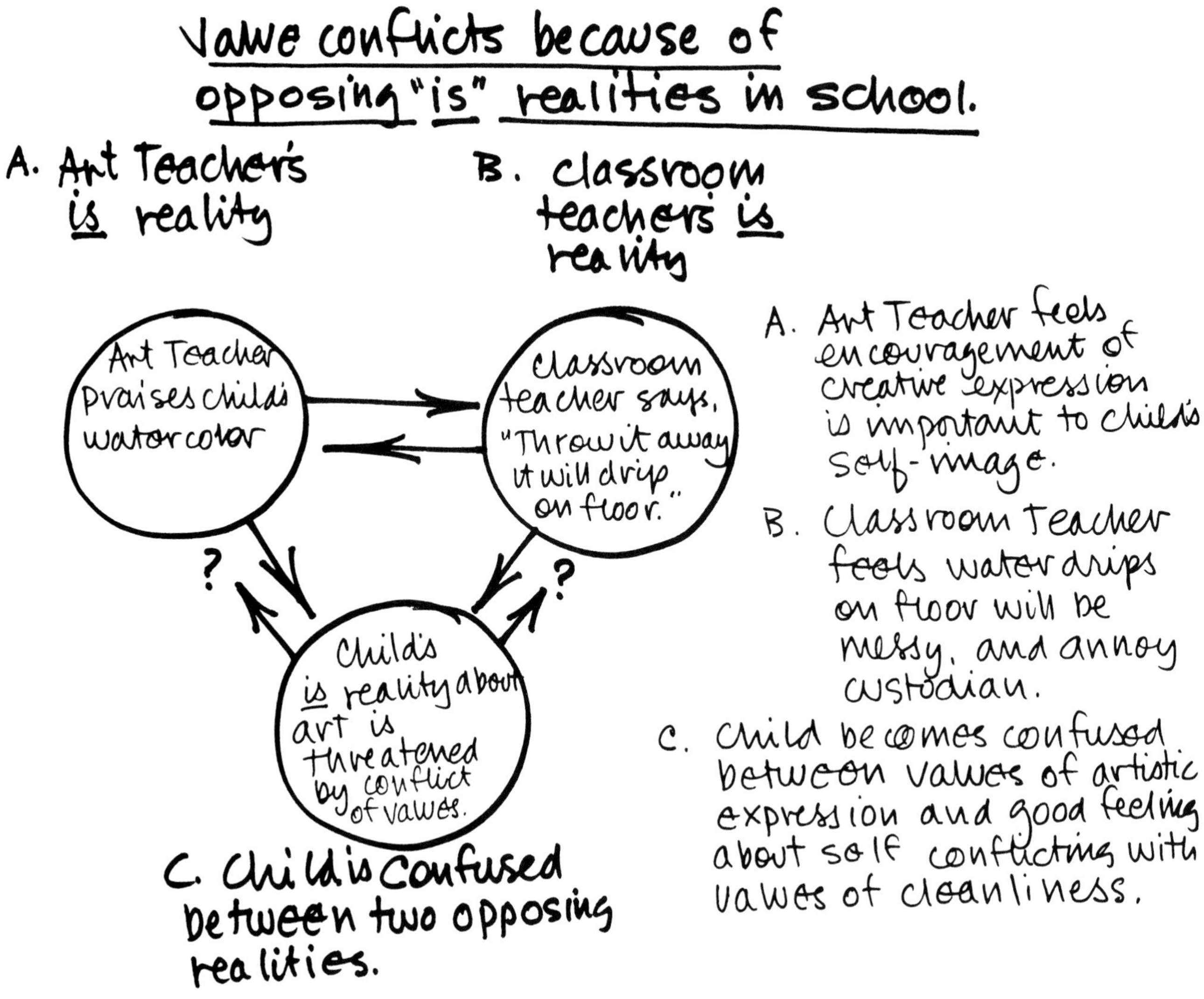

Vawe conflicts because of opposing "is" realities in school.

A. Art Teacher's is reality

B. classroom teacher's is reality

Art Teacher praises child's watercolor

classroom teacher says, "Throw it away it will drip on floor."

?   ?

Child's is reality about art is threatened by conflict of vawes.

C. Child is Confused between two opposing realities.

A. Art Teacher feels encouragement of creative expression is important to child's self-image.

B. Classroom Teacher feels water drips on floor will be messy, and annoy custodian.

C. Child becomes confused between vawes of artistic expression and good feeling about self conflicting with vawes of cleanliness.

Figure 4.3   Value conflicts because of opposing is realities in school.

form to stereotypical images of the majorities' natural or good behavior. Even when misjudging the situation and behaving wrongly, it is important to know "He (or she) meant well."

Stage 4—oriented towards authority, fixed rules, and doing one's duty. Individuals show respect for authority, and maintain social order for its own sake.

Postconventional level (about sixteen years and up):

Stage 5—oriented towards contracting with some legalistic and utilitarian overtones in terms of general rights and standards agreed upon by the whole society. Individuals may be aware of relative values and opinions aside from those democratically and constitutionally agreed upon. They may follow legal procedures of consensus to change the law, and maintain the official view of the United States government as grounded in the Constitution.

Stage 6—oriented toward decisions of conscience, self-chosen ethical principles, abstract rules (such as the

golden rule), and categorical imperatives, rather than the Ten Commandments. Individuals follow principles of justice, reciprocity, equal human rights, and respect the dignity of human beings as individual persons.

According to Kohlberg and the study team, the age relationships are approximate, since they are based on the largest percentage of children's ages for a specific level. The range is somewhat greater. For example, seventy percent of the ten-year-old middle-class urban boys questioned were at the preconventional level, while thirty percent moved to the conventional level. None were at the postconventional level. At thirteen years, fifty percent had moved to the conventional level, while five percent moved to stage 5 of the postconventional level, and less than five percent moved to stage 6. However, at sixteen years of age, about thirty percent reached stage 5, and eight percent reached stage 6 of the postconventional levels, but forty-five percent remained at the conventional level, and twenty-three percent remained at the preconventional stage.

Kohlberg's cross-cultural studies indicated that a greater difference was evident between socioeconomic levels than between different cultures. Movement could stop at any level, but progress was made through the same sequence of stages. Middle-class children advanced more rapidly and went further toward moral judgments than children in the lower economic working-class groups. Religious orientations (Catholics, Protestants, Jews, Buddhists, Moslems, and atheists) showed no important difference. They still followed the same stages. Kohlberg raises some questions about whether stage 5 is a step to stage 6, or if each is an alternate stage and more or less terminal.

Kohlberg's team experimented with moral discussion classes. They found children in earlier stages tended to move forward when confronted with the views of children just one stage beyond them. Children in the stage beyond understood the stage below, but no longer accepted the arguments of that stage. Children and adolescents can be encouraged, or lead, to move to a new stage by verbalizing their conflicts or confusions. It is not the purpose of this chapter to give examples of such discussions. Raths, Harmin, and Simon (1966); Simon, Howe, and Kirschenbaum (1972); and Weinstein and Fantini (1970) provide practical suggestions for classroom use in developing values, but they are not related to the arts and humanities as such. Chapter 6, on the core monument is designed to give the reader themes for dealing with values and human needs found in arts and humanities subject matter.

Major Social Values

What, then, are those values which confront children with confusions and conflicts as they grow into adulthood? During a time of changing values, do they really change or is it the priorities we give them which change? For answers we might turn to those sociologists who have concentrated on social values, and the cultural environment that either sustains them or encourages their change. The major value configurations of a people or a country, or within a given period of time, reflect those aspects of an organized cultural environment considered most essential by that people or country, or within that period of time. As cultural environments change, the balance between dominant and subordinate value qualities may also shift.

The sociologist Robin M. Williams, Jr., identified fifteen major value orientations that have developed through the course of United States history:[4]

1. Achievement and success
2. Activity and work
3. Moral orientation
4. Humanitarian mores
5. Efficiency and practicality
6. Progress
7. Material comforts
8. Equality
9. Freedom
10. External conformity
11. Science and secular rationality
12. Nationalism—patriotism
13. Democracy
14. Individual personality and the countervalues
15. Racism and related group superiority themes

Some closely related values reinforce each other. Such values as achievement and success, activity and work, moral orientation, efficiency and practicality, progress, and material comforts comprise six of the fifteen values. Together they make up the most continuous single frame of reference for establishing value priorities in the growth of the United States—the Puritan (or Protestant) Ethic. Efficiency and practicality are closely related to science and rationality. Material comforts demonstrate achievement and success through activity and work.

Other values conflict with one another. Equality, freedom, and individual personality conflict with external conformity, which by its very terminology suggests the existence of an internal nonconformity. Democracy has elements of both types. Although it symbolizes freedom in many minds, democracy encourages external conformity through majority rule.

The one value most persistent, yet most difficult to maintain, is equality. Along with individual personality it conflicts with the countervalue of racism and superiority themes which give privileges or deny rights to individuals through the chance of birth into a particular ethnic group or socioeconomic class. It is listed as a "countervalue" since it most sharply opposes all other values listed above it. It nonetheless remains highly valued in terms of race and religious beliefs, a form of the egocentrism suggested by Piaget.

Science and secular rationality, and the scientific predicability related to them, are currently influencing our educational systems through the twentieth-century predeterminism of B. F. Skinner. In *Beyond Freedom and Dignity* (1971) he succeeds in combining the values of efficiency, practicality, and progress with science and secular rationalism.

The arts however can be related to freedom (of expression), and individual personality. Through the humanities the arts can be identified with humanistic mores and moral orientation. Material comfort, a resultant symbol of achievement and success is identified in this value structure with leisure time, which conflicts with the more predominant value of activity and work. The same can be said of such leisure-time activities as the performing arts, music, dance, and theater. However, the artisan was identified with activity and work until his handcrafting skills were replaced by factory

4. Robin M. Williams, Jr., *American Society: A Sociological Interpretation,* second edition, revised. Copyright 1960 by Alfred A. Knopf, Inc., pp. 417-68.

machines. Artisans became factory workers. During the mid-nineteenth century the painter began to be viewed as a hardworking, dedicated individual having a noble but impractical occupation, and starving in a garret. Since artists and performers occupations did not really sustain even these values, they were looked upon, from the standpoint of group superiority standards, as being generally immoral and without values of any sort.

Art, Humanities, and Traditional Values

Milton Rokeach, the social psychologist, has studied American belief structures and value systems for many years. In his *The Nature of Human Values* (previously referred to) he has provided a slightly different set of values, and studied the priorities given them. Rokeach defines a value as "an enduring belief that a specific mode of conduct or end-state of existence is personally or socially preferable to an opposite or converse mode or end-state of existence." He goes on to define a value system as an "enduring organization of beliefs concerning preferable modes of conduct or end-states of existence along a continuum of relative importance."[5]

Rokeach also identifies two types of values, *terminal* and *instrumental*. Terminal values concern desirable end-states of existence, and consist of two subtypes, *personal* and *social* values. Personal values are self-centered and intrapersonal end-states, such as salvation and peace of mind. Social values are society-centered and interpersonal end-states, such as world peace and brotherhood. People tend to vary their priorities on personal and social terminal values. Their behavior varies accordingly. (See the list in the next column.)

Instrumental values concern desirable modes of conduct, and also consist of two subtypes, *moral* and *competence* values. Moral values refer to modes of behavior and are directed toward interpersonal (social) interaction, which, when violated, lead to pangs of conscience. Competence values are personal, self-actualizing values, which, when violated, cause feelings of shame about personal inadequacy rather than guilt at wrongdoing. Moral behavior is considered honest and responsible, whereas competent behavior is considered logical, intelligent, and imaginative.

Rokeach designed a survey consisting of eighteen terminal and eighteen instrumental values. Eighteen seemed to be about as many items as an individual could arrange in order of rank while still retaining a sense of the whole system. His list contains several values identified by Williams as major social values. Unlike Williams's purpose, his was to identify priorities according to socioeconomic, age, sex, racial (white/black), educational, and religious differences. His range is therefore broader than the list by Williams, since it also includes minor values. Several can be specifically related to the arts and humanities. Terminal values related to the arts and humanities are a world of beauty (beauty of nature and the arts), a sense of accomplishment (lasting contributions), pleasure (an enjoyable leisurely life), self-respect (self-esteem), and wisdom

Value Survey Basic List[6]

Terminal Values

A comfortable life (a prosperous life)
An exciting life (a stimulating, active life)
A sense of accomplishment (lasting contribution)
A world at peace (free of war and conflict)
A world of beauty (beauty of nature and the arts)
Equality (brotherhood, equal opportunity for all)
Family security (taking care of loved ones)
Freedom (independence, free choice)
Happiness (contentedness)
Inner harmony (freedom from inner conflict)
Mature love (sexual and spiritual intimacy)
National security (protection from attack)
Pleasure (an enjoyable, leisurely life)
Salvation (saved, eternal life)
Self-respect (self-esteem)
Social recognition (respect, admiration)
True friendship (close companionship)
Wisdom (a mature understanding of life)

Instrumental Values

Ambitious (hardworking, aspiring)
Broad-minded (open-minded)
Capable (competent, effective)
Cheerful (lighthearted, joyful)
Clean (neat, tidy)
Courageous (standing up for your beliefs)
Forgiving (willing to pardon others)
Helpful (working for the welfare of others)
Honest (sincere, truthful)
Imaginative (daring, creative)
Independent (self-reliant, self-sufficient)
Intellectual (intelligent, reflective)
Logical (consistent, rational)
Loving (affectionate, tender)
Obedient (dutiful, respectful)
Polite (courteous, well-mannered)
Responsible (dependable, reliable)
Self-controlled (restrained, self-disciplined)

(a mature understanding of life). Others, such as social recognition, freedom, and inner harmony are associated with arts goals but not limited to them. Although most of the above values are found as goals and objectives in arts and humanities curriculum guides, wisdom does not seem to be among them.

Instrumental values most attributable to the arts and humanities are: imaginative (daring and creative), broad-minded (open-minded), capable (competent, effective), and independent (self-reliant, self-sufficient). Other instrumental values listed by Rokeach, such as clean (neat, tidy), and logical (consistent, rational), might be given low priority ratings by art teachers, but high ratings by classroom teachers and principals. The reader may question this list of arts related values, or make changes in it.

5. Rokeach, p. 5.
6. Rokeach, *Nature of Human Values*, p. 28.

Rokeach and his research teams surveyed over 7,500 individuals—students from elementary through graduate school in various academic fields, and hippies, at all income levels, and among different races. He has provided an elaborate set of charts showing RHO correlations, median scores, and rank orders. Among the instrumental values, *honesty* ranked first by almost every category, except for the hippies, who ranked it second, and *imaginative* first. Almost all other categories ranked *imaginative* lowest at the 17 and 18 levels—except for college graduates and those in academic fields who ranked it between 3 and 10.

Among the terminal values, *a world at peace* was constantly ranked first or second in all categories except for college students who ranked it 10, perhaps in reaction to not having been drafted. *A world of beauty* was ranked consistently low, 14, 15, and 16, with a few around 11 and 12. The hippies and liberal artists rated it 8 and 5. In view of our increasing concern over the ecological imbalance, pollution, and the quality of life, the need for education to raise a world of beauty to a higher value becomes accordingly evident. On the school age list, the eleven-year-olds ranked it seventh, but it declined to seventeenth place by college groups and remained there for adults. Rokeach attributes this to the socialization process which "destroyed the young adolescent's initial appreciation of beauty by replacing it with other values that are deemed more important."[7] *A sense of accomplishment* was ranked first by the biological, physical, and social scientists, and second by those in liberal arts. Among the eleven-year-olds, it ranked sixteenth, which Rokeach interprets with the child's lack of sufficient maturity to know about it or recognize it as a value.[8]

For a selection of composite rank scores from those categories which may interest elementary art and classroom teachers the most, see Table 4.1. It lists rank scores according to age, and educational levels, income, sex, and race. Careful study will indicate that the greatest differences are between low and high income levels, and in racial differences as they reflect income level and equality. Terminal value differences for the income category are greatest for *a sense of accomplishment, wisdom, a comfortable life,* and *salvation*. Instrumental value differences for the income category are greatest for *broad-minded, clean,* and *responsible*. It is not clear whether by "clean (neat and tidy)" the high value placed on that category by the lower-income and the black respondents was in terms of health or aesthetic order. The indication is that a high value is placed on a visual order and spatial arrangement. Within the ghetto, this is also a high value of Puerto Rican migrants to mainland cities. This has considerable importance in setting standards or determining values when middle-income teachers are in lower-income, or inner-city, schools. In reverse, teachers rising from lower-income backgrounds teaching in upper-middle-class schools will also be confronted with a different value system.

It may be well to note in particular the responses to those value priorities related to the arts and humanities by school children, especially the eleven- and thirteen-year-olds who are most likely taught by the elementary teachers using this book. Among the instrumental values, *imaginative* ranked sixteenth and seventeenth, *broad-minded* was fifteenth and sixteenth, *capable* was eleventh and ninth, *independent* was twelfth and fourteenth, and *intellectual* was seventeenth and fifteenth, respectively. Among the eleven- and thirteen-year-olds, terminal values such as *a world of beauty* ranked seventh and twelfth, *a sense of accomplishment* was sixteenth and thirteenth, *pleasure* was thirteenth and tenth, *self-respect* came in fourteenth at both ages, *wisdom* was tenth and then seventh, while a *comfortable life* ranked eighth both times. This points to a middle or low priority for those values relating to the arts and humanities.

The reasons for ranking some values high and others low are contradictory. *Equality* ranked second by black people may indicate a desire for something they do not have, but strive for. Ranked eleventh by the white people it may indicate equality as being taken for granted, and therefore not valued. It may also reflect a white inclination to keep it low, so as not to feel guilty when it is not given to minority groups. Low ranking may also indicate lack of knowledge about or experience with a particular value, such as *intellectual, imaginative,* or *a world of beauty*. As a result, it would not be considered important, and therefore would not be wanted.

If one purpose of the arts and humanities in the elementary schools is to develop moral, ethical, aesthetic, and humanistic values, then the teacher must be prepared to do a remedial job first, and seriously consider the low esteem in which the children may first hold some of these values. To what extent our traditional values are changing, or can be changed, remains to be seen. It is the future toward which we are reaching—and teaching.

Current Values: Status Quo or Quo Vadis?

During periods of stress or conflict, such as wars and depressions, or during times of plenty, the priorities placed on specific values change their hierarchical order. How the values are interpreted also changes. At present, we are passing through a period of great social change and radical transition. At least, the prevailing belief of the times, lead by Marshall McLuhan (1962), Philip E. Slater (1970), Alvin Toffler (1970), and Charles E. Reich (1970), among others, would have us believe so. Although their observation of accelerated speeds in all aspects of our lives may be considerably hampered, as it was in the winter of 1973-74, with a fuel and energy crisis, we may nevertheless, despite

7. Ibid., p. 78.
8. Ibid., p. 62.

TABLE 4.1
TERMINAL AND INSTRUMENTAL VALUES
Consolidated Rank Order

Based on charts from, M. Rokeach, The Nature of Human Values. (Page references in parentheses)

TERMINAL VALUES	AGE (p.76)				SEX (p.57)		INCOME (p.60)							EDUCATION (p.64)							RACE (p.67)	
	11	13	15	17	M	F	UNDER 2,000	2,000-3,999	4,000-5,999	6,000-7,999	8,000-9,999	10,000-14,999	15,000-OVER	0-4 YRS	5-8 YRS	SOME HIGH SCHOOL	COMPLETE HIGH SCH.	SOME COLLEGE	COMPLETED COLLEGE	GRADUATE SCHOOL	WHITE	BLACK
World of Beauty	7	12	14	16	15	15	14	14	15	15	15	15	13	16	14	15	15	15	15	12	15	16
Sense of Accomplishment	16	13	12	10	7	10	12	12	9	10	8	6	5	13	12	11	9	6	4	4	8	11
Pleasure	13	10	17	15	17	16	16	17	16	11	17	16	18	14	16	17	17	16	18	18	17	17
Self-Respect	14	14	10	17	6	6	8	4	5	7	6	4	7	7	8	5	5	5	6	6	5	6
Wisdom	10	7	6	4	8	7	10	9	8	5	7	5	4	11	11	8	6	4	4	2	6	8
World at Peace	1	1	1	1	1	1	1	1	2	2	2	2	1	1	1	2	2	2	1	1	1	1
A Comfortable Life	8	8	12		4	13	6	7	7	6	11	13	15	3	6	7	12	13	15	15	12	5
An Exciting Life	11	9	13	13	18	18	18	18	18	18	18	18	16	18	18	18	18	18	16	14	18	18
Equality	6	4	4	2	9	8	5	8	6	9	5	9	6	12	9	9	7	8	8	7	11	12
Family Security	3	2	3	6	2	2	2	2	2	2	1	2	2	2	2	1	1	1	5	5	2	4
Freedom	2	3	2	3	3	3	4	3	3	3	3	3	3	4	3	3	3	3	3	3	3	3
Happiness	5	6	7	5	5	5	7	6	4	4	4	4	8	5	5	4	4	10	10	10	4	7
Inner Harmony	12	17	15	9	13	12	13	13	13	13	13	11	11	9	13	13	13	9	9	9	13	12
Mature Love	9	11	11	11	14	14	17	16	14	14	14	14	12	17	15	14	14	11	11	11	14	14
National Security	15	15	9	17	10	11	11	12	11	10	8	11	8	10	10	10	10	12	13	13	9	13
Salvation	18	18	18	18	12	4	3	5	11	8	9	12	14	8	4	6	8	11	14	17	16	15
Social Recognition	17	16	16	14	16	17	15	15	17	16	16	17	17	15	17	16	16	17	17	16	7	9
True Friendship	4	5	6	8	11	9	9	10	10	12	10	10	10	6	7	12	11	12	7	8	10	10

Art & Human-ities related Values [bracket spanning: World of Beauty, Sense of Accomplishment, Pleasure, Self-Respect, Wisdom]

Source: Based on charts from Milton Rokeach, The Nature of Human Values. Page references appear in parentheses on columnar headings.

Based on Charts from, M. Rokeach, The Nature of Human Values.
(Page references in parentheses.)

INSTRUMENTAL VALUES	RACE (p.68) BLACK	RACE (p.68) WHITE	EDUCATION (p.65) GRADUATE SCHOOL	COMPLETED COLLEGE	SOME COLLEGE	COMPLETE HIGH SCHOOL	SOME HIGH SCHOOL	5–8 YRS.	0–4 YRS.	INCOME (p.61) 15,000–OVER	10,000–14,999	8,000–9,999	6,000–7,999	4,000–5,999	2,000–3,999	UNDER 2,000	SEX (p.50) M	F	AGE (p.77) 11	13	15	17
Imaginative	18	18	10	15	17	18	18	18	18	15	18	18	18	18	18	18	18	18	16	17	18	18
Broadminded	8	5	3	3	4	4	8	7	10	4	4	4	6	8	8	5	4	5	15	16	14	6
Capable	5	10	9	9	7	11	11	13	11	4	4	11	8	4	2	10	8	12	11	9	8	7
Independent	10	13	7	7	9	12	14	14	15	8	7	7	11	11	14	14	11	14	12	14	10	8
Intellectual	16	15	11	11	12	16	16	16	16	7	15	15	16	16	16	16	15	16	17	15	15	14
Ambitious	2	3	5	4	3	3	3	3	3	3	3	3	3	3	3	3	2	4	10	4	3	2
Cheerful	12	12	14	14	14	9	9	8	5	14	12	10	12	9	9	9	12	10	3	12	13	15
Clean	3	8	16	17	16	13	14	4	4	5	5	5	5	8	8	10	9	8	6	8	9	11
Courageous	7	6	4	5	7	6	7	6	13	12	5	8	5	5	4	7	5	6	8	10	7	5
Forgiving	5	4	6	12	13	7	4	4	2	6	6	5	4	4	2	3	6	2	5	6	5	10
Helpful	6	7	8	8	5	5	5	7	4	8	8	8	7	6	6	4	7	7	4	3	6	9
Honest	1	1	1	1	1	1	1	1	1	1	1	1	1	1	1	1	1	1	1	1	1	1
Logical	17	17	14	14	17	16	10	10	6	13	16	16	17	17	17	17	16	17	18	18	17	16
Loving	15	9	18	18	18	18	15	15	14	18	17	15	15	11	11	12	14	9	2	2	2	3
Obedient	14	16	17	16	14	15	16	14	15	16	14	17	15	13	11	14	17	15	14	13	16	17
Polite	11	14	2	17	16	16	11	15	12	13	16	15	15	14	13	15	13	13	7	7	11	13
Responsible	4	2	13	2	2	2	9	9	9	3	3	3	3	3	3	3	3	3	9	5	4	4
Self-controlled	9	11	13	13	6	8	12	8	8	11	9	9	9	9	9	12	10	11	13	11	12	12

Arts & Human-ities Related Values (Imaginative, Broadminded, Capable, Independent, Intellectual) such setbacks, find acceleration in some areas, even though there may be deceleration in others.

Robin M. Williams, previously discussed has given us a set of criteria by which we can identify major social values, and judge the quality or degree of their change:

1. *Extensiveness of the value* in the total system. What proportion of the population and its activities manifest, the value?

2. *Duration of the value.* Has it been persistently important over a considerable period of time?

3. *Intensity* with which the value is sought or maintained as shown by effort, crucial choices, verbal affirmation, and by reactions to threats to the value; for example, in promptness, certainty, and severity of sanctions against the threat.

4. *Prestige of the value carriers*, that is, of those persons, objects, or organizations considered to be bearers of the value. Culture heroes, for example, are significant indexes of values of high generality and esteem.[9]

This brief set of criteria might be adapted to the classroom for the purpose of trying to evaluate value change or growth, when provided with appropriate behaviors and responses. Beyond the classroom, the various examples of changing values mentioned by McLuhan, Slater, Toffler, Reich, and others might be adjudged in terms of Williams's criteria to determine if the present cultural changes indicate potential long-range and major value changes. This is particularly important in testing the extent to which the subordinate values, counterculture values, and alternate cultures (which are more artistically and humanistically oriented) will become the major cultural and social values of the future. They are certainly extensive, intense, and have prestigious leaders within their own mythology and frame of reference. Only time, and observing the young people as they pass their own thirty years of age criterion, will provide a basis for assessing their durability.

In the meantime, their children, along with all the others of the lower, middle, and upper classes in the elementary classrooms, will be the focus of the arts and humanities—and reading, writing, and so on—including the type of instructional emphasis you provide. It is here, that you, the art or classroom teacher will influence the future. Well prepared or not, your influence will leave its mark on 20 to 30 children each year for from one to twenty or more years—on from 20 to 600 or more future adults. The humanities are essentially historically oriented. The challenge put to the teachers of the humanities is to use them for assisting young people in establishing appropriate values for the future, not merely to maintain and further rigidify those of the past.

Reinforcing Activities

1. Evaluate the fifteen major social values of Williams and/or the Eighteen Terminal and Eighteen Instrumental Values of Rokeach and add those personal values which you think are missing. Compare in class discussion.

2. Rank in order of priority the fifteen major social values of Williams and/or the Eighteen Terminal and Eighteen Instrumental Values of Rokeach. What does this tell you about your own set of values when compared with Table 4.1.

3. Compare your set of values with those categories with which you personally identify, and/or will teach children who represent them. Do you find a conflict or agreement in values between you and the composite rank score for others in your categories. Can you expect conflict between your values and those expected from the children you teach?

References

ALLPORT, GORDON W. *Becoming: Basic Considerations for a Psychology of Personality.* New Haven: Yale University Press, 1955.

KAHLER, ERICH. *The Disintegration of Form in the Arts.* New York: George Braziller, 1968.

KOHLBERG, LAWRENCE. "The Child as a Moral Philosopher." *Psychology Today* 2, no. 4. (1968):25-30.

McLUHAN, MARSHALL. *Understanding Media: The Extensions of Man.* New York: McGraw-Hill Book Company, 1964.

RATHS, LOUIS E.; HARMIN, MERRILL; and SIMON, SIDNEY B. *Values and Teaching: Working with Values in the Classroom.* Columbus, Ohio: Charles E. Merrill Publishing Co., 1966.

REICH, CHARLES. *The Greening of America.* New York: Random House, 1970.

SIMON, SIDNEY B.; HOWE, LELAND W.; and KIRSCHENBAUM, HOWARD. *Value Clarifications: A Handbook of Practical Strategies for Teachers and Students.* New York: Hart Publishing Co., 1972.

SKINNER, B. F. *Beyond Freedom and Dignity.* New York: Alfred A. Knopf, 1971.

SLATER, PHILLIP E. *Pursuit of Loneliness: American Culture at the Breaking Point.* Boston: Beacon Press, 1970.

TOFFLER, ALVIN. *Future Shock.* New York: Random House, 1970.

WEINSTEIN, GERALD, and FANTINI, MARIO D., eds. *Toward Humanistic Education: A Curriculum of Affect.* New York: The Ford Foundation, Praeger Publishers, 1970.

9. Ibid., pp. 409-10.

5

Human needs
and the human ideal

In the previous chapter human values were discussed. Human needs are different from human values, but the two are interrelated in that they are unique to the human situation and are subject to humanistic persuasions. Although humanistic literature and curriculums may use the combined phrase "human needs and values," the differences between them are not often defined. In chapter 4 specific human values were defined and identified. In this chapter some human needs will be identified.

Needs, when strong enough, motivate action. They are, as Rokeach suggests, cognitively transformed into values. The need for dependence and conformity may be transformed into values such as obedience, loyalty, or respect for elders. Aggressive needs may be transformed into values of ambition, honor, family, or national security, while the need for sex is transformed into values of love, spiritual union, and intimacy (Rokeach 1973, p. 20).

All living organisms, humans, and infrahumans have life-sustaining needs. Plants need sunshine, water, and nutriment from the earth, and they propagate their species. We are discovering too, that they need music and conversation. Animals need food, water, and rest or sleep, and they propagate their species. But humans, unlike other animals, set up laws, codes of behavior, and procedures by which to fulfill their needs in socially responsible ways. To certain limited extents, animals also establish patterns of behavioral characteristics, pecking orders, territorial imperatives, and social contracts within and outside of their species. We hesitate to call these value systems.

We humans are also separated from infrahumans by our faculty of imagination and our ability to think in terms of abstractions. By virtue of our imaginative power we can establish images or concepts of ourselves outside of ourselves. We can see ourselves in terms of a time-space continuum. We can separate parts of ourselves from nature, our minds, intelligence, imagination, or conscience. We have an awareness of our birth and an expectancy for death, and therefore of our limitedness. We are aware of the problem of being alive which moves beyond our instincts for survival.

"But," as Erich Fromm puts it, "inasmuch as man is human, the satisfaction of these instinctual needs is not sufficient to make him happy. They are not even sufficient to make him sane."[1] From the condition of his existence, man has developed particular human needs which go beyond his animal needs. Identifying these

needs has been the centuries-old quest of humanistic philosophers and, more recently, of humanistic psychologists. How individuals satisfy these needs varies with the way they each respond to limitations and conflicts with themselves, and the values of the cultural environment in which they live.

Fromm: Human Needs and Conflicts

In *The Sane Society*, Erich Fromm identifies and describes five basic human needs. They can be applied to curriculums in the humanities, and to specific human values. See chapter 6 for humanistic-related themes. Fromm defines human needs in terms of conflicts or active polarities within the individual.[2]

1. *Relatedness* is the need to be part of nature, a part of the world, of the local surrounding environment, society, or culture. It conflicts with *narcissism*, the need to be free and isolated. The need to be close conflicts with the need to be independent. Fromm finds the resolution of this conflict in mature love.

2. *Transcendence* is the need to rise above or achieve beyond the nature of the passive person. It results in a conflict between *creativeness* and *destructiveness*. Each answers the need for transcendence, but when the will to create is frustrated or cannot be satisfied, it is replaced by the will to destroy.

3. *Rootedness* is the need to belong to a place or the source of life (mother, soil, home). It results in a conflict between degrees of *brotherliness* and the unhealthy relationship between family members. One aspect of rootedness is the drive to return to the natural state, to become one with nature, again, as before birth. To prevent this, all manner of taboos are established controlling son-mother/daughter-father relationships and suicide. Brotherliness is a oneness with others for social unity and survival of the pack. Rootedness is manifested in religious belief, myths of creation, and a sense of territoriality. Brotherliness is manifested in the evolution of societies, patriarchal systems, nationalism, and primogeniture.

4. *A sense of identity* is the need for *individuality* which conflicts with *herd conformity*. The constant quest

---

1. Erich Fromm, *The Sane Society* (New York: Holt, Rinehart and Winston, Inc., publishers for the United States and Canada and the open market territory outside of The British Commonwealth, 1955), pp. 31-32.

2. Ibid., pp. 33-66.

of answering "Who am I?" "What am I?" is found in the individual's struggle for self-image. It resists the urge or desire to conform or find identity (security) within the crowd.

5. *A frame of orientation and devotion* is the need to obtain reason over irrationality. Fromm finds conflict in the human confrontation with the world of unpredictable natural phenomena; that is, our responses to the bombardment of sensory perceptions and sensations, and the mystery of our own imaginations and imagery. To give them order and reason, to create a balance between reality and illusion, we had to give ourselves a point of view from which to relate to them. To do this, we have created religious systems, philosophical systems, and disciplines of inquiry to which we can devote ourselves.

There is a logical relationship between these five human needs and the previously discussed fifteen major social values of Williams, and Rokeach's terminal and instrumental values. The conflicts between need polarities reflect conflicts within individuals when confronted by different value systems, as for instance: the need for a frame of orientation has lead to science and secular rationality. The need for a sense of identity leads to the individual personality in conflict with external conformity, success, and achievement, and may also lead to racism and related group superiority themes. The need for rootedness is the basis of nationalism and patriotism. The need for transcendence encourages freedom, equality, and progress. The need for relatedness gives rise to moral orientations, humanitarian mores, and democracy, but raises a conflict with freedom. The very complexity of human needs and resultant conflicts in achieving their fulfillment seems to require a small cluster of values for each one within a particular society.

More complex than the matter of identifying human needs and values is the problem of describing the types of human beings who manifest the most positive aspects of such values, and how to help children grow into them. In this, we are dealing with human variables, as well as anticipating those individual characteristics needed for a rapidly changing future culture which has as yet unidentified requirements and conflicts within the human psyche.

Individual and Social Character

Fromm describes a sane society as one which corresponds to man's needs when they have been objectively ascertained through the study of man. He distinguishes between the individual character and the social character within a single human being, very much as Rokeach distinguishes between personal and social terminal values. The individual character maintains its uniqueness and private personality, while the social character contributes to and helps maintain the needs and functions of society. Human beings, in that each is a part of society, have within themselves both individual and social characters.

As social structures and other cultural factors change, the social character must also adapt and change. It is a product of the interaction of the ideological and sociological factors of a period. The industrial value of the nineteenth-century socioeconomic structure required value orientations exemplified by the Puritan Ethic. Its survival depended on making a social character whose inner drive was compatible with and directed toward maintaining the aims of that society.

Both the ideological and sociological factors of a culture must be understood if the social character for that period is to be understood. Accordingly, both factors in our future culture and the changes leading to their characteristics must be anticipated if the social character which is needed to maintain that culture can be described and developed. Our current educational systems and those social institutions influencing human growth need similar insight into the ideological and sociological factors of the future culture if they are going to develop a human personality capable of sustaining that culture. The real end result or goal of the humanities in education should be the "truly human" human being, one who has learned to balance the individual character with the social character, or personal values with social values. Fromm's value systems center on moral objectives, humanistic mores, and freedom (not narcissistic freedom so much as a socially conscious freedom) revealed in the centuries-old dialogue between free will and determinism. In *The Sane Society,* Fromm writes more about the social character than about the individual. He writes of a humanistic utopia, but differently than B. F. Skinner, who also writes in utopian terms.

Skinner: Programmed Human Beings

In *Beyond Freedom and Dignity,* B. F. Skinner describes a twenty-first-century determinism based more on scientific research and behavioral psychology than on a Calvinistic predestination. Although sustaining the Puritan Ethic, Skinner conceives of a godless, mythless society relating aspects of automation to behavioral conditioning. He seems to lack faith in the ability of human beings to somehow muddle through.

Skinner does not deal with such humanistic terms as relatedness, devotion, transcendence, rootedness, and identity, but is nevertheless concerned with similar concepts. He discusses freedom in terms of types of control and resistance to control, transcendence in terms of escape, relatedness in terms of an emotion which reinforces two individuals, while love is "mutual reinforcement," and loneliness results from the absence of a particular reinforcing individual. For Skinner, religion is a controlling agency both in the singular medicine man of primitive tradition and in the organized "church" of civilizations. Individuals turn to religion for ethical and moral controls on their behavior, rather than, as Fromm suggests, from a humanistic need for a frame-of-orientation and devotion. Skinner seems to associate human needs with emotions to which individuals respond with various repertories of reinforcing techniques.

"Repertories" are individual storage banks of habits and behavioral responses. "Reinforcers" are rewards and punishments leading to appropriate and inappropriate behavioral responses. Skinner's experimental analysis of human behavior is intended to "strip away the functions previously assigned to autonomous man and transfer them one by one to the controlling environment." The resulting image is "not a body with a person inside, but of a body which is a person in the sense that it displays a complex repertorie of behavior." He very rightly indicates that the result is unfamiliar. "The man thus portrayed is a stranger, and from a traditional point of view he may not be a man at all."[3]

In spite of this, Skinner still writes about man controlling his own evolution, which is an existential point of view. Yet he dismisses the existential concept of man, viewing it as something future society must do without if it is to survive. Skinner and Fromm both speak of preserving mankind and human life on this planet, but do so from opposing points of view. They speak in terms of collective concepts, societies, cultures, and utopias. They do not deal with the type of human being, the entity, which makes up this collective utopia with sufficient clarity to enable teachers and educational program-builders to identify the kind of individuals or human beings who are the result of their educational systems. In Skinner's philosophy, there is no place for humanistic literature, especially that of André Gide, who in *The Counterfeiters* and *Lafcadio's Adventures* (Caves du Vatican) deals with the gratuitous, unmotivated act. However, in Lafcadio Hearn's tale of the tidal wave, we have an old man who might be called a Skinnerean "hero," because he "programmed" the villagers to save themselves from a danger they did not see. (See Humanistic Exemplar: "The Wave.")

The Human as Existential End Product

If our society and culture are to survive, then provisions must be made in our school programs for creating the types of individuals best suited to be our end products. This does not mean students with potential for college entrance or with salable skills. These are not humanistic aims, but the aims of guidance programs. It means students as human beings interacting with other human beings in an international, intercultural, intersocioeconomic, and interpolitical world society. Within this definition, the aims and purposes of the humanities in the schools, broadly stated, and at their most dynamic should be:

1. to develop the humanistic potential of each and every student
2. to help each student fulfill his or her own personal needs and values in terms of the social values of the prevailing culture, based on the knowledge and awareness of what the richest aspects of being human means

3. to contribute to the survival, rather than the destruction of the human enterprise of the future, through a humanistic rather than robotized denial of the human being as an entity.

Humanistic psychologists such as Abraham Maslow, and Rollo May, and the analytical psychologist, Carl G. Jung focus on the individual as a unique being who acts as a dynamic force within a larger sociocultural construct, rather than as a social character or a repertoire of behavioral responses. Although their terms may vary, each describes a human ideal as one who is mutually healthy and who functions with an inner security and direction in relation to society.

Maslow: Self-Actualizing Man

Abraham Maslow (1968, 1971) describes his ideal individuals as *self-actualizing.* Without exception they are involved in causes outside themselves, follow personal callings or devotion to intrinsic values and the values of being. One way or another they are creative. He identified eight behaviors leading toward self-actualization.[4]

1. Self-actualizing people experience "fully, widely, selflessly, with full concentration and total absorption, without self-consciousness." At this moment of experiencing, they are "wholly and fully human."

2. The self-actualizing process is one in which the choices aid progress in growth processes, while other choices may lead to regression. Refraining from stealing, and being honest rather than lying, are growth choices. They move away from fear toward courage. They move out to new experiences.

3. Self-actualizing people rely upon their own impulses and inner workings to achieve sensory responses.

4. Self-actualizing people, when in doubt, are honest instead of dishonest (a growth choice). They take responsibility for their own actions, behaviors, and decisions.

5 Self-actualizing people are aware of the self, and make increasingly better choices that are constitutionally right for them. They come to know their own destiny, mission, or calling, or who their spouse will be. Maslow suggests, "One cannot choose wisely for a life unless he dares to listen to himself, his own self, at each moment in life, and to say calmly, 'No, I don't like such and such.'"

6. Self-actualizing people use their intelligence and become smarter by "going through an arduous and demanding period of preparation in order to realize [their] potentialities." They work well to do the things they want to do, to be first-rate, or as good as they possibly can be.

3. B. F. Skinner, *Beyond Freedom and Dignity,* copyright © 1971 by Alfred A. Knopf, Inc., pp. 199-200.
4. From *The Farther Reaches of Human Nature* by Abraham Maslow. Copyright © 1971 by Bertha G. Maslow. Reprinted by permission of The Viking Press, Inc., pp. 45-50.

7. Self-actualizing people try to set up conditions which will provide peak experiences. A peak experience is a transient moment of self-actualization in which total involvement in an activity provides its own joy and sense of achievement. When such people move out of themselves, they feel more integrated with themselves than at any other time. They use the peak of their powers almost effortlessly, free of inhibiting blocks to their (creative) working processes. They are more aware of the joy of the experience; more a pure psyche than a thing of the world. The peak experience can be, but is not always, a major turning point in the growth process.

8. Self-actualizing people are those who find out who and what they are, what they like or dislike, what is good or bad for them, where they are going, and where their mission calls them. They know their defenses, are open to themselves, and find courage to give up their defenses.

One such defense Maslow describes as *desacralizing,* which young people employ to turn off the values and virtues of their parents and the older generation after having learned to mistrust these values and virtues or having found their elders to be hypocritical. Hypocrisy is viewed as a conflict between *ought* and *is,* talking about honesty and bravery but lying and being afraid to stand up against opposing beliefs or others. Young people "desacralize" their parents' values and virtues by reducing the older generation to concrete objects, refusing to see them as they might be, would like to be, or in terms of symbolic values. Self-actualization means the giving up of this defense mechanism and learning, or being taught to *resacralize.*[5]

Maslow coined the two nonce words "desacralize," and "resacralize," to define the acts of depriving an item, person, or concept of its sacredness, and then to reinstate it. In view of this, an additional aim of the humanities in the schools should be to help children and young people recognize the balance between human weakness and human strength, and the conflicts between human needs, values, and virtue which keep people from adhering to them. Within Maslow's definition, self-actualizing people are less likely to have a conflict between their actions and their *ought* value systems. It may well be that young people who desacralize the most are those whose parents were not self-actualizing.

A literary example of this can be found in John Galsworthy's double trilogy on the Forsyte family. Soames Forsyte was not self-actualizing, and his daughter Fleur broke from him. Young Jolyan, Soames's brother, was self-actualizing, and in allowing his son freedom of choice kept his loyalty. Irene, the anima figure between Soames and young Jolyan, was self-actualizing and a free spirit.

May: Self-Affirmative Man

Rollo May, in *Love and Will,* deals also with mentally healthy individuals, but refers to them as *self-affirmative.* He is not, however, as systematic as Maslow about describing personality characteristics. May's self-affirmative person cares and is involved with the world and the activities of people. To be *related to the world* means "to love and will the world as an immediate spontaneous totality." *To will the world* means "to create it by our decision, our fiat, our choice, and we love it, give it affect, energy, power to love and change us as we change it."[6] *To will* means "to bring about." *To love* means "to embrace through personal involvement."

May interprets the interworking of love and will as the acceptance of the daimonic in ourselves—as "any function which has the power to take over the whole person." The daimonic refers to such archetypal functions of human experiences as sex, eros, anger, rage, and the craving for power. It can be a creative force, but becomes evil (destructive) when "it usurps the total self without regard to the integration of that self, or to the unique forms and desires of others and their need for integration."[7] The individual's personal daimon guides him (or her) in particular situations. Originally, in Latin *daimon* translated into "genii" (of "jinni"). Through the Romans the word came to mean genius, or a spirit which presided over the destiny of an individual. According to May, genius comes from the Latin, *genere,*[8] thus genius means to beget, generate, or to have high mental endowments or talents.

Jung: Individuation

Carl G. Jung identifies the process of achieving individual wholeness as *individuation.* It results from the individual coming to terms with his or her own inner center (psychic nucleus), self, or unconscious personality. Jung named this recognition and confrontation with the inner self as, "The realization of the shadow" because it was sometimes personified in dreams. The male sees a male shadow; the female sees a female shadow. The individual may confront the shadow through a deeply honest self-examination which may take a long period of time and require therapy.

The shadow does not operate alone but is backed up by other aspects of the personality. In the male, this is called the *anima,* or female factor, the *yin* originating in the influences of the mother image. In the female, this is called the *animus,* or the male factor, the *yang* originating in the influence of the father. The *anima* personifies all feminine psychological tendencies in a man's psyche, "such as (his) vague feelings, moods, prophetic hunches, receptiveness to the irrational, capacity for personal love, feeling for nature, and . . . his

5. Ibid., p. 49.
6. Rollo May, *Love and Will* (New York: W. W. Norton & Company, 1969), p. 324.
7. Ibid., p. 123.
8. Ibid., p. 125.

relation to the unconscious."[9] The *animus* personifies all masculine psychological factors in the woman's psyche, her deep convictions, "enterprising spirit, courage, truthfulness, and in the highest form, spiritual profundity."[10]

Both the anima and the animus can be either negative or positive, creative or destructive in their effect on the individual. They act as mediators between the person and his or her ego and self. They act as guides to the inner world, revealing conflicting aspects of the individual's psychic center.

The humanities provide a rich source of anima/animus personifications. Dante's Beatrice, the Mona Lisa, and Jeanne D'Arc are positive anima figures, while the Greek Sirens, Circe, H. Rider Haggard's *She*, Puccini's *Turandot*, Scarlett O'Hara, the femme fatale—all are negative anima figures. Ivanhoe, King Arthur, most prince charmings, and Steve Canyon are positive animus figures; while Heathcliffe, Bluebeard, the death angel in "Death Takes a Holiday" are negative animus figures. Movieland has created its own mythological anima/animus personifications in Greta Garbo, Marlene Dietrich, Jean Harlowe, and Marilyn Monroe, in John Barrymore, Rudolph Valentino, and Clark Gable. Within our own personal lives, we have private anima/animus personifications drawn from parents, friends, and acquaintances who might maintain a dream relationship to our psychic center much as the Duchess of Towers became the destructive dream anima in George DuMaurier's *Peter Ibbetson*.

Jung describes four stages by way of which mythologies and cultures reflect the development of anima/animus personifications through the collective unconscious: *Stage 1*, the sexual and primitive anima (Eve), or the male physical power in primitive state (Tarzan); *Stage 2*, the romanticized aesthetic love, still sexual anima (Cleopatra, Helen of Troy), or the initiating romantic planned action (Shelley, Mozart's *Don Giovanni*); *Stage 3*, the rising of love to a spiritual devotion by the anima (the Virgin Mary), or the bringer of the word (logos) by the animus (Khalil Gibran); *Stage 4*, the transcendence of wisdom—even the most holy and pure—the sublime anima (Mona Lisa), or the wise guide to spiritual truth (Mahatma Gandhi).

Individuals who struggle and confront their personal anima/animus personifications long enough and deeply enough bring about changes in their unconscious through their new discovery of the self. In our discovery and acceptance of the real self we identify our true self-image. Individuation is the process of realizing and overcoming our shadows, recognizing the nature of our negative anima/animus, and adapting our true self to the roles we must play before the various faces of society. Jung calls the mask or the role we play in different social situations and encounters with others, the *persona*. It is the role we play, mask we wear, and part we continually enact. Individuals who have achieved the stage of individuation are able to identify their inner selves in terms of their social surround. They

accept the necessary mark or *persona,* and wear it effectively.

Jung defines the *persona* in terms of the social self, "a complicated system of relations between the individual and society, fitting by enough a kind of mask designed . . . to make a definite impression upon others, and . . . to concern the true nature of the individual."[11] For its own surety, society expects and demands that all individuals play the parts or roles assigned to them. The public or career mask must be irrevocable and consistent. The private life is what happens behind the mask.

Jung speaks from the European upper-middle-class society in which he grew up during the last quarter of the nineteenth century. Aspects of our present culture, the last quarter of the twentieth century, question the needs and reasons for masks. Humanistic awareness groups attempt to remove masks. Part of our current cultural dilemma results from conflicts between traditional and presently popular social roles as demonstrated in behavior and dress. Educational goals vaguely represent social needs; however, just preparing children going through the K-12 assembly line to wear the mask or maintain the persona of the college entrance professional, the technical-vocational apprentice, or business school secretary is no longer enough. The differences between the black tie, the white collar, or the blue collar became increasingly more ambiguous as the forty-hour workweek became thirty-five hours long and promises to become even shorter. Until recently, society (or the Puritan Ethic) had not accepted the creative or performing artist as a product of the system.

The Needs of Now

Now, however, we must decide upon the type of human being our future society needs. If we want our children to be human beings as well as doctors, lawyers, mathematicians, scientists, factory workers, or voters who can read, then quality human beings are the end products of courses in the humanities. Individual personality characteristics develop from birth. Social institutions such as schools have an influence only after children become a part of them; consequently, the positive (or negative) influence of schools on children begins when they enroll. High school and college is *too late* to begin forming humanistic personalities.

Each teacher must decide what this humanistic human being is going to be. Such individuals have been

9. Marie-Louise von Franz, "The Process of Individualism," in *Man and His Symbols,* ed. Carl G. Jung (Copyright 1964 by Aldus Books Limited, London; reprint edition, Doubleday and Company, New York, 1969), p. 177.

10. Ibid., p. 195.

11. THE COLLECTED WORKS OF C. G. JUNG, ed. by G. Adler, M. Fordham, and H. Read, trans. by R.F.C. Hull, vol. 7, *Two Essays on Analytical Psychology* (copyright 1973 and © 1966 by Bollingen Foundation), reprinted by permission of Princeton University Press: p. 203.

presented above as the self-actualizing individual of Maslow, the self-affirming individual of May, and the achiever of individuation suggested by Jung.

Never has the teacher, educator, school psychologist, or social worker been placed in such a position or dilemma. Even in an age when we have accepted the existential belief that we can control our own destiny, we are confronted with the conflict between free will and technological determinism. The teacher's role is now one of creating ideal individuals for the future, people who will survive the uncertainties of scientific and technological progress, transition, air pollution, wars, pestilence, plagues. That is the *star child* at the end of *2001: A Space Odyssey*.

Maslow, as a humanistic psychologist, identified the future role of the arts in education in developing future human beings when he wrote:

Another conclusion I seem impelled toward . . . is that creative art education, or better said, Education-Through-Art, may be especially important not so much for turning out artists or art products, as for turning out better people. If we have clearly in mind the educational goals for human beings that I will be hinting at, if we hope for our children that they will become full human beings, and that they will move toward actualizing the potentialities that they have, then, as nearly as I can make out, the only kind of education in existence today that has any faint inkling of such goals is art education . . . not because it turns out pictures but because I think . . . it may become the paradigm for all other education. That is, instead of being regarded as the frill, the expendable kind of thing which is now is, if we take it seriously enough and work at it hard enough and if it turns out to be what some of us suspect it can be, then we may one day teach arithmetic and reading and writing on this paradigm. So far as I am concerned, I am talking about all education. That is why I am interested in education through art —simply because it seems to be good education in potential.[12]

Maslow is identifying an educational process leading to self-actualizing individuals. Skinner, in *Walden Two*, deals with the collective society. The function of school programs is not one of creating utopias so much as it is of developing the type of individuals who make up

society. Describing those individuals in order to recognize them when they have been formed, or the degree to which they have developed is the next major task of the teacher and, in particular, the future teacher of the humanities.

Reinforcing Activities

1. Describe, for yourself, the ideal individual needed for the future. Use, if you wish, suggestions provided in this chapter. If they do not appeal to you, use other examples from literature you have read and find more acceptable.

2. List or mentally note specific characteristics and how to recognize them.

3. In rap sessions, discuss and compare your concept of the ideal individual with others in the class. How can you help children in your system obtain the ideal personality?

4. Analyze yourself in terms of the self-actualizing, self-activating, individuated, or existential individual described in this chapter.

5. How close are you to being a self-actualizing person as you go about your activities and interact with your students, other teachers, and administrators? In which students do you reinforce positive factors the most? How? In which students do you reinforce negative factors the most? How?

References

Maslow, Abraham H. *Toward a Psychology of Being.* 2d ed. New York: Van Nostrand Reinhold, 1968.
Rokeach, Milton. *The Nature of Human Values.* New York: The Free Press, 1973.
Skinner, B. F. *Science and Human Behavior.* New York: Macmillan Co., 1953.
———. *Walden Two.* New York: Macmillan Co., 1948.

12. Maslow, *The Farther Reaches*, pp. 57-58.

6

Core monuments
in the humanities

If social values and human needs are to be the basis for a humanities curriculum, then the subject matter should relate directly to them. In this chapter Fromm's five human needs will be used as the focus for humanistic themes in the elementary classroom. These themes will center around what the author considers *core monuments*.

By "core monument" are meant those works of art, literature, and other products of creative human enterprise and natural phenomena, the study of which make it possible to more readily grasp humanistic themes. They may not be great works of art such as the "key monuments" considered essential to the study of art history (Janson 1959). Nor are they quite the *aesthetic exemplars* suggested by Harry Broudy (1966) since the objective in focusing our attention on them is not to study aesthetics, or the work of art itself, so much as to use it to study human needs and values in an interdisciplinary classroom setting. In using the term "core monuments," the author has drawn on the key monument and aesthetic exemplar concepts, but has injected them with the core curriculum concepts of the 1930s and 1940s.

Core Monuments Identified

Romeo and Juliet is an excellent core monument for the teenage student, inasmuch as Romeo was about fifteen years old, and Juliet about thirteen. Besides being an introduction to Shakespeare, it deals with teenage problems: love-hate conflicts, teenage marriage, elopement, duty to parents, and the generation gap. It provides a basis for discussing the differences between teenagers of the Renaissance and those of today.

It can also be used for *comparative aesthetics,* by which is meant using a single work created in one art form and comparing it with adaptations to the aesthetic structures of other art forms. Usually such works are of literary origin, as for instance *Romeo and Giulietta*, a novella of the Italian Renaissance, written about 1530 by Luigi da Porto (Levtow and Valency 1960). Shakespeare adapted it, as *Romeo and Juliet*, to play form to fit the confines of the Globe Theater stage, and to suit his audience. Each presentation since has required some revisions and adaptations in staging to suit the ever-changing audience. Each of three different film versions required very definite changes because of the progressively greater flexibility, the spatial coverage, and the

time-sequencing of the film media. It has also been adapted to opera, ballet, and symphonic compositions in which the dramatic action must be reflected in the music and dance. The Broadway musical, *Westside Story* updated the setting of *Romeo and Juliet*, but maintained the essential story line. The balcony scene, which becomes a love duet in opera, a pas-de-deux in ballet, was the song "Maria," sung below a fire escape in the musical.

Another core monument example is the legend of the Holy Grail, though it is not characterized by any single work. As a theme, it embodies man's search for truth, and the struggle for purity against all temptations. It is a medieval legend, found in both Teutonic and Anglo-Saxon literature. It has been told in opera (Wagner's *Parsifal*), poetry (Tennyson's "Holy Grail," from *Idylls of the King*), and depicted in paintings and tapestries as well. The film versions, and the musical "Camelot," tend to deal more with King Arthur and the Knights of the Round Table. They omit the grail aspect, although the allegiance to truth and honor remain.

Mary Shelley's *Frankenstein* is a core monument around which to study man's drive to be a creator, to assume the role of God. It has its origins in such concepts as the homunculus, the golem of Hebraic folklore, and its counterpart, the contemporary computer, HAL, in *2001: A Space Odyssey*. In the literature, man's presumption at trying to imitate God by creating a living being through other than natural procreation usually meets with disaster; the mechanism is not perfect. It is the failure of the created being that gives these tales their moral orientation.

The "Bayeux Tapestry" can also be used as a core monument. It records a historical event, demonstrates man's drive for immortality by leaving his image and a record of his achievements in art, and the thrust for superiority by warfare and invasion. As an art object, it exemplifies a key art monument of historical importance and includes potential for teaching stitchery and tapestry making, linear narrative sequencing, visual symbols and problems in deciphering ancient alphabets.

A core monument might also be a natural phenomenon such as the rainbow (to be discussed later in this chapter). But, the core monument is not so much a theme or concept as it is the vehicle or product through which humanistic themes, concepts, values, and needs have been expressed and can be studied by others. Mythology, folklore, and fairy tales are rich with core monument vehicles exemplifying human needs and values because they extend from the darkest origins of man's collective unconscious, and sustain it.

William Irwin Thompson, in *At the Edge of History*, (1971) proposes that history and historical facts are the real myths and that myths are the real history. Myths grow from within the human being as those things they want to believe. They have their own kind of truths, and are saying, "This is the way we want it to have been."

Folklore and Myths as Scientific Resources

When Heinrich Schliemann was ten years old (1852) his father gave him a book on the Trojan Wars, Odysseus, and Agamemnon. For some years before that, his father had read to him and told him fairy tales, fables, and legends which to Heinrich's imagination had their own reality. Thus it began. For him, they were more than just stories, and for the rest of his life Heinrich dreamed of finding Troy, the source of a wealth of legends. In 1870 he realized the first of his dreams and began the excavations which changed historians' facts and attitudes about the ancient past and Greek legends.

These stories had been told and read to Heinrich at an early age, when his mind and imagination could still come alive merely by hearing the stories. They can be told and read to children at the kindergarten and first-grade levels, and later might be read again or in conjunction with social studies and science units in order to reinforce their humanistic value and be discussed in terms of their historical value.

Since the discovery of ancient Troy, archeologists and historians have used legends, folklore, and myth to find the truth of the past, the origins of man and cultures. Some circles of scientific inquiry accept ancient tales and legends as a score to the past, others tend to dismiss them. Through his imagination, man found a way to hold onto the past by intermingling myths and legends with actual truths. They are prescientific sources with which archeologists, geologists, and historians among others seek out the otherwise overlooked clues to the past. Psychologists, especially those following Jungian thought, turn to fairy tales, folklore, legends, and myths to understand the human psyche in terms of the collective unconscious.

Other scientists disregard such sources. In the 1950s Immanuel Velikovsky published a series of books (*Worlds in Collision* 1950; *Ages in Chaos* 1952, and *Earth in Upheaval* 1955) dealing with celestial cataclysms. He used ancient texts and folk narratives, legends, and myths from Egyptian, Hebrew, Polynesian, Central and South American, theological and other sources. The American Association for the Advancement of Science still does not acknowledge his theories as important enough for investigation, because his sources are humanistic rather than scientific. But studies from the International Geophysical Year, and results from Mariner II and Pioneer V space flights indicate his predictions are more than just fantasy and imagination. In 1960, Velikovsky published *Oedipus and Akhnaton* using ancient Egyptian texts and Greek plays to prove that Akhnaton was the real life prototype for the Oedipus myth.

The relationship between human needs and fairy tales, folklore, legends, and myths is not so obscure that some suggestion cannot be made to help the teacher get a point of view on the basis of which to make a selection from among the various stories. They can be used for much more than just entertainment or development of reading and comprehension skills.

1. Need: Relatedness vs. Narcissism

The human need for relatedness can be associated with such social values as moral orientation and humanitarian mores. Fromm observes that the love of individuals for each other is one aspect of the need for relatedness, for identifying with and being with another person. Love implies care, responsibility, respect, and knowledge. It takes various forms: romantic love, chivalric love, parental love, spiritual love, and brotherly love. Agape or Christian love is that felt for all mankind. Adversely, narcissism is love of self out of proportion to love for others. It gets its name from the Greek myth of Narcissus, who, loved by many, could only find the reflection of himself to love. The healthy individual usually has some degree of narcissism, but not disproportionate to that love, care, and concern felt for others. In fairy tales such as "Beauty and the Beast" and "The Frog Prince," it is when the heroine feels compassion and love for the animal that the bewitching spell is cast off and the beast becomes a prince charming.

Society has established institutions which center on relatedness, marriage, humanitarian enterprises, philanthropies, charities, and welfare organizations. By setting aside specific days for caring and giving (Valentine's Day, Thanksgiving, and Christmas), our culture helps us to reinforce our relatedness to others.

An elementary humanities program could be designed around the humanistic purposes and historical origins of holidays. The following classifications may be of some help.

1. *Days of group giving and sharing* wherein individuals give to and receive from others, the exchange of tokens of mutual friendship and love. St. Valentine's Day, Christmas, Chanukah, and wedding anniversaries are four such days in the Judeo-Christian culture. Ancient customs also included New Year's Day for mutual exchange of gifts symbolically wishing others prosperity. It was thus observed through the Elizabethan Age, until the Puritans preached that, along with Christmas trees and St. Nicholas, it was a form of paganism. Toward nationwide gift-giving holidays our charities make concerted efforts to provide for the needy.

2. *Days for individual recognition* help satisfy the narcissistic needs of the individual. These are the days when one receives from others, without return gifts, such as on birthdays. Mother's Day, Father's Day, and the less commercialized Children's Day reinforce relatedness in

the family unit. Special recognition is accorded individuals at times of achievement and success, such as for Bar Mitzvahs, first communions, graduations, debuts, and retirements, which are our contemporary culture's forms of rites of passage.

3. *Days of thanksgiving and commemoration* reinforce relatedness to social values, ideas, and worthy concepts often of a nationalistic nature. They are often feast days and holidays, and may continue from ancient origins giving thanks to a supreme spiritual being, or commemorating the dead. In the United States, Thanksgiving is such a day, but through family gatherings it reinforces familial relatedness. The telephone companies, greeting card companies, and floral telegraph groups all focus on maintaining familial relatedness across the miles.

National commemoration days sustain the memory of great events and heroic deeds, along with one's relatedness to the past, such as, El cinco de Mayo, Fourth of July, Bastille Day, or Columbus Day. We remember past heroes on their birthdays (Washington, Lincoln), memorialize the assassination of great leaders (Martin Luther King, Jr., or John F. Kennedy), or other days of infamy (Pearl Harbor Day, Hiroshima). We celebrate the ends of wars and commemorate those who died in them (Memorial Day, Veteran's Day), and reinforce brotherliness and the struggle for peace (United Nations Day).

In May, the ancient Greeks observed *Lemuria,* a ceremony to pay homage to the dead, or for the Romans to lay restless spirits to rest, not unlike our own Memorial Day in May.

Such days reflect national and public relatedness by renewing such values as nationalism, patriotism, freedom, and democracy. Martin Luther King, Jr., Day is used to renew values of equality and the struggle against racism. In Communist countries May Day celebrations recognize progress, success, and achievement. In the United States we celebrate them on Labor Day, along with activities and work by (paradoxically to the Puritan Ethic) taking the day off from work. In England, it is the Bank Holiday.

4. *Days of renewal,* such as New Year's Day, reorient our relatedness to the recent past by reviewing its events and dedicating ourselves to the future. They are cyclical in nature and continue the myths of the eternal return, the contact with the first time (Eliade 1954).

Most New Year's Days, whether they are on January first, in February (Chinese New Year) or September (Rosh Hashanah) are days for making new resolutions, paying back debts, and establishing rituals for future prosperity. The Japanese make cakes to offer the sun and moon. In some places in India new foods are eaten, new clothes worn, and cattle decked in flowers. Some American Indian tribes would extinguish tribal fires, ceremoniously scatter the ashes, and then relight them. Such customs and rituals reflect some aspect of renewal, prosperity, and establishment of a relatedness to time.

Such larger cycles as decades, centuries, and millenniums receive special recognitions as anniversary dates and renewals of the past. The bicentennial of the United States provides another such rallying point for rediscovering our national heritage and renewing its purposes in the present generation of young people.

The millennium, which denotes a period of one thousand years, is a much more rare celebration. Our next one, the year 2000, will be witnessed by most of today's school children, and hopefully many of us—their teachers and parents. How will we all receive it? The last millennium, 1000 A.D., occurred when the Renaissance began its dawn over the Dark Ages. In some parts of central Europe during the late 990s, people faced the year 1000 with fear and trembling, hysteria, and suicides, perhaps, in belief of Revelation 20:7-8, "And when the thousand years are ended, Satan will be loosed from his prison and will come out to deceive the nations which are at the four corners of the earth, that is, Gog and Magog, to gather them for battle; their number is like the sand of the sea" (Revised Standard Version). They saw the end of the world, the great eschatology.

The annual renewal cycle was conceived differently by agrarian and pastoral societies. The ancient agrarian societies (Babylonian, Mesopotamian, Egyptian, Grecian, Roman) celebrated spring, the vernal equinox, as the beginning of the New Year with appropriate myths. The Greek myths of Persephone, for instance, relate that the daughter of Demeter (goddess of crops and fertility) came up from Hades, the underworld where she had resided for the six winter months, to walk the earth and bring sunshine. Derivative of this is the Easter celebration of the Resurrection, in the Christian tradition, and the Jewish Passover, of which it historically was a part. The Easter bunny and painted eggs are acculturations of the hare, the ancient pagan symbol for fertility. (For related arts activities see: Appendix A: From the Author's Memory Bank: Easter and Passover.)

Ancient pastoral societies of northern and central Europe based their New Year and renewal cycles on cattle and livestock. The Druids recognized Baltane, about May first, as the New Year when the livestock and cattle were let from the houses, barns, and folds to feed on pastoral grasses. The Celts, on the other hand, recognized Samhein, about November first, as the New Year. The New Year of each was six months separated from that of the other. Each was preceded by a night when witches, goblins, ghosts, and demons rode the night wind on fantastic beasts, rather than on broomsticks, a more recent adaptation. Under Christian adjustments to pagan rituals, the night before Samhein became All Hallow's Eve (Halloween, the night before All Saints Day). The demons were either leaving their tombs, deserted homes, castles, and other hiding places, to ride the summer night's winds on Walpurgis Night (night before St. Walpurga's feast day), or they were trying to get into the homes, barns for winter shelter against which the people barred their doors and windows on Halloween. One other such night is St. John's Eve, June

23rd, the night before Midsummer's Day (John the Baptist's natal day), June 24th. On each of these nights, the demons of the underworld and the deeply troubled, unrested spirits rode night winds. Those of St. John's Eve, by Russian tradition, gathered on Bald Mountain to await the transmogrification of Satan, depicted in music by Moussorgsky's *A Night on Bald Mountain.* The same eve, in English fantasy, fairies and elves were brought to story form in Shakespeare's *A Midsummer Night's Dream.*

On October 31st, the night before All Holies, or All Saints Day (now Halloween, in our present-day tradition), bonfires were lit in the village to keep the demons away. Children went from door to door, asking, "Give us a peat," a coal to put on the village fire. All that remains of these pastoral New Years in our present culture are children dressed as demons and goblins, in homemade or discount store plastic masks and cheesecloth costumes, operating from door to door as a minor-league protective racket called "Trick or Treat." (For related activities see: Appendix A: From the Author's Memory Bank: Moussorgsky's, *A Night on Bald Mountain,* and Halloween).

2. Need: Transcendence (Creativeness vs. Destructiveness)

Fromm describes transcendence as the human need to move or change the present state of being, either by creating or destroying, toward love or hate. Values related to transcendence are achievement and success, activity and work, progress, material comforts, and freedom. Escape is a form of transcendence. Hallucinatory drugs, intoxicants, and other devices to alter states of consciousness are all methods of achieving transcendence.

The values and human needs related to transcendence have a complex interaction in fairy tales, folklore, myths, and fables which defies simple classification. Some folk and fairy tales have themes extending back as far as twenty-five hundred years before Christ (Von Franz 1970, p. 3). Such stories have provided a more exacting moral and ethical base than did much of the Christian teachings. In Eastern cultures transcendence is the end result of a life of meditation and achieving a oneness with the universe. In the cultures of the Western world it is a result of free will and determination.

Daedalus and Icarus escaping from their labyrinthian imprisonment by flying with wax and feather wings exemplify the ultimate in Western thought on the human need for transcendence and freedom. Richard Bach's *Jonathan Livingston Seagull* is our contemporary contribution to symbolic transcendence. Other cultures gave the world levitating saints, werewolves, and vampires.

The werewolf and the vampire are each of ancient origin. The werewolf represents man's need for transcendence over his animal nature. The vampire represents man's desire to transcend death, and is counter to the spiritual transcendence promised in the Christian religion. Both the werewolf and the vampire are negative, destructive products from a prescientific folklore.

More recent examples of man's struggle to overcome his animal origins are found in Edgar Rice Burrough's *Tarzan of the Apes* and Robert Louis Stevenson's *Dr. Jekyll and Mr. Hyde.* Both are products of the late Victorian culture, following the influence of Darwin's *Origin of Species.* Tarzan, really Lord Greystroke, is raised by a near-human family of apes after his own parents die in the African jungles. Mr. Hyde, revealed as part of man's animal nature, is identified in atavistic ape-like descriptives. Tarzan is a positive figure, while Mr. Hyde is a negative destructive figure.

Such tales provide a basis for humanistic study and classroom discussion when occasions, such as movies, television, and comic strips cause an interest. They are very much a part of our popular culture.

Fairy tales also deal with aspects of transcendence, or changing the present state of things, often ending with "they lived happily ever after." Since the same tales were told in different countries over long periods of time they maintain variations reflecting differences in the various cultures. They might be read first to children for pleasure, but they can also be compared. The more popular tales might be compared for transcultural differences, since at least one version would be quite well known. They might be compared for factual samenesses and differences, and for variations in the story line. At the upper elementary level, following Kohlberg's stages of moral development, they might be discussed for differences in their moral and ethical aspects.

Cinderella, for instance, transcends the hearthstone with the spells of her fairy godmother, escapes to the ball, returns, and is finally rescued by the Prince, who takes her away from domestic chores and mean stepsisters. In the version by Charles Perrault (seventeenth century, France), the stepsisters are forgiven and she finds them husbands. In the version recorded by the brothers Grimm (nineteenth century, Germany), called "Ashenputtel," the dead real mother and turtle doves play a magical role not found in the French. Each of the stepsisters cut off parts of their feet to be able to fit into the slippers. At the wedding, they carry Ashenputtel's train, but the turtle doves fly in and perch on their shoulders. On the way to the altar the birds pluck out one eye of each stepsister, while on the return, they change shoulders and pluck out the remaining eye of each. Such a comparison can lead to a discussion of punishments, retribution, and forgiveness. The author discussed the story with his son (about 8 years old at the time), who felt that the stepsisters did not deserve that much punishment just for being bad-tempered and mean. He thought that since parts of their feet had already been cut off, they had been punished enough.

Other differences, the turtle doves, pumpkins, fairy godmother, the ball repeated three successive nights are all cultural variations on the Cinderella theme. Another version, adapting the Perrault's tale to the late Victorian English culture was written and illustrated by Arthur Rackham. The contemporary American version is Walt Disney's animated film with considerable hocus-pocus and rambling among the household pets. The Rodgers and Hammerstein television musical version had to cut the number of balls attended, and translates some narrative into song and duets. When available on the television or local movie houses, Cinderella in its various versions might be discussed for its humanistic and *comparative aesthetics* overtones.

The feminine need for transcending domestic chores, filial injustice, and work-a-day poverty has remained constant in our cultures. In the United States, the soap opera fed this need; now women's liberation is making an actuality out of what has long been limited to the wishful imagination. Until now, the suppressed female depended upon the male, Prince Charming, for escape on a white horse. At the adult level, Gustave Flaubert's *Madame Bovary* was a destructive symbol of the struggle to change the present state of things, while in Charlotte Brontë's *Jane Eyre*, Rochester's arrival on a horse lead to a more positive change in her state of being. How much of this can be discussed with a class or should be discussed with groups of elementary school children depends upon the children themselves, upon the teacher's knowledge of the children—their needs, and the situation—and local attitudes about women's liberation.

Fairy tales frequently tell of three sons going forth to seek their fortune. Each succeeds through trickery, cleverness, wisdom, or industry. There is an ecological lesson in the tale of the three pigs who build their houses of straw, sticks, and bricks. It is also a slight allegory on the development of architecture. The "Grasshopper and the Ants" provides a moral about work and play reflecting the Puritan Ethic. Tales of goodness overcoming evil in our society may no longer provide realistic morals, but can still provide thematic sources for discussion of man's need for material comfort, freedom from work, and the type of transcendence found in reading fantasy, attending movies, the theater, and concerts. Though they may be temporary forms of escapism, they can help us change our present state of being. Thus the arts, particularly the performing arts, are more than leisure-time pursuits. They are creative, rather than destructive, forms of transcendence, even as puppet shows and student-produced school plays. (For related activities see: Appendix A: From the Author's Memory Bank: "Jack and the Beanstalk," K-6.)

3. Need: Rootedness and a Sense of Identity (Ourselves as Heroes and Heroines)

Fromm identifies these as separate needs. They have been combined here because they seem interrelated. The need for rootedness, to establish one's hereditary identity—to return to one's personal origins, seem to be a part of the search for identity. Fromm describes the need for a sense of identity as a conflict between in-

dividual action and herd conformity. In terms of William's major social values, this suggests individual personality and freedom in conflict with democracy (the majority rules) and external conformity. In Kohlberg's levels of moral development, the conflict exists between the conventional and postconventional levels.

The sense of identity goes hand in hand with our self-image, and self-identification. To help us identify ourselves we have devised numerous techniques from classifications of sex, skin color, national heritage, and religious beliefs, to astrological charts, zodiacal signs, and psychological types (Jungian, Adlerian, and so on). We have designed family trees, tartans, and heraldic devices to establish family identity and rootedness.

With the sense of identity, the *individual* gains a sense of being an *individualist*. The two are not the same entity, although they are essentially the same word. The individual may be a part of the herd, the individualist may be in conflict with the herd. The individualist also differs from the nonconformist, who must not conform on any issue which represents the herd or the establishment. The individualist may at times conform, because it seems right to do so. It may be an external conformity, however, concurrent with maintenance of an internal nonconformity. Both nonconformists and individualists can be looked upon by others as natural heroes who can lead to creative or destructive transcendence or change of the present state of being. Another goal of the humanities in schools may well be to develop the individual as a positive hero or heroine.

Hero and birthright myths are types of identity myths. The search for identity is found in tales of brothers who set off to find their fortune. They face the reality of themselves through a series of tasks and challenges, sometimes given them by old people along the road. At the adult level they are found in Hervey Allen's *Anthony Adverse*, John Steinbeck's *East of Eden*, Henry Fielding's *Tom Jones*, or the rejection of the search for rootedness in the gratuitous personality found in André Gide's *The Counterfeiters*. The Oedipus myth deals both with rootedness, and with its negative factor.

Many such tales and myths have core monument potential in their similarity with other such stories. In the tradition of the Hercules legend, tasks such as his are punishments for having committed a crime, usually accidental but nevertheless punishable. Children might discuss punishments as character-building tasks, rather than as spankings and deprivations.

Theseus and Arthur Pendragon ("King Arthur") establish their birthrights through sword-and-stone challenges. Alexander established his right to conquer, not by untying the Gordian knot, but by slashing it with his sword. Isaac and Esau exchange birthrights, and both are punished. Lot, Noah, Utnapishtim and Deucalion each withstand temptations, and/or the jeers of the populace and so survive the wrath and destruction of the gods. Lot survives the fall of Sodom and Gomorrah, while Noah, Utnapishtim, and Deucalion each survive the ancient flood in the Hebrew, Babylonian, and Greek tales of the flood. (For related activities see: Appendix B: Humanistic Exemplars: "Noyes Fludde" and Project CREATE.) These tales also relate to rootedness, since they end with a form of renewal of the human race, and the repeopling of the earth.

Tales of migration and exploration deal with rootedness and transcendence. The early biblical histories trace the migration of the wandering tribes of Israel, and the exodus from Egyptian enslavement under Moses's leadership. Explorations and the discovery of new lands under the leadership of charismatic individuals can be found in the histories of all peoples. The westward migration of Europeans and American pioneers, the eastward migration of Orientals, Amerindian migrations to various parts of the Western hemisphere, the migrations of southern black people to northern cities, of Puerto Ricans to mainland cities, of Mexicans to southwestern cities were all part of a need to improve a state of being existing at the time. Those who moved out first resisted herd conformity. Whether the leaders were Columbus, Daniel Boone, Lewis and Clarke, Cortez, or the unknown first pioneers, they led the way out for others to follow. (For a humanistic approach to Columbus Day see: Appendix A: From the Author's Memory Bank: Columbus.)

4. Need: Frame of Orientation and Devotion (Reason vs. Irrationality)

In our need for a frame of orientation from which to view the strange phenomena of our world and our place in it, we have created from our imaginations belief systems encompassing our past, present, and future. From our need to explain puzzling and sometimes violent natural phenomena we created reasonable solutions linked to our concepts of a supreme spiritual being or beings. To sustain and reinforce our solutions, we founded religions around a god, or gods and goddesses, and established religious hierarchies. Each had its own set of truths, its own reasons and reasoning.

We also created science as a secular rationality, as a systematic means of investigating the same natural phenomena. Conflicts developed between science, religion, and philosophy; and between scientific proof through rigorous and sometimes technological methods, and truths resulting from rational explanations. Conflicts between one's religious beliefs and those of another were somewhat resolved by placing the others in the realm of mythology and superstition. With the advent of science, it was said of most religions that each was originally based on superstition and mythology. One man's truth became another man's myth.

Study units in classroom humanities can deal with the balance between myths and science, folklore and anthropology, or they can compare the folklore and myths of diverse cultures and peoples as they seek to explain similar natural phenomena.

For making these studies with some degree of order, it is suggested that the following five headings be used as a guide: (1) origins of natural phenomena, (2) origins of animal characteristics, (3) myths of creation, (4) the quest for an identification with space, and (5) the conflict between good and evil. Each of these groups has subject matter which can lead from irrationality to science and secular rationalism. For possible stages in programming this sequence, see the final section of this chapter, "From Mythology to Scientific Inquiry in Classroom Humanities." (For a bibliography of resources for teachers' backgrounds and student reading see: Appendix C: Resources for Elementary Core Monuments in the Humanities.)

Origins of Natural Phenomena

There seem to be three aspects of the natural environment which most concerned the ancients and primitive man: the stars and constellations, rainbows, and fire (and knowledge/imagination).

Constellations and Stars   The configurations of the stars in constellations have fascinated human beings throughout the ages. Those configurations were a source of wonder and mystery. Through their own abilities men were able to bring visual closure or design to a specific grouping of stars which were identified in humanistic terms—as animals, man-made objects, or heroes and heroines. Some groupings were associated in similar ways by diverse cultures widely separated geographically and temporally from one another. For example, the Pleiades, inspired similar tales of laughing, dancing children rising to the sky told by various pre-Columbian Indians of South America, by the Iroquois of North America, and by the ancient Greeks (from whence we derived the name *Pleiades*).

Constellations and the movement of the sun, moon, and stars across the sky have been the basis for recording time, seasonal transitions, and cycles of renewal. The phases of the moon are still used to determine religious holidays such as Easter, Passover, and the Jewish and Chinese New Years.

The same heavenly bodies were visible to all peoples throughout the development of the human race. The use of folklore to interpret them provides a rich source of imaginative inquiry prior to the study of the solar system in scientific terms. As a rule, these stories deal with individuals and animals which, following some adventure on earth, ascended to the heavens. As we discover that stars are gases and distant suns, that the new stars at the births of famous heroes are novas, and the planets are really rocks and stones and physical elements, the fantasy may go, but we still must have that first fantasy, that childhood suspension of disbelief.

Locating the constellations in the sky, as an exercise in visual perception, requires visual analysis, ground figure differentiation, and visual closure. The process of visualizing the mythological and zodiacal symbols in their respective configuration requires visual synthesis and the projection of a visual image to give it rational meaning.

The Rainbow The rainbow is a natural phenomenon entirely limited to the vision mode. It does not give heat as does the sun, nor can it be landed on by astronauts. As one approaches it, it disappears because the position of the viewer to the sun and the rain which produces it changes beyond the range of being able to see the refraction of light.

Human beings, in giving the rainbow meaning, established myths, folklore, and superstitions about it. The biblical account uses the rainbow as a covenant from God to Noah after the flood bringing peace. To the Scandinavians and Polynesians it was a bridge between heaven and earth. But to the Burmese, it was an evil omen bringing death to whomever it covered. To the Zulu, it was an evil but sacred snake. For the Greeks, Iris, the wife of Zephyrus, was the goddess of the rainbow. In current movie and television, Dorothy finds the Land of Oz, "somewhere over the rainbow." Among seafaring men and agrarian peoples it is a weather predictor, "Rainbow in the morning, sailor's (farmer's) warning, rainbow at night, sailor's (farmer's) delight."

The rainbow has all the elements needed to make it a core monument. It can be seen, painted, interpreted in various tales and stories. A scientific rule or principle for observation can be identified. There is a scientific as well as a mythological rationalism for its existence, and it can lead to the study of optics and color theory. The prismatic effect of the rainbow can be recreated with soap suds, and by the use of the spray nozzle of garden hoses. The sequence of colors in the rainbow are quite definite; children can demonstrate their cognitive knowledge of the rainbow by painting it in a picture but using their imaginations to paint the rest of the landscape or scene. The color theories of Sir Isaac Newton and Goethe might also be studied as part of the science or art history units. Children might write poems about the rainbow, describe it in essays, or tell how they feel when they see a rainbow in the sky, or how it would be to ride a rainbow.

Fire, Knowledge, and Imagination These three are grouped together because various myths link the giving of fire to mankind along with the giving of knowledge and/or the imagination. They are considered the gifts of God. Fire was especially sacred to ancient peoples and primitive societies. It was one of the four basic elements: earth, air, fire, and water. The domestication of fire was their most important discovery. They used it for warmth, cooking, religious rituals, and protection from wilderness, animals, demons, and the unknown. It was so sacred that in some legends and tales the bringer of fire was punished. Zeus punished Prometheus for giving mankind both fire and knowledge. He was tied to the rocks of the Caucasus Mountains, and each day a raven came and ate out his liver, but it grew back only to be eaten again the next day. Coyote, in Paiute Amerindian legends, was given the fire by a "trickster," who stole it from the gods, and he brought it to mankind, but it singed his fur, giving it a yellow

streak. Deities representing fire were identified with Apollo (Greek), Helios (Roman), Ra (Egyptian), Loki (Scandinavian), and Mother Ut (Mongolian).

Our use of fire represents a major turning point in the development of the human species. Claude Lévi-Strauss, in the *Raw and the Cooked* (1969), has focused a stage in his study of anthropoogy through mythology on its significance. Fire symbolizes god, life, purification, and resurrection. The "Eternal Flame" keeps alive the memory of heroes, on the tombs of John F. Kennedy and the Unknown Soldier. It is carried in Olympic games. In fiction, H. Rider Haggard's *She* gains eternal life by standing in the blue flames of Kor.

Knowledge and the imagination were also mysteries to early peoples, together providing the link between them and the gods. Human beings were punished for finding it. The Genesis story does not tell how Adam and Eve discovered fire. But, by eating of the forbidden tree of knowledge, they were sent from the Garden of Eden, to prevent them from eating of the tree of everlasting life and so becoming even more like God.

We still wonder about the origin of the imagination in human beings. The other animals, infrahumans, do not have it. A new mythology is developing in a scientific age concerned with the origin of the imagination. In Arthur C. Clarke's *2001: A Space Odyssey* the imagination is sent to earth as a black monolith from a planet in outer space. Its vibrations affect a certain species of ape which demonstrates it's newfound ability by using the bone of a dead animal as a weapon.

More recently, Erich von Däniken, in *Chariots of the Gods*, proposes that the imagination and the source of knowledge was our heritage from ancient astronauts who impregnated the female of the near-human species. Although relegated to science fiction by some, these are contemporary humanistic solutions to age old questions which methods of scientific inquiry and secular rationalism still cannot explain.

Origins of Animal Characteristics

This is an appropriate subject for kindergarten and first-grade children when animals are being studied. Folk tales from peoples who are close to the animal world contain stories of how animals get certain characteristic features; or such peoples give animals human personality traits. How the elephant got its trunk, the leopard its spots, the loon its necklace, or Anansi the spider got his tales extend from primitive peoples close to the wilderness. Rudyard Kipling's *Just So Stories* relate some of them. Tales like these can be found in the folk literature of African, Afro-American, Puerto Rican, Mexican, Amerindian, Eskimo, Japanese, Chinese, and Hawaiian peoples, and can be used in classes with children from these nationalities or races. Animal stories of this kind are to be found as nature tales in remote and rural white American cultures (more than in cities and towns).

After reading such tales to the children, or after the children have read them, the teacher might help them choose an animal (their pets, possibly), and study them to find something unique or special about the animal. They then might make up a story about how it happened. What was the animal like before it happened? How did the event change the animal's behavior? They might also draw the animal before the changing event took place, and afterwards. If an animal is available for class observation, it might be used, if not, then the children could rely on their visual memory.

Myths of Creation

To answer such questions as, "What is Man?" "Where did he come from?" human beings created their most deep-seated myths. These are the towering questions they asked the universe. Scientists still ask these questions. Much religious dogma is the result of answers formulated through ancient myths.

The study of the myths of creation also provide insight into the basic differences between cultures. Joseph Campbell, in *Myths to Live By* (1972), suggests that the Eastern and Oriental myths of creation show humans and animals as pouring forth from the gods. The myths of Western cultures have gods creating humans separately. Such essential differences may also effect attitudes about the treatment of all living things and the natural environment by peoples so differently oriented in their concepts of the creation of human, infrahuman, and plant life. Lynn White, Jr. (1969) suggests that the Judeo-Christian religious tradition stemming from the *Book of Genesis*, in which man is given dominion over all the animals, fish, and plant life, has led to the ecological crisis of today. It is an orientation not found among peoples whose relation to the earth is more tempered towards interacting with it, feeding it, and nourishing it, so that it may return life.

Quest for an Identification with Space

As long ago as the second century, Galen, a Greek physician and philosopher, and other earthbound human beings had dreamed of flying and speculated on traveling to the moon. In the eighteenth century, Baron Münchhausen told of taking two trips to the moon. Once by climbing up a fast-growing Turkish beanstalk, and again by accident when his sailing ship was caught by a great wind and blown to the outer atmosphere. During the last half of the nineteenth century, Jules Verne popularized space travel with *From the Earth to the Moon* and a *Trip Around the Moon*. H. G. Well's *War of the Worlds* brought space traffic in our direction. Flash Gordon and Buck Rogers gave space travel a comic strip reality in the 1930s. Such stories of space travel, and of constellations and stars formed as a result of human beings and demigods ascending to the heavens to become stars, are manifestations of the human desire to transcend the earth.

Mythology and science fiction have prepared the human mind for the possibility of spaceflight, or for being at one with the universe. Astrology uses the universe, the position of stars and constellations, to determine the fate of human beings. These all seem like aspects of the same need or humanistic enterprise, to identify with outer space. The most recent popular image of being at one with the universe, in Western culture at least, is as the ultimate, the Star Child.

With space exploration an actuality, the seeking of new answers to age-old questions returned to the foreground of human consciousness. The question of flying saucers and unidentified flying objects remains persistently unanswered. Officially, military scientists refute them, while the popular imagination wants to accept them. In 1959, Carl G. Jung interpreted flying saucers and U.F.O.'s as manifestations from the collective unconscious of a god image during a generally godless and scientific age created to oversee our actions.

Another manifestation of our continuing need for a frame of orientation and devotion, but consistent with a scientific space age, are the theories considering gods as ancient astronauts. Such theories have been made popular through the visits to small planets by the crew of the Starship Enterprise, in *Star Trek*. The idea that earth was visited by visitors from outer space, and we are their descendants, gives us a rootedness to space that we have not had before.

Von Däniken, to prove his theories, used the Mayan murals and bas-reliefs, ancient stone pyramids, observatories, and rock paintings (by the Bushman) in South Africa and (by the aborigines) in the Kimberly district of Australia as examples. He located the arrival points of the visitors from outer space on the Southern Hemisphere, Africa, America, and Australia. It was they, he claimed, who taught and directed the construction of pyramids, mural painting, and bas-relief carving, planned giant landing strips for spacecraft, impregnated the near-human women with the seeds of the imagination, and left, promising to return. Von Däniken, in using archeology, anthropology, and art history to support his theory, is applying forms of secular rationalism to make them acceptable. Whether true or not, the myth of the eternal return as modern folklore is thus reinstated.

Conflict Between Good and Evil

The presence of evil in the world, and the conflict between good and evil, have various mythological origins. In the biblical tradition, the archangel Lucifer, one of Jehovah's creations, is exiled from the heavenly hierarchy for attempting to be equal to God. Adam and Eve, through the serpent identified as the Devil, are tempted to eat the forbidden fruit. Dialogues between God and the Devil can be found in the *Book of Job*, and in Milton's *Paradise Lost*.

The human conflict with good and evil was personified through legends wherein Satan, or his counterparts, tries to tempt the earthly descendants of the Godhead (Jesus, Siddartha, and Gautama). Tales of the struggles of saints with temptations fill the long histories of most religions, and are seemingly endlessly depicted in the arts—whether St. Anthony being plagued by evil demons, or St. George slaying the dragon.

In fairy tales, the conflict is often between good and bad human beings, such as the victimization of the innocent and pure (Snow White, Cinderella, Beauty) by evil stepsisters, stepmothers, or witches and wizards along the road. In some instances particular individuals have been considered the prototype for the character, such as Giles de Rais, traditionally accepted as the original Bluebeard.

Recent research into the folklore and archives of Transylvania revealed that a historical prototype for Bram Stoker's *Dracula* (1897) had, indeed, existed. He was Vlad Tepes (Vlad the Impaler), son of Vlad III, Dracul. As son of Dracul, he was called *Dracula*. He lived between 1431-76, was a Prince of Wallachia, a duchy in the Transylvanian regions of the Carpathian Mountains in Hungary. However, he was not a vampire in the traditional sense. Elizabeth Bathory, the "Blood Countess" was more a source for tales dealing with vampirism. She was a Hungarian contemporary of Vlad Tepes. The werewolf, also of ancient origin, had a European prototype in Petrus Gonsalrus from the Canary Islands. He lived in Paris and Munich, married and had two daughters, who, like their father, had features somewhat wolf-like, and were covered with hair (McNally and Florescu 1972).

Most of the tales of evil individuals or beings predate, by hundreds of years, their historical prototypes. But it seems to be the doings of these human beings, whatever they may have been, that transpose the folklore into contemporary literature and the cinema. As grotesque, bizarre, or horror stories, such tales as *Dracula, Frankenstein, Dr. Jekyll and Mr. Hyde,* and others of that ilk, play a part in the fantasy world of children because of their presence on the home screen and the movies. Accordingly they can be discussd in terms of the conflict between good and evil, use of Christian symbolism (crosses and silver bullets) to overcome evil, or comparing various versions of the same tale, or the film version, with the original book, as with *Dr. Jekyll and Mr. Hyde.*

The search for the sacred rather than the profane truths are found in the Arthurian and Grail legends, and provide a richly constructed core monument. The legends embody a host of tales dealing with King Arthur, his Knights of the Round Table, Sir Lancelot and Guinevere, Merlin, and Mordred are most familiar. Less familiar is the story of Percival, chosen to find the Holy Grail, which Lancelot fell short of achieving.

As a tale symbolizing the struggle or quest for a spiritual transcendence, it is a matrix of Anglo-Saxon, Teutonic, pagan, classical, and Christian sources. This symbolism—the fisher-king, the grail, the perilous chapel, the sword and the stone—requires a deeper analysis than is appropriate at the elementary level. But the many retellings for children (see Appendix C: Resources) can provide the basis for later involvement beyond merely the events at Camelot.

The Holy Grail, believed to be the chalice from which Jesus drank and blessed his apostles at the Last Supper, was passed down into history through Joseph of Aramathea. It continues to be sought on Glastonbury Tor, by archeologists and historians in quest for the reality of King Arthur.

Not limited to England, the Grail legend also has a strong Germanic origin through the legend of *Parzival* (Parsifal, or Percival). The Germanic tradition also includes a countersymbol, representing the antichrist. It is the spear of Longinus, believed to have been used by him at the Crucifixion to pierce the side of the Christ as he hung on the cross. It is also believed to contain occult powers used by Adolf Hitler—to be the real source of evil demonic energy behind Nazism and the Third Reich (Ravenscroft 1973).

The German version, *Parzival,* by Wolfram von Eschenbach, a ninth century Minnesinger, was Richard Wagner's source and inspiration for his opera, *Parsifal,* which includes both the Grail and the spear. The English version, *Le Morte d'Arthur* by Sir Thomas Malory (about 1469), is a gathering of many tales and legends, the Arthurian being considered Breton, and the Grail Welsh, and includes related tales in the Mabinogeon, a collection of medieval Welsh tales.

Arthurian tales have been depicted in medieval illumination, Celtic mosaics, tapestries, bas-reliefs, and sculpture, and retold in allegorical epic poetry (Edmund Spenser's *The Faerie Queene*); romantic poetry (Alfred Tennyson's *Idylls of the King*), and in various children's versions by Andrew Lang, Howard Pyle, and a new cycle by Constance Hieatt, and illustrated by N. C. Wyeth (see Appendix C: Resources). From T. H. White's *The Sword and the Stone,* Walt Disney made an animated film, and the team of Lerner and Lowe wrote the Broadway musical, *Camelot.* Numerous Hollywood versions—some good, others like tin-suited westerns of spurious value—have helped make the Arthurian adventures even more familiar.

The Grail legends are more in line with the humanistic traditions discussed here and are worthy of study. Similar to the quest for transcendence and the salvation aspects of the Grail legend is John Bunyan's *Pilgrim's Progress* (1678-84), a Puritan, working man's allegory of the struggle of the Christian pilgrim to resist greed, despair, the house of the beautiful, and the advice from strangers, Mr. Worldly-Wiseman, among others, along the way. It was a popular home document on the proper moral conduct for reaching the Celestial city. It is more middle and working class in its orientation than the Arthurian and Grail legends.

For all of their universality, the tales of Arthur were not as popular for the folk and the working classes as for the upper classes and aristocracy. The folk found Robin Hood a more amiable hero. He was more of a rogue and stole from the rich to give to the poor. Except for ballads and narratives, children's verses and stories, and Hollywood film and television versions, Robin Hood has not had the appeal for the fine arts that King Arthur has had through the centuries. However, Robin Hood might get a more lively discussion under way in the inner city than would the search for the Grail.

From Mythology to Scientific Inquiry in Classroom Humanities

An elementary humanities program might be designed to deal with these sources of folklore, legends, and myths in three phases. The purpose would be not just to teach mythology, but to open up children's fantasies and imagination with them—and help them realize that myths are more than just make-believe. They provide an important heritage and link in man's quest for knowledge. Not every tale, myth, or legend read at a lower level need be carried to scientific inquiry, nor is it possible that they are all prescientific explanations of natural phenomena. Those which are might follow the route to scientific definition such as rainbows, or thunder and lightning.

The three phases might be included in a single study unit, or studied individually throughout a school year, or over a total kindergarten—grade six program. The three-phase aspect is based on using the same subject matter or story three ways—each time giving it a different point of view, adding new concepts concerned with it, or relating it to other materials and subject matter. The students may then have a chance to let the importance of the legends or myths, each backed with a lengthy heritage, grow within them.

Phase 1 deals with the fairy tale, myth, legend, or folktale as a pleasurable thing, to be read and enjoyed for itself, for its fancy and fantasy. The teacher might ask convergent questions afterwards about its content, descriptive details and sequence of narrative events to reinforce it in the mind of the students, and test for listening and comprehension skills, and the like. The teacher might ask divergent questions to help the children express feelings and responses to the story, the events, liking or not liking what happened to certain characters, and trying to explain why they felt that way.

Phase 2 involves a reintroduction or telling of the same tale to learn more about it as a story. This may involve analyzing it for its identifying characteristics as a myth, legend, folk or fairy tale. J.R.R. Tolkien (1966) has identified certain characteristics of fairy tales: (1) they must be straightforward, as really happening, not excused as being dreams; (2) they must have interaction between human beings and animals, fairies, and non-human beings; and (3) they must have some sort of moral orientation. He does not provide criteria for evaluating myths, legends, and folklore, but his criteria for fairy tales can be applied to those stories of unidentified origins which may extend back to prescientific times and have been recorded by such as the Brothers Grimm, Hans Christian Andersen, or Perrault, from old tales; or applied to stories written as pieces of fairy tale literature, such as "The Happy Prince" and "The Selfish

Giant" by Oscar Wilde, "The Goblin Market" by Christina Rosetti, or by those by J.R.R. Tolkien (1966, pp. 3-84). He has been less precise in describing the specific characteristics of myths, legends, and folktales as differing from those of fairy tales.

At this phase, similar tales might also be compared for likenesses and differences in content, structure, and moral outcome. On a comparative basis they might be classified as myths, legends, folktales, or fairy tales.

Phase 3 involves the possibility of reading the story a third time in terms of a correlated curriculum, relating it to a science unit, social studies or history unit, in studying natural phenomena or specific humanistic concerns, and values. Also important at any time is discussion about how these stories, myths, legends were used by the people. Were they part of religious rituals, designed for adults first, only to become in time nursery tales? Were they told by elders and wise men, sung as ballads by troubadors, parts of actual histories—or were they narrated and passed by recitation from generation to generation, or were they first written as literary pieces? All food for thought!

At any phase, described above, fairy tales, folklore, myths, and legends can be illustrated, dramatized, pantomimed, danced, made into movie-panel sequences, narratives, illustrated as comic books with dialogue included in the balloon, murals for decorating the school walls, or applied in day-to-day classroom art activities. Plays might include original songs and lyrics by the children. (For an example see: Appendix A: From Memory Bank: "Jack and the Beanstalk," K-6.)

References

ASHE, GEOFFREY, ed. *The Quest for Arthur's Britain.* New York: Frederick A. Praeger, 1968.

BROUDY, HARRY S. "Aesthetic Education in a Technological Society: The Other Excuses for Beauty." *Journal of Aesthetic Education,* Spring 1966, Inaugural Issue, pp. 13-23.

CAMPBELL, JOSEPH. *Myths to Live By.* New York: Viking Press, 1972.

DA PORTO, LUIGI. "Romeo and Giulietta." In *The Palace of Pleasure: An Anthology of the Novella.* Edited by Harry Levtow and Maurice Valency. New York: Capricorn Books, 1960.

ELIADE, MIRCEA. *Cosmos and History: The Myth of the Eternal Return.* New York: Harper & Row, Publishers, 1954.

FRAZER, SIR JAMES G. *The Golden Bough* (one volume abridged version). New York: Macmillan Co., 1960.

JANSON, H. W., ed. *Key Monuments of the History of Art.* New York: Harry N. Abrams, Inc., 1964.

JUNG, CARL G. *Flying Saucers: A Modern Myth of Things Seen in the Sky.* Translated by R.F.C. Hull. New York: Harcourt Brace Jovanovich, 1959.

LÉVI-STRAUSS, CLAUDE. *The Raw and the Cooked: Introduction to a Science of Mythology.* vol. 1. Translated by John Wightman and Doreen Wightman. New York: Harper & Row, Publishers, 1969.

MALORY, SIR THOMAS. *Le Morte D'Arthur.* (Everyman's Library, vol. 1.) New York: E. P. Dutton & Co., 1947.

McNally, Raymond T. and Florescu, Radu. *In Search of Dracula, a True History of Dracula and Vampire Legends.* Greenwich, Conn.: New York Graphic Society, Ltd., 1972.

Ravenscroft, Trevor. *The Spear of Destiny.* New York: G. P. Putnam's Sons, 1973.

Thompson, William I. *At the Edge of History: Speculations on the Transfer of Culture.* New York: Harper & Row, Publishers, 1971.

Tolkien, J.R.R. "Tree and Leaf: On Fairy Stories." In *The Tolkien Reader.* New York: Ballantine Books, 1966.

Velikovsky, Immanuel. *Oedipus and Akhnaton, Myth and History.* Garden City, N. Y.: Doubleday & Co., 1960.

———. "My Challenge to Conventional Views in Science" (and related articles). In *Pensee-Student Academic Freedom Forum* 4, no. 2 (1974):10-14 passim.

Von Eschenbach, Wolfram. *Parzival, a Romance of the Middle Ages.* Translated by Helen M. Mustard and Charles E. Passage. New York: Random House, Vintage Books, 1961.

Von Franz, Marie-Louise. *An Introduction to the Interpretation of Fairy Tales.* New York: Spring Publications, The Analytical Psychology Club of New York, 1970.

White, Lynn, Jr. "The Historical Roots of Our Ecological Crisis." In *Subversive Science: Essays Toward an Ecology of Man.* Edited by Paul Shepard and Daniel McKinley. Boston: Houghton Mifflin Co., 1974.

7

The cognitive domain
and its uses in the arts

The next three chapters will deal with a currently fashionable and surprisingly workable system for classifying educational objectives. It is called the "Taxonomy of Educational Objectives," or more popularly, "Bloom's taxonomy," because Benjamin S. Bloom was the chairman of a committee of college examiners who first met informally at the American Psychological Association Conference in Boston, 1948, and identified those objectives. The committee was looking for a framework that would promote an exchange of test materials, ideas about testing and evaluating, and eventually become valuable for the improvement of curriculum design.

They identified three domains of learning: the *cognitive*, the *affective*, and the *psychomotor*. Their classification was similar to that of the "faculty" psychologists of the eighteenth and early nineteenth centuries who identified *knowing, feeling,* and *doing* as the three ways, or faculties, of learning. Each of the three domains describes a specific approach to learning. They interact and affect one another, but can be analyzed separately for a better understanding of each.

(1) The *cognitive domain* is concerned with knowledge: comprehending it, applying it, analyzing it, synthesizing it, and evaluating it. The cognitive domain usually has educational priority in our school systems and institutes of higher learning. It is the domain most traditionally recognized by the public, and was the first one of the three about which a handbook was published by the committee of college and university examiners who determined them (Bloom 1956).

(2) The *affective domain* is concerned with interests, attitudes, and loyalties, the acceptance and rejection of concepts, beliefs, judgments, and appreciations, values, and personality characteristics. As such it is usually given additional priority by those working in the arts, and acknowledged as highly important in our school systems and institutions of higher learning. It is also the most difficult to evaluate and was the second domain about which a handbook was published by the committee (Krathwohl 1964).

(3) The *psychomotor domain* is concerned with muscular and motor skills, manipulative abilities in using tools, implements, materials, kinesthetic activities, and skills involving neuromotor coordination. It attains its maximum priority in teaching penmanship, and in developing skills in art, sewing, industrial arts, physical education, and instrumental music. The committee could not find sufficient information on this field to enable it to prepare a handbook on the psychomotor domain. It is not as highly rated in the academic institutions as the cognitive and affective domains. As yet a handbook covering this area has not been published. However, Anita J. Harrow did compile the research and published *A Taxonomy of the Psychomotor Domain* (1972). Another psychomotor taxonomy was defined by Dr. R. H. Dave, head of the Department of Curriculum and Evaluation, National Institute of Education, New Delhi, India: *Developing and Writing Behavioral Objectives* (Armstrong 1970, pp. 33-34).

Each of the domains is designed in terms of a hierarchy of learning skills. It is a continuum from simple to more complex learning skills. For the individual accomplishing these cognitive, affective, and psychomotor skills, it is like climbing a ladder. (See figs. 7.1, 8.1, and 9.2.) The lowest level of each domain's hierarchy is the lowest rung on the ladder (1.00). Each domain has five major rungs, except the cognitive domain which has a sixth rung (6.00) on evaluation. This does not mean that evaluation only takes place in the cognitive domain, but that evaluation is an intellectual cognitive process even when applied to evaluating learning in the affective and psychomotor domains.

The Cognitive Domain Hierarchy

1.00 KNOWLEDGE

This category, first step on the Cognitive Hierarchical Ladder, deals with factual information, data, methods, and specifics which usually depend on memory-recall processes. Such knowledge or information can usually be presented, researched, and remembered through verbal (written or oral) tests. Knowledge has three subcategories:

1.10 KNOWLEDGE OF SPECIFICS uses recall to deal with (**1.11**) *Terminology* and (**1.12**) *Facts* such as dates, events, sizes, locations, titles, and so on. These can be applied to the arts and humanities as terms dealing with art, music, literature, drama, and dance; and the dates and titles of works and historical periods in the arts, and the names of their creators.

1:20 KNOWLEDGE OF WAYS AND MEANS OF DEALING WITH SPECIFICS is knowing how to organize, study, judge, and criticize specific knowledge. There are five levels (each more advanced than the preceding one). Knowledge of: (**1.21**) *Conventions,* such as knowing the characteristics of animals, symbols,

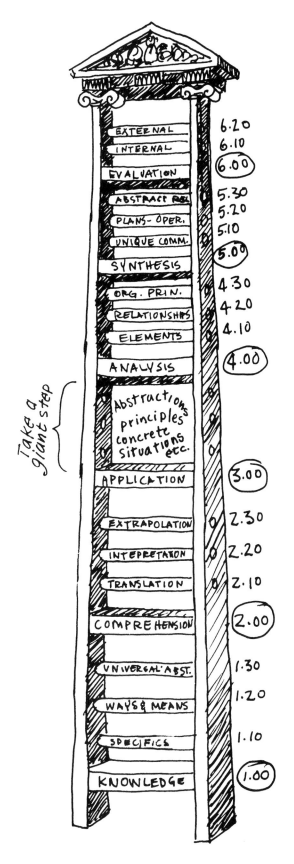

EXTERNAL	6.20
INTERNAL	6.10
EVALUATION	(6.00)
ABSTRACT REL.	5.30
PLANS - OPER.	5.20
UNIQUE COMM.	5.10
SYNTHESIS	(5.00)
ORG. PRIN.	4.30
RELATIONSHIPS	4.20
ELEMENTS	4.10
ANALYSIS	(4.00)
Abstractions principles concrete situations etc.	
APPLICATION	(3.00)
EXTRAPOLATION	2.30
INTERPRETATION	2.20
TRANSLATION	2.10
COMPREHENSION	(2.00)
UNIVERSAL ABST.	1.30
WAYS & MEANS	1.20
SPECIFICS	1.10
KNOWLEDGE	(1.00)

Take a giant step

Figure 7.1 The cognitive hierarchical ladder. Read upward.

art media, and other natural and man-made phenomena so as to identify them, use them, and present ideas about them; (1.22) *Trends and Sequences,* such as knowing trends and processes, following directions, recognizing sequences according to time, and identifying similarities and differences when making comparisons; (1.23) *Classifications and Categories,* such as knowing sets, classes, divisions, and arrangements in a particular subject matter, and being able to group, sort, or classify objects, terms, and concepts about the arts, periods of arts, history, color and design theories, dance styles, songs and musical compositions, types of narrative forms; (1.24) *Criteria,* such as knowing facts, principles, and opinions for making judgments about things. In the arts, using aesthetic criteria, and proper terminology when criticizing or evaluating student or professionally produced works of art, music, dance, theater, or creative writing; (1.25) *Methodology,* such as knowing how to make things in art, do cursive writing, mix colors, clean a paintbrush, hold a musical instrument for proper playing, throw a ball, write a sentence, and so forth.

1.30 Knowledge of Universals and Abstractions, such as knowing about major schemes and patterns used in organizing things and ideas. These are the overall structures, theories, and generalizations dominating a field of study, mathematics, science, the humanities, art forms, or other subject matter. There are two subcategories, knowledge of: (1.31) *Principles and Generalizations,* such as knowing practical abstractions which help summarize observations and data for explaining or describing something, predicting an outcome, or deciding the appropriate action in problem solving; (1.32) *Theories and Structures,* such as knowing the interrelationships between principles, generalizations, and theories in order to have a comprehensive view of a subject area. This might involve knowing theories about art production, color mixing, ecological balance, movement education, Orff or Kodály music techniques, or the aesthetic structure of different art forms.

At the knowledge level, it is possible to evaluate how much the student has learned of each category or subcategory with questions, either written or oral, directed to the specific level being tested. Knowing specific facts, ways and means of dealing with facts, and universals and abstractions in a specific field does not mean one comprehends or is able to apply this knowledge. One can memorize and recall this knowledge, but to be able to do more than record or pass a test with it requires a higher level of cognitive learning.

2.00 Comprehension

This category, second step on the Cognitive Ladder, identifies the lowest form of understanding. We understand what is being communicated without relating it to other uses, or seeing potentials for further implications. Comprehension has three steps or subcategories:

2.10 TRANSLATION is demonstrated by the care and accuracy with which a communication or bit of knowledge is paraphrased, or rendered from one language to another. Quality of translation is based on its accuracy or faithfulness to the original in both sense and feeling. In art, copying another picture is the lowest level of indicating comprehension, since it requires visual perception but no understanding of what the lines or shapes mean.

2.20 INTERPRETATION is demonstrated by explanations and summaries about a communication, symbol, or visual statement, often found useful in attempting to provide necessary clarifying information. Telling what a painting means, expressing a specific emotion in art or dance, illustrating a story, and explaining the meaning of visual symbols are forms of interpreting.

2.30 EXTRAPOLATION is demonstrated by extending beyond the communication to suggest further implications, consequences, corollaries, and effects, to predict trends and tendencies beyond the given data. Predicting how a photograph will turn out from the settings in a camera, using aesthetic principles in creating a work of art, or writing a story using metaphors and allegories after having them identified might be forms of extrapolation in the arts.

There are similarities between extrapolations and *application*, the next step in the cognitive domain. Comprehending knowledge is an intermediate step to applying it.

3.00 APPLICATION

This is demonstrated by selecting the proper abstraction, rule, and principal method, strategy, or the like, to achieve a certain purpose or solution to a problem. The student might learn the step-by-step procedure for doing something (which is cognitive at the methodology level), but must comprehend the logical sequence (extrapolation) before applying it. In chapter 6 we discussed core monuments. Understanding the principle behind them, by the reader, indicates how well he or she will be able to apply them in planning a humanistic study unit. There are no specific subcategories for the application level. In the art-making process, the student's ability to apply art methods and techniques are demonstrated through the psychomotor domain, but the knowledge of the methods and techniques can be tested using verbal techniques in the cognitive domain.

4.00 ANALYSIS

This, the fourth major step on the Cognitive Ladder, extends beyond knowing, comprehending, and applying, to the ability to look into the whole of a theory, principle, or concept and break it down into separate parts

and note their interrelationships. As shall be seen in chapter 14, analysis is a creative mental process. As such, it is not limited to this level of the cognitive domain, but might be used for comprehending and applying knowledge. When used to interpret nonverbal or sensory information and data, analysis takes place via the psychomotor domain. For example: interpreting visual symbols or visual data in a work of art or in the natural environment is part of visual analysis. Auditory analysis is the ability to interpret or give meaning to sounds, such as identifying instruments in an orchestra by their sound, or birds by their songs. Gustatory analysis is the ability to identify the ingredients in a particular dish or combination of foods. All are sensory modes. Such analysis is through the psychomotor domain, although the intellectual process is identified in the cognitive domain. Analysis has three subcategories:

4.10 ANALYSIS OF ELEMENTS. Elements are basic to all communication of a phenomenon. Basic facts, terminology, and so forth are considered elemental. In art, the elements of design are: line, color, texture, shape, and form. The individual, at this level, can use these terms and identify these elements when looking at a work of art, natural object of visual content. Music and dance have other elements.

4.20 ANALYSIS OF RELATIONSHIPS. This takes the analysis of elements one step further: it calls for an ability to judge whether or not the five elements relate successfully to one another, and thus work together. A teacher at this level may be able to determine whether the subject matter of a lesson is taking hold with a particular group of children after analyzing the content of that lesson in terms of the ability of the students. In the arts the individual can make comparative statements about different elements within a work, or relationships of elements between different works and art forms, such as in comparative aesthetics.

4.30 ANALYSIS OF ORGANIZATIONAL PRINCIPLES. In the arts, organizational principles are the aesthetic criteria (counters) used to evaluate or criticize a painting, building, symphony, sonata, jazz improvisation, dance, play, opera, and so forth. Each art form has its own organizational structure and principles. In art: contrast, repetition, balance, dominance, and subordination would be considered principles of design. They are the rules which govern the use of the five elements. The analysis of the relationship between the elements of design and the principles of design constitute art criticism. Innovations in the arts require new principles for critical analysis.

Analysis provides the basis for separating parts (elements, relationships, and organizational principles); but, another, quite closely related mental process, is an important factor in completing the learning process. That process is *synthesis*.

5.00 SYNTHESIS

This is the process of pulling the various elements—concepts, theories, relationships—once analyzed, back together again to give them new meanings, gain new theories, or make new products. Synthesis must take some specific form. A collage is a synthesis of many materials. Our national anthem is a synthesis of two diverse elements, a poem, *The Star Spangled Banner* by Francis Scott Key, set to a popular tavern song of the time, "Anacreon's Hymn." Synthesis has three subcategories:

5.10 PRODUCTION OF A UNIQUE COMMUNICATION. The objective of producing a unique communication is to present a new idea, feeling, theory, or experience to others. Creative self-expression—assuming the end product to be a personal unique communication—operates at this level of synthesizing. It may indicate a personal response to an event, such as Picasso's mural, *Guernica,* as a part of the affective domain; but, such an expression is still the synthesis of a unique communication. It results from having analyzed the elements, and from the interrelationship of materials with the feelings and ideas to be communicated (expressed) and needed to produce a unique, personal statement. Such a statement can be an original work in any of the arts, an improvisational dance, an essay, a poem, a sculpture, or a painting or mural.

5.20 PRODUCTION OF A PLAN OR PROPOSED SET OF OPERATIONS. This is a longer, more extensive procedure than that of making a single unique communication. Picasso made many sketches, drawings, and worked and reworked the symbols he wanted to use in his *Guernica.* He planned its composition, determined its color or lack of it, synthesized and then resynthesized until it said about war what he wanted it to say. Long-range products—murals, plays, school programs, films—require the setting up of plans of operations, gathering together the materials, getting with other teachers on the team, getting the children to work as a team, and fitting all this into a school schedule. This is a process of synthesizing a plan or proposed set of operations. Such planning can be done by children, teachers, the principal, or by all of them together.

5.30 DERIVATIONS OF A SET OF ABSTRACT RELATIONS. This results in ideational productions rather than material or sensory productions. The individual begins with specific known data or phenomena, analyzes and synthesizes it, and more or less extrapolates from it to produce new meanings, explanations, theories, or classifications. He or she may use basic propositions, theories, or symbols to deduce new propositions, theories, or relations. A person with training in one field or discipline can produce a new or unique solution to a problem which was previously unanswerable in another. The knowledge Louis Pasteur brought from animal husbandry to chemistry to discover his antitoxins is such a synthesis of knowledge.

The use of major social values and human needs to help formulate the goals and objectives of a school humanities program is a synthesis of abstract relations. The Taxonomy of Educational Objectives is itself a set of abstract relations.

The final step in Bloom's hierarchy is evaluation. Although it is placed at the top, evaluation can take place at any level along the continuum. Most written and oral tests evaluate specific knowledge. To evaluate comprehension and the ability to apply knowledge, and to analyze and synthesize, specific tests should be devised which are addressed to the descriptives and criteria of each level.

6.00 EVALUATION

This is the process of making value judgments about ideas, theories, works, projects, solutions, and methods, according to specific standards or criteria. When appraising for values of a qualitative or quantitative nature, the criteria may be determined by the student or teacher, or can be preestablished and standardized. Evaluation has two subcategories:

6.10 JUDGMENT IN TERMS OF INTERNAL EVIDENCE. The internal evidence within a product, work of art, or theory are those elements which are consistent, have logical accuracy, and are free of particular internal flaws when viewed as a whole or complete entity. This requires coherence of organization and an inner unity which resists the need for change. When analyzing relationships, we might ask, "Do all the elements work together on their own?"

6.20 JUDGMENT IN TERMS OF EXTERNAL CRITERIA. Such criteria are predetermined rules or standards and theories. The principles of design are the criteria for judging a work of art. A student may have a certain idea in mind when creating a work of art, which is his or her own external criteria. Success or failure depends on how close the end result comes to the original concept or idea. The teacher in giving assignments should have some set of external criteria available in order to more effectively describe the assignment. It is generally the internal concept of the product, idea, or tested item which, when equated or compared with the external criteria, gives the evaluation results, test score, or critique. Evaluation in the learning process is most effective when it is checked, at specific stages, against the cognitive, affective, and psychomotor hierarchies. The last two will be discussed in chapters 8 and 9.

Reinforcing Activities

Draw two vertical lines, one for each of two subject areas you are studying in college, or teaching in school. Choose one subject you like most, and one you like least; or one you do well and one you do not do well. Mark off the lines with levels of the cognitive hierarchy (as in fig. 7.1, The Cognitive Ladder.) Analyze your level of knowledge in both subjects in terms of reading the textbooks, memorizing and recalling specific knowledge, comprehending them, applying them, and analyzing and synthesizing your knowledge about each. What does this tell you about your cognitive skills in both subjects? Is there a relationship between your level on the cognitive hierarchy and your interest?

References

ARMSTRONG, ROBERT J. et al. *Developing and Writing Behavioral Objectives.* Tucson, Ariz.: Educational Innovations Press, 1970.

BLOOM, BENJAMIN S., ed. *Taxonomy of Educational Objectives: The Classification of Educational Goals, Handbook I: Cognitive Domain.* New York: David McKay Co., 1956.

HARROW, ANITA J. *Taxonomy of the Psychomotor Domain.* New York: David McKay Co., 1972.

KRATHWOHL, DAVID R.; BLOOM, BENJAMIN S.; and MASIA, BERTRAM B. *Taxonomy of Educational Objectives: The Classification of Educational Goals. Handbook 2: The Affective Domain.* New York: David McKay Co., 1956.

8

The psychomotor domain and its uses for the arts

Of the three domains, the psychomotor is the one most relevant to instruction in the arts, since the arts call for procedures for doing things—painting, carving, dancing, singing, playing musical instruments, and so on. To do them well requires specific cognitive knowledge, the skills to do them, and the desire and commitment to learn them. Thus, the cognitive and affective domains each play their parts in learning by way of the psychomotor domain. However, the close relationship between the cognitive knowledge of ways and means, and applying that knowledge through the psychomotor domain seems to place these in juxtaposition. After dealing with the psychomotor hierarchy, I shall attempt to show in chapter 10 the interplay of the affective domain on both the cognitive and psychomotor domains.

Traditionally the art-talented child was described as one who could draw or paint representationally very well. The accuracy of a drawing, when compared to the subject it represented, made the object the external criteria for evaluating talent. Lowenfeld, in *Creative and Mental Growth* (1947), helped break down this stereotyped and Renaissance-oriented concept by introducing the visual-haptic theory to art education in this country. Visually oriented children, who are objective about their subject matter, draw what they see and experience with representational accuracy. Haptically oriented children, who react subjectively to what they see or experience, draw it according to their emotional and other sensory responses. Their drawing may look out of proportion, and show incorrect attempts at inner perspective. Such children are classified as poor in art. Since even small children have learned to accept representational accuracy as external criteria for artistic ability, haptic children may think of themselves as untalented or poor in art.

The visual-haptic theory is a continuum, not a dichotomy. Children have to some degree both visual and haptic orientations. The large majority are in the middle sector. Both the visual and haptic, or intellectual and emotional, or mental and sensory responses of children should be developed in them as part of the motivation for an expressive type of art activity, such as drawing, painting, modeling, or sculpting.

As a result of current processes in clarifying, defining, and describing student behavior, drawing might now be defined as the ability to delineate a visual stimulus or mental image with a certain degree of accuracy and satisfaction. Lack of this ability might be defined, to use the terms of learning disabilities, as the result of a visual-perceptual learning dysfunction, such as visual dyslexia, wherein an individual may see a visual stimulus accurately, but be unable to integrate it into a similarly correctly delineated symbol. Such individuals may also have difficulty making figure-ground differentiations or maintaining visual memory. They might respond with other sensory perceptions and imagery that the individual with highly developed visual abilities does not have. There may even be a relation between strong hapticity and visual perceptual learning dysfunctions, but the author does not believe this has been researched. Hapticity may also be found to be the result of the dominance of the expressive, emotive (right) side of the brain over the intellectual, cognitive (left) side of the brain.

When we consider art in the domain of manipulative, psychomotor, and neuromotor skills, we are dealing with a much wider range of skills than drawing and painting. It includes writing, lettering, hammering, nailing, sewing, playing a musical instrument, ball, or tiddly-winks, and driving a car, skiing, or swimming. In art, the ability to draw representationally is no longer the only criteria for identifying the gifted and talented. Criteria based on creativity and skills in manipulating many materials, tools, and equipment, developing a rich, visual vocabulary (knowing many ways to draw a large array of subject matter), expressing ideas and emotions in visual symbols and techniques, and being able to think both two and three dimensionally reduces "drawing representationally" to only one of many criteria for artistic talent.

The Psychomotor Domain Hierarchy

The psychomotor domain has not been so thoroughly written about in the taxonomical literature as have the cognitive and affective domains. Various approaches have been suggested, but Anita Harrow's *Taxonomy of the Psychomotor Domain* (1972) is perhaps the most comprehensive and recent. It has considerable value to writing of student performance or behavioral objectives. Some aspects of her classification system may be of more concern to clinical study than our concern here. Her groups range from nonvoluntary reflex actions through nondiscursive communication movements to which she attributes the expressive and interpretive movement. Her area of skilled movement lends itself to consciously learned skills with which the classroom

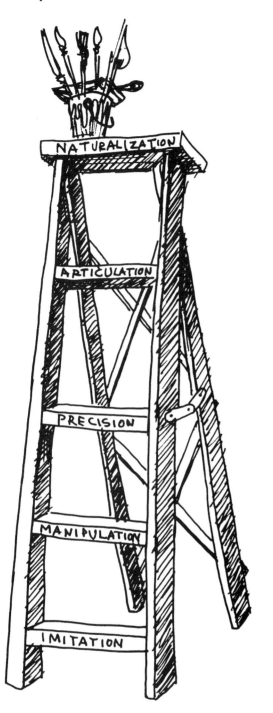

Figure 8.1   The psychomotor hierarchical ladder. Read upward.

teacher is concerned, but I find the psychomotor hierarchy of R. H. Dave (1970) more adaptable to the learning process.

Dave's five-stage hierarchy consists of: (1.0) Imitation, (2.0) Manipulation, (3.0) Precision, (4.0) Articulation, and (5.0) Naturalization (see fig. 8-1). Dave's hierarchy also provides categories of recognizable growth from one stage to the next, which is not entirely the case with Harrow's classification system. His psy-

chomotor hierarchy can also be applied to the mental processes, that is, the metamotor or "psycho" half of the term "psychomotor." The mind, in learning a new technique or skill, might go through the same stages from imitation to naturalization as those described for motor skills For instance, we may first learn a foreign language by imitating sounds. In conversation we may manipulate (2.0) sounds, foreign words, and phrases with a high degree of trial-and-error experimentation. As we become more sure of foreign nuances and vocabulary we make less errors and become more precise (3.0). At the articulation level (4.0), we are able to communicate in a foreign language and create our own thoughts and phrases with little or no error. At the naturalization level (5.0) we tend to think in the foreign language. It is no longer a process of thinking in one language and translating mentally into another. The process described here is mental, and only motor in the pronunciation of foreign words.

A similar analogy might be made about writing. The process of writing is psychomotor, as is typing; but, the skill or style of making a sentence, then creating a paragraph, is a mental process before it gets to the hand and muscles doing the actual "writing" or typing. The child learning to "write" a complete sentence first learns the rules of sentence structure and syntax, follows specific examples, and through some trial and error achieves the ability to *think* of a complete sentence (a mental process) before putting it down on paper (a motor process). Dave's psychomotor hierarchy seems applicable to both.

1.0 Imitation

This is the process of doing exactly as someone else is doing (either following instructions or of one's own free will), following a leader, copying or imitating observable acts or behaviors. At first imitation might be crude and imperfect, but with enough satisfaction of response it is repeated and the skill developed into a stereotype. Manuscript lettering and cursive writing are psychomotor skills usually taught by having the children imitate specific lines and directions in the order numbered on the Zaner-Bloser, or other, charts. Coloring books and workbooks with coloring-in activities operate at the imitation, manipulation, and precision levels without going to the articulation level. In the arts, origami is taught through the imitation, step-by-step method. Some basic nonexpressive skills in art, such as folding a straight edge, cutting, pasting, and threading a needle, can be taught through imitation. Other arts skills might be taught at the imitation level, but can be experimented with, such as tying macramé knots, centering and throwing a pot on a wheel, fingering on a musical instrument, or learning the steps and choreography of a dance. Eventually these can lead to creative expression.

2.0 Manipulation

At this stage the learner experiments and tries various ways of doing the same skill. He or she may experiment or manipulate techniques first learned through imitation, or may begin trying something without a formal set of instructions. Children learning cursive writing may try their own techniques rather than those on the chart. Left-handed children may need to manipulate and experiment sooner than right-handed children usually do in order to learn the same skills.

Art teachers usually prefer to begin at the manipulative level of some techniques for the use of certain types of art materials and media, rather than at the imitation level. They might begin a demonstration on watercolors, poster tempera, or colored chalk with a few ideas of wetting paper, applying the media or twisting and turning the tool, holding it lightly or applying pressure, but will leave it up to the students to figure out their own ideas—to experiment. People who teach themselves certain skills often begin at the manipulative-experimental trial-and-error level, even when the directions are written out for them in a manual or on a box. Teachers who withhold any instruction of a medium often leave the students stuck at the manipulative-experimental level.

3.0 Precision

At this stage the learner has eliminated most of the errors made at the manipulative-experimental level. The learner who began imitating a technique or skill, but did not improvise or experiment with it, can also reach the precision level, but in this case, they just become more efficient and exact in doing that particular skill (such as coloring in an outline). A child's cursive writing may not take on any variations or personality characteristics but continue to look like the charts even into the third and fourth grades. In the arts, as children show more confidence in painting, drawing, cutting, and printing, or dancing and singing, they, and the teacher, become more certain that each product or performance will be free of mistakes, errors, or degrees of failure. The learner is more quick and efficient in that particular skill at the precision level.

4.0 Articulation

At this level, the skill has been learned well enough to be consistent, and to allow the learner to express or communicate a personal concept, or try something special and fancy with the skill. In cursive writing, as a personal expression or wish to demonstrate his or her individuality, the child may try special ways of making letters, dotting i's with circles, adding curlicues, and so forth.

This does not mean to imply that even at the imitation, manipulation, and precision levels the learner has not tried to articulate or communicate a special statement or idea in a particular medium, art form, or technical skill; but, at the articulation level, confidence and abilities are secure enough so that the learner can try something new, communicate a new personal idea, or express a feeling about something and have it succeed with some degree of efficiency and/or accuracy.

5.0 Naturalization

In this the final stage, the learner has developed a high degree of proficiency and skill, and performs without expending much psychic energy or conscious effort. At times, the skill is routinized to the point of becoming almost automatic, and performance is accomplished with ease and smoothness. At this level the child may write a sentence or composition and concentrate more on what he or she is saying than on the formation of letters. The writing will, nonetheless, be accurate and legible. In art, the learner might be interrupted by the teacher or another student, and still reply without interrupting the painting, carving, dancing process, musical instrument, or whatever else is in progress.

These stages, like most hierarchies or continuums, follow in sequence, but the learners may not move from level to level at like speeds. A learner might, for example, stop at a stage along the way in unpursued skills, while moving on to the naturalization (final) stage in other skills. To achieve precision, articulation, or even naturalization in any skill requires *repeated opportunties* to use that skill.

Depth vs. Breadth Approaches to Learning Skills

There is somewhat of a continuous dialogue going on over the matter of the *depth* versus *breadth* approach to teaching art. The depth approach is that in which the learner concentrates on a particular skill or study area with repeated experiences or opportunity to learn from it. The breadth approach is that in which the learner has a wide range of experiences but not much opportunity to repeat any of them in order to acquire ability in depth. The breadth approach is most frequently used in elementary art by those art and classroom teachers who are always trying to find something new or different to do for an art lesson. The children are often conditioned or programmed to expect every art lesson to be something not done before.

Research conducted by Edward Mattil, Kenneth Beittel, and Robert Burkhart on the depth approach has some significant implications for the hierarchy of the psychomotor domain (Burkhart 1962). They investigated the depth versus breadth methods with ninth-grade art students using watercolors, but their conclusions have significance for elementary art classes.

They found that at least twelve lessons and experiences with watercolors were necessary before the average student had sufficient control of the materials to use them successfully in expressing personal concepts or original visual statements. This might be interpreted to mean that at least twelve experiences were necessary before the average ninth grader in the experiment could reach the articulation level. Such experiences had to be close enough together to minimize forgetfulness and skill regression. It is also necessary to repeat and review the cognitive information about what to do before each activity.

The child who does watercolors one week, crayons

the next, builds a toothpick structure the third, and so on will not learn to do any of them much beyond the imitation level, or the manipulation-experimentation level. In his own teaching experience, the author found this to be true. The following practices from his memory bank, which he worked out for himself, may prove helpful to his readers.

For clay modeling, each of the kindergarten children and the first and second graders were supplied with at least one-quarter pound of Plasticine. This they kept in small half-pint milk cartons, in their desks or cubbies. It was used frequently, to model human figures, usually of themselves playing games or saluting the flag, for example; or as a group activity which could be set up on a tabletop. With the support of the classroom teacher, children who had difficulty doing their manuscript letters, cursive writing, or numbers were not given penmanship drills, but Plasticine to work with. This helped develop the muscle and motor control necessary for writing.

Before giving the students self-hardening clay for pottery they had had three weeks of making pots in Plasticine: the first week a pinch pot, the second a pot pressed over a form, the third a coiled pot. On the fourth week they were given the self-hardening clay to make a pot, selecting their own method. One reason for this was the limited budget, since Plasticine could be reused. A bucket of balls of Plasticine was usually kept in the author's stockroom, wrapped in plastic suit covers saved from the dry cleaner's. This kept it from getting too firm. The bucket was also placed near the radiator, so that the Plasticine would remain pliable (though not too soft)—hardening clay gets harder and dries while it is being worked. The children thus learned the techniques first on a material they were familiar with, rather than having to learn new techniques while struggling with a new fast-drying material.

Other times, at about the third-grade level, during the spring, they learned about drawing trees. This was a three-week unit, planned to breakdown their stereotypes of trees. Since the tree was subject matter, rather than a new medium technique, it was kept constant, but the medium was changed. Each week the group went outdoors to the trees around the school building. This was done in the springtime, after the leaves had started to come out, but before the trees were so covered with leaves that the structure of the branches could not be seen.

For the first week the class concentrated on the details of the trees: bark texture, places where the branches and twigs grow from each other, different sizes of each, the smell, touch, and taste of the leaves as well as how they look. On the first lesson the students drew with twigs dipped in bottles of black india ink. They were to concentrate on just the small details. Paper was nine-by twelve-inch white drawing paper. For drawing boards—a few pieces of masonite, cut to size, and shirt cardboards over notebooks.

The second week the whole tree was studied, and the sizes of the larger older branches on the bottom were compared with those of the higher smaller branches and twigs on the outer edges. That day the group returned to the same trees that had been drawn in india ink the previous week, but this time they used watercolors. The colors, root structure, and general characteristics were discussed. The students painted on twelve- by eighteen-inch white drawing paper.

The third week, the trees in the landscape were studied. Before leaving the classroom, the group had looked at two reproductions: Van Gogh's *Peach Trees*, and his *Vegetable Gardens* (The Blue Cart)—and had talked about foreground, middle ground, and background. When outdoors, far enough away to see the trees in their relation to each other and the school building, the class observed and discussed differences in size, shape, sunlight, shadow; and located the foreground, middle ground, and background. This time crayons and colored pencils were used because the composition was more complex.

For the transfer of learning it was necessary to ask questions each week about what they had learned the previous weeks. In this way they were enabled to reinforce their learning, from one concept to the next, by incorporating it into each succeeding experience of drawing or painting the trees. By asking questions, those who remembered were able to verbalize and thus remind those who forgot, or stimulate their own memories.

Each of these examples represented an attempt to teach a particular art-making experience in depth. Both are related to the psychomotor domain—one modeling, the other rendering a tree. In one case the medium (clay) and the subject (bowl) were kept constant, but the techniques changed. In the other, the media (ink, watercolor, crayon) changed but the subject matter (tree) was kept constant as the concepts about it became more complex. Since this was done at the third- and fourth-grade levels, the students had had enough previous experience using pen and india ink, crayons, and watercolors to make additional instruction in those media unnecessary. They could, therefore, concentrate on the different aspects of the subject matter itself.

Reinforcing Activities

1. Select a skill you have had or recently learned (such as driving a car: parking, turning, backing, and steering) and trace the various stages of your learning according to the five stages of the psychomotor domain.

2. Consider the nature of the cognitive knowledge given you pertaining to that skill you used in activity 1 (above). Compare, if you can, the correlation between certain levels in the cognitive domain with those of the psychomotor domain as your skills increased.

References

BURKHART, ROBERT C. *Spontaneous and Deliberate Ways of Learning.* Scranton, Pa.: International Textbook Co., 1962.

HARROW, ANITA J. *Taxonomy of the Psychomotor Domain.* New York: David McKay Co., 1972.

LOWENFELD, VIKTOR. *Creative and Mental Growth.* New York: Macmillan Co., 1947.

9

The affective domain
and its uses in the arts

The affective domain is concerned with attitudes, interests, loyalties, values, taste preferences, acceptances, and rejections which make up the individual personality. Like the cognitive and psychomotor domains, it too progresses along a hierarchy of which the major levels are: (1.00) Receiving (Attending), (2.00) Responding, (3.00) Valuing, (4.00) Organization of values, and (5.00) Characterization by a value or value complex (Krathwhol, Bloom, and Masia 1964). Refer to figure 9.1, the Affective Domain Hierarchical Ladder.

Individuals who, professionally, are most in accord with themselves may be those whose work, jobs, or careers are most in balance with their personality characteristics at the 5.00 affective level. Reinforcing acts aid the individual, whether socially acceptable or rejected by society, to achieve the top of the affective domain. A negating factor may terminate the individual's progress along the affective hierarchy at any point, but satisfaction at the response level may be the most sensitive positive factor. Examples of negating factors are teachers who pat a child on the head during music and say, "Don't sing, Johnnie. It might be better if you just hum." Or in art, to say, "You make such a mess when you paint, Frankie, wouldn't you rather use the coloring-in sheets?"

The Affective Domain Hierarchy

In the affective domain there are five levels, each with several sublevels. They are:

1:00 RECEIVING (Attending)

This first level concentrates on sensitizing the individual or learner to an awareness of the subject matter, and a willingness to receive information about it. In education this is called motivation; in the business world it is called advertising and selling. Receiving and attending has three subcategories:

1.10 AWARENESS. This, the lowest level of the Affective Domain Hierarchy Ladder merely means for the individual to be aware, to be cognizant of the fact that a thing or phenomenon exists without having much information about it, and to accept, reject, or make value judgments about it. So-called "Environmental Awareness" programs are titled after this level, but the people who plan them are seeking commitments to the preservation of the environment (**3.30** *Valuing*) rather than merely an awareness that

ecology and natural preservation exist. At this level, students **1.10** *Awareness* may recognize that a picture can be called "art," that a carving is a statue, that some buildings are called architecture while others are not, or that some dances are called ballet. It is not necessary to experience a thing or activity to be aware of it.

1.20 WILLINGNESS TO RECEIVE concerns the willingness of the individual to receive information about a particular subject or phenomenon. The teacher's motivation or disciplinary acts, and prizes and awards, are usually designed to encourage the child to want to listen, learn, and/or receive information. Students at the **1.20** level may pay attention during teacher demonstration, assignment description, or lectures and discussions without taking part in them. In art they will be in their places and willing to receive materials.

1.30 CONTROLLED OR SELECTED ATTENTION. At this level students control their expression of interest, ask questions, show alert body language. By attending to other activities in spite of the teacher asking for their attention, students can also demonstrate a selected interest in things and activities elsewhere in the room, or outside the window. As children remember some data, but forget others, they demonstrate a selected interest in the subject matter of the data remembered.

2.00 RESPONDING

This level is demonstrated by active response, rather than passive acceptance and attention. Since the arts are essentially *doing* learning activities, they require almost immediate response and overt involvement in a way that neither listening to a teacher nor reading a book does. Response has three subcategories:

2.10 ACQUIESCENCE OF RESPONDING. This is still somewhat passive—the student does not volunteer, but will do as asked; complies with requests without a sign of conviction that the response is important. Some art students will pass out materials, go through the movements in a dance, sing, or make an object in art, without indicating the slightest preference for doing the requested activity over another. They might even resist doing it and ask to do something else, showing a preference for something else, and then acquiesce and do the assignment when told they must do it rather than the other.

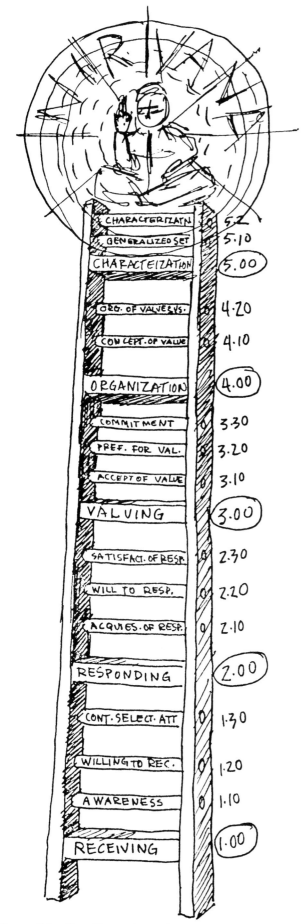

Figure 9.1 The affective hierarchical ladder. Read upward.

2.20 Willingness to Respond. This is the beginning of a preferred interest in an activity, similar to controlled or selected attention (**1.30**) at the top of the receiving-attending level. These children may be the first in the art or music room, get their reading and other books off the desk ready for an art lesson before being asked to do so. They may volunteer when volunteers are asked for. They may begin drawing, humming or singing, moving in dance steps—before the demonstration or instruction begins.

2.30 Satisfaction in Response. This is the first evidence of positive emotional response by the individual to the stimulus, motivation, or the learning activity itself. Although it might occur in earlier affective stages, Krathwhol and committee placed it here as a reminder of the importance of the emotional response to affective behaviors (Krathwhol, Bloom, and Masia 1964, p. 18). Students feeling secure in their cognitive knowledge of a subject and its techniques, and the manipulation skill (psychomotor) necessary to apply them, move very well into the level of satisfaction of response to specific arts and other class activities. Students at this level may ask to mat, mount, or frame an art product, put it on display, and show it to others, to sing a new song, or to show a dance movement to their parents or classroom teacher, if taught by a special teacher. They will ask to repeat or do more activities of a similar nature, or when given free choice select the activity (art, music, dance, gym, and so forth) which gives them the most satisfaction of response.

3.00 Valuing

At this level individuals move beyond looking for repetitions of satisfactory responses to placing a sense of value or personal worth on the favored activity or phenomenon. Their behavior in this regard will be consistent enough for others to know they place a value on the arts in general, or a single art form in particular. Their values may reflect or conflict with the values of others. Valuing has three subcategories:

3.10 Acceptance of a Value means internalizing a value, or a valued activity, enough to be consistent in response to it, and be recognized by others as valuing it. Such recognition can also reinforce the individual's self-image in connection with the valued activity. Students in the arts will want to be involved in their favored activity (drawing, painting, dancing, making music, or writing) most of the time, and spend much of their leisure time at it. They may ask for special privileges, go to the art or music room during lunch, recess, or elective activities. They may bring in news items or articles on their favorite arts subject for current events. In fact, they may be related to hobbies in their intensity.

3.20 Preference for a Value. More than just hold a particular value for, or interest in, one or more of the arts, the student, at this level, will give them favored priority over other activities, perhaps take special classes outside of school, or openly pursue more arts activities. Evidence may be demonstrated by pictures placed not only in the room at school, but at home as well by the types of arts books, art materials, records, music, instruments, dance clothes, and the like requested for birthdays and at Christmas; and the inclination to save money to buy related materials. Besides leisure time, they may ask for special time or privileges in order to work at their favored subject, or see movies about artists, dancers, or musicians and composers over again. If the original stimulus did not come from their parents, students at this level may get their parents involved.

3.30 COMMITMENT. Once this level is attained, there is little evidence of value confusion. Individuals interested in the arts may try to win converts. At the gang age (nine to eleven years), or later, they may try to organize arts clubs or groups, or seek out others with similar interests. How much commitment children may have for anything other than playing may call for further study. Children can be quite intense about their commitments, but those commitments are not always long-lasting.

For some children, childhood commitments grow into lifetime occupations. George Bellows, the American painter of the Ash Can School, knew as a boy in public elementary school in Columbus, Ohio, that he would probably be an artist. Sometimes he fought the other boys to prove he was not a sissy for liking art. At age ten he discovered sandlot baseball and faced a conflict about art. He resolved it by drawing pictures of the other kids playing ball, but his interest in sports remained throughout his life. As an adult, paintings of boxers (*Stag at Sharkey's, Dempsey and Firpo,* and *Both Members of This Club*) represent three of his most important works (Braider 1971, pp. 5-6). Henry Moore, the contemporary British sculptor, who was the seventh son of a Yorkshire miner, knew by the age of eleven that he wanted to be a sculptor, although his sociocultural environment was scarcely conducive to this field of endeavor. Between the ages of nine and thirteen, Virginia Woolf, with the help of her brother and sister, published a neighborhood newspaper, the *Hyde Park Gate News.* By the age of thirteen, she had experimented with writing in the style of Nathaniel Hawthorne and in the Elizabethan style (Bell 1972, pp. 40-57). Isadora Duncan, by the age of twelve, had a calling to be a great dancer. The Brontë children (Charlotte, Emily, Anne, and Branwell) lived a life of childhood fantasy and make-believe with stories written in a series of lost but legendary juvenilia based on a set of Branwell's toy soldiers, called "The Twelves." Whether they were geniuses, or just creatively gifted and talented, it seems their commitments began before they were twelve years old.

Students in the public schools with strong art interests may choose books because of their pictures or illustrations, use leisure time to draw, or ignore other assignments to do art. Around the age of twelve or thirteen when the average child loses an interest in drawing as a means of communication these children will continue, and their interest tends to increase. At the commitment level, the individual may want to test his or her art-making abilities with others, or make contact with the professional world. They may send in coupons to correspondence art schools, enter the "Draw Me" contests in magazines, or copy comic strip and animated cartoon characters and send them to the original artist. Children developing commitments to other art forms, academic enterprises, or career orientation may show similar behavior patterns related to their own area of interest.

4.00 ORGANIZATION

The need for organizing values into a system arises with commitment. A value priority helps resolve internalized conflicts by identifying those which will dominate others. Organizing a value system may require cognitive analysis and synthesis of conflicting interests Because organizing a value system is an internalizing process, the student's or individual's processes in this respect may not all be overt or outwardly observable. Organization has two subcategories:

4.10 CONCEPTUALIZATION OF VALUE. This level begins when the child or individual must make a choice between two or more alternatives which may be simple or complex. Children, for example, might be confronted with value conflicts when they trade one object, a baseball card—a collector's item—for another. Teachers and parents help by giving children limited choices to make, and can also provide opportunities to broaden their learning, aesthetic, and other experiences. At the commitment level, the child's (or the individual's) internalization process originates in the need for a personal value system rather than an outside force. Students conceptualizing values about the arts may ask questions about the importance of the arts in society, or the value of a career in the arts, or what parents, teachers, or others really think about artists, dancers, composers, writers, and so forth. Unfortunately, in our society, the attitude "art is sissy stuff" may raise value conflicts for boys at the gang age or at the puberty stage in relation to their heterosexual growth characteristics and, according to Erik Erikson, realization of an acceptable job or societal role orientation.

4.20 ORGANIZATION OF A VALUE SYSTEM. At this stage the individual brings together a complex of disparate values, fitting them into an ordered relationship of harmonious internal consistency. The value system (ideally, but not always realistically) functions in a dynamic equilibrium that responds to the most salient influence of the time. Values can also be synthesized into a new value system, which, being of a higher order, provides the basis for philosophical discourse (Existentialism, Neoplatonism, Christianity, Communism, etc.). Students, or other individuals, at this level try to balance their interest and activities in art with other preferred and school-assigned activities; they evaluate their decisions and choices in terms of their own value systems to see if they work, and form judgments about relating their interest in art to parental attitudes and career decisions. They try to decide, in their own terms, what arts mean to them—to evaluate their strengths and weaknesses in various creative art processes and forms (in relation to those with which they have had experience), and to compare their talents with the talents of others who have had similar art experiences; or, they may test their talent against competition in poster or school art competition.

5.00 CHARACTERIZATION BY A VALUE OR VALUE COMPLEX.
Thus, the final rung of the Affective Domain Ladder is reached by individuals who have lived with their organized value systems long enough to have no feeling of being threatened when their values are challenged. As a durable philosophy of life, this level is usually not achieved until after the individual's formal education has ended. It is achieved best through an interaction with the higher levels of the cognitive domain. For individuals professionally dependent on their manipulative skills (painters, surgeons, dentists, sculptors, movie stuntmen, acrobats, musicians, opera singers, dancers, and so on), achieving the upper levels of the psychomotor domain (articulation and naturalization) are essential for attaining the top levels of the affective domain if pleasure is to be derived from their work. Not all people reach this level of personality characteristic, but such individuals are very likely self-actualizing (according to Abraham Maslow), self-affirming (according to Rollo May), or self-idealizing (according to Carl Rogers). The characterization level has two subcategories:

5.10 GENERALIZED SET. This level indicates that the individual operates with an internal consistency in reference to his values and attitudes in a usually unconscious behavior response. The individual has a predisposition to respond to circumstances, challenges, and phenomena in a consistent way, according to clusters of attitudes held together by a common core of abstracted values. The generalized set cannot, therefore, be achieved in a single study unit, semester course, or fully accomplished by the average teacher. All that can be safely stated as an objective is that the student will (hopefully) find a direction toward particularly identified social, aesthetic, and humanistic values.

In terms of these goals, full-time art, music, and physical education teachers, if they are in a single school long enough, are better able to oversee the aesthetic, sensory, kinesthetic, and humanistic needs of each individual child, because they are the only teachers to have regular contact with the same children for as long as six or seven years. Classroom teachers, even in open units and teams, are limited to one or two years of a child's growth, and their interest is usually more the cognitive-academic and verbal growth than it is the affective-psychomotor, nonacademic, nonverbal growth of the child.

In either case, the teacher's role in helping children achieve a generalized set at the characterization level is in assisting them to approach problems objectively, willing to change their minds when facts indicate a change is in order, to accept their own subjectivity, irrationality, and contradictions in their growing selves, and to discover consistencies within themselves as important factors in the direction they are growing. Such activities include helping students identify their taste preferences (at that particular period in time or level of aesthetic growth), the do's and don'ts of personal behavior in terms of their parents' generation and their peer authorities in their own generation, and attitudes toward work-play, leisure time, and recreational time.

5.20 CHARACTERIZATION. This is the peak of the internalization process and the top rung of the affective hierarchical ladder. This includes the total "of one's view of the universe, one's philosophy of life, one's *Weltanschauung* = a value system having as its object the whole of what is known or knowable (Krathwhol, Bloom, and Masia 1964, p. 170)."

The artist (painter, sculptor, dancer, poet, composer, etc.) is fully integrated between his or her approach to art and that to life. It may be demonstrated in the selection of subject matter, work and practice habits, living and working environment, and human relationships. The humanity of George Bellows was evident in his painting, the attitudes of Isadora Duncan in her selection of dance interpretations, and so forth. The sudden change of Paul Gauguin from a stockbroker to an artist imbued with wanderlust is not surprising when one considers that his youth was one of having grown up in Peru, and his friendship with the Impressionists began before he made the break with middle-class morality and the establishment. In his novelette, "Childhood of a Leader," Jean-Paul Sartre (1948) tells of the development of the existential personality characterizing Lucien Bouffardier who tried many changes of identity and considerable role-playing before he finally realized his own unique personality.

Krathwohl equates the **5.20** characterization with positive attitudes toward society and humanism, citing Socrates, Christ, Lincoln, Gandhi, and Einstein as examples. In the same way, the social individual of Fromm, the self-affirming individual of May, and the self-idealizing individual of Carl Rogers are positive contributors to society and the human condition. Archie Bunker in "All in the Family" is a fully-realized characterization of a personality type. Even his first name suggests arch-conservatism. While a bunker, other than representative of Bunker Hill and the American Revolution, is also a box, can or other receptacle, or an enclosed gun implacement. In golf, a bunker is an obstructive ridge with a sand trap in front of it. Not only is he a complete **5.20** characterization of the stereotyped arch-conservative working-class personality, but his name reinforces his image.

The antisocial individual also goes through the same stages of awareness of crime, satisfaction of response to criminal acts, valuing the results, organizing a life-style to make them successful and remain undercover, and finally a personality characteristic. Within the lives of John Dillinger, Al Capone, and Adolph Hitler, it should be possible to detect the various levels of the affective domain in their antisocial development. The stages in the affective domain can be the same whether the individual ends up in prison, or as a painter.

In a way, play is, for children, a philosophy of life around which their conduct, values, behavior, and attitudes all focus. Conflict occurs more between play and school, the adult world of work, and other social institutions, than among children themselves. By turning learning activities into games, play, and fun activities, the educational system is adapting itself to this aspect of childhood personality characterization. A purpose of the humanities in the schools in this regard is to develop in growing children positive humanistic characteristics of a social rather than antisocial nature, and contribute to that objective with an attempt to maintain a balance between play and work.

Affective Growth of the Artist

In the arts, such uniquely lived lives as those of Emily Dickinson, Emily Brontë, Pablo Picasso, Vincent Van Gogh, Lafcadio Hearn, Martha Graham, or Yukio Mishima, to name but a few, lend themselves to analysis according to the hierarchy of the affective domain. Their lives do not provide a clear-cut answer to the question "Is the artist made or born?" which has been accorded a wide range of dialogue in the arts to consider that both possibilities may apply.

For teachers in and of the arts, only one answer seems consistent within their profession, "Yes, a child can be made to grow up to be an artist." How this is done is still a problem of arts education, as is the question as to whether or not it is the purpose of education to encourage children talented and gifted in the arts to become artists. The author's answer to both questions is the same. It is as much the role of the schools to help develop the creative artistic potential of children who might choose the arts as a profession or career, as to develop potential doctors, lawyers, business people, teachers, factory workers, auto mechanics, and so forth.

How this is done has been suggested by B. F. Skinner in a most succinct statement presented at a series of lectures in the Guggenheim Museum in 1969, on the theme, "The Future of Art" (Skinner 1970). His thesis

is very much like that outlined above in the affective domain, in which each encounter by the individual in either looking at or making a work of art is followed by or is in itself a reinforcement making the next stage of the development possible.

In dealing with art and leisure, Skinner observes that leisure is not only essential for viewing and appreciating art (as discussed in chapter 3), but also for making art. He states in effect that artists need leisure to develop, think, and allow creative ideas and techniques to come about. To achieve this, they will live in a garret or remain among the so-called unemployed, avoiding or disregarding distracting commitments and socially imposed obligations.

Skinner relates the extent to which art is accepted in the culture to the degree that it reinforces what the artist tries to put into it and what the public turns to it for. He equates the increased appreciation in monetary value as more realistic in a materialistic society than appreciation in spiritual values. He also considers it a misfortune that art, music, and literature are taught in the schools as "mysteries, to which effective methods of instruction are held not to apply."[1]

For structuring the arts programs in the schools, Skinner recommends that the first stages, which can be equated with the receiving-attending stage of the affective hierarchy, be cheap, quick, and easy. Art teachers, limited by budgets, time, and materials, are already forced to operate as Skinner suggests. Reinforcements should be generous. Teachers might help the students in their need to reinforce themselves. Constant praise without helping the students evaluate and reinforce themselves according to their own criteria can reduce the effectiveness of such praise. Better materials should, he suggests, "be introduced with care as the instruction proceeds."[2] The dedicated artist is in Skinnerian terms, "the product of a series of probably accidental but happy program of successes."[3] Although the terminology is Skinner's, the procedure and situation in art education are very much as he indicates.

Interlacing the Cognitive, Psychomotor, and Affective Domains

Krathwohl, in attempting to show the interrelationship between the cognitive and affective domains, has designed two continuums and had them aligned side by side—corresponding stages juxtaposed with one another (Krathwohl, Bloom, and Masia 1964, pp. 49-50). Since he had no hierarchy defined for the psychomotor domain, it is not included.

The author considers that the interaction between

---

1. B. F. Skinner, "Creating the Creative Artist," in *On the Future of Art,* sponsored by the Solomon R. Guggenheim Museum (New York: Viking Press), p. 71. Copyright 1970, B. F. Skinner. Reprinted by permission.
2. Ibid., pp. 73-74.
3. Ibid., p. 74.

the cognitive domain and the psychomotor domain affects the individual's growth along the affective domain. This has been illustrated in the "taxonomical tennis shoe." (See fig. 9.2.) As an example, we might consider the first steps in learning to drive a car. It is a recently acquired psychomotor skill, common to most of us and, therefore, perhaps easily remembered.

We learned the cognitive data about driving rules, the sequence of acts in starting the car, some suggestions for steering the car, some suggestions for parking. We tried them out behind the wheel. Although willing to receive information and try, it was some time before we derived satisfaction from our driving. Having learned the rules and comprehended them, we applied them through the psychomotor domain. To get our driver's license, we took a written test (cognitive) and a driving test (psychomotor). Depending upon our ability to steer, park at an angle, park parallel, back up, and so on, we developed certain affective likes and dislikes about driving as a daily activity. (Auto stunt men, however, have taken the car to the communication level of a unique statement, and as part of their personality characteristics.) The psychomotor levels from imitating the instructor at the early stages, through manipulation and experimentation, leads to the precision stage, at which point we are able to pass the driving test. Gunning a car, expressing annoyance to another driver in passing, or gracefully curving around an empty space in a shopping center parking lot are ways of using the car to articulate a feeling or statement. We have reached the naturalization stage when we drive home from a faculty meeting, ruminating about what was said or not said, and arrive in our respective driveways wondering how we got there, stopped, signaled, and did all the other driving procedures without being aware of having done any of them.

Self-Expression in the Three Domains

Perhaps the most elusive creative factor to fit into the taxonomy of educational objectives is self-expression. One difficulty lies in a tendency to identify it with a single domain, usually the affective, rather than to see how it relates to all three domains. It is the author's belief that expression is most fully operant through an interaction between the three domains at the following levels: the Cognitive, (**5.1**) Synthesis: A unique communication; the Affective (**2.3**) satisfaction in response; and the Psychomotor (**4.0**) articulation.

Expression is usually about something. It is a feeling, idea, concept, reaction, or response to a specific act, event, or phenomenon which affected the individual enough for an expressive (emotional or subjective) statement to be made as a response. The response is affective, but the analysis which might precede the act of expression to determine the most appropriate symbology, medium, or art form to communicate the statement is cognitive, while the final statement, a synthesis of feeling response and media or techniques, is (it is

hoped) a unique and personal communication. A long-felt commitment may result in the wish to express a particular feeling about something through an art form, or some other way, but expression begins at the response level. It may reflect a momentary commitment, but it does not need to be long-lasting to be strongly felt at the time the expression is made. Whether the individual is making a painting, dancing, making music, sculpting, writing or talking about what is being felt and expressed, it is an articulated communication. Accordingly, the psychomotor aspects of self-expression are placed at the articulation level, although attempts to express feelings can be attempted at the manipulation and precision levels. Some methods or expressive symbols might be imitated from others, but these are not unique communications.

When evaluating self-expression, it may be well to look at the finished product with external criteria for each of three domains.

Reinforcing Activities

1. Refer to the vertical lines you drew for the activities at the end of the chapters on the cognitive and psychomotor domains. Mark off the five affective stages. Use the same two or more courses identified previously. Locate your affective levels for each course and compare them with your notations on the cognitive and psychomotor domains. Is there a relationship between amount of cognitive knowledge, level of difficulty in the doing, and your affective liking or rejecting of the course?

the small society   **by Brickman**

(Photo: Hank Londoner, Photographer)
© Copyright Washington Star Syndicate, permission granted by King Features.

2. What criteria do you use when relating value to (a) distance, (b) time, and (c) cost?
   a. How far will you walk (or drive) to
      _____ see a favorite type of movie or movie star?
      _____ visit a friend, or expect them to visit you?
      _____ eat out?
      _____ meet other students in a tavern or gathering place?
   b. What is your time limit for
      _____ studying courses you like most?
      _____ studying courses you like least?
      _____ preparing study units in reading, mathematics, social studies, art, music, physical

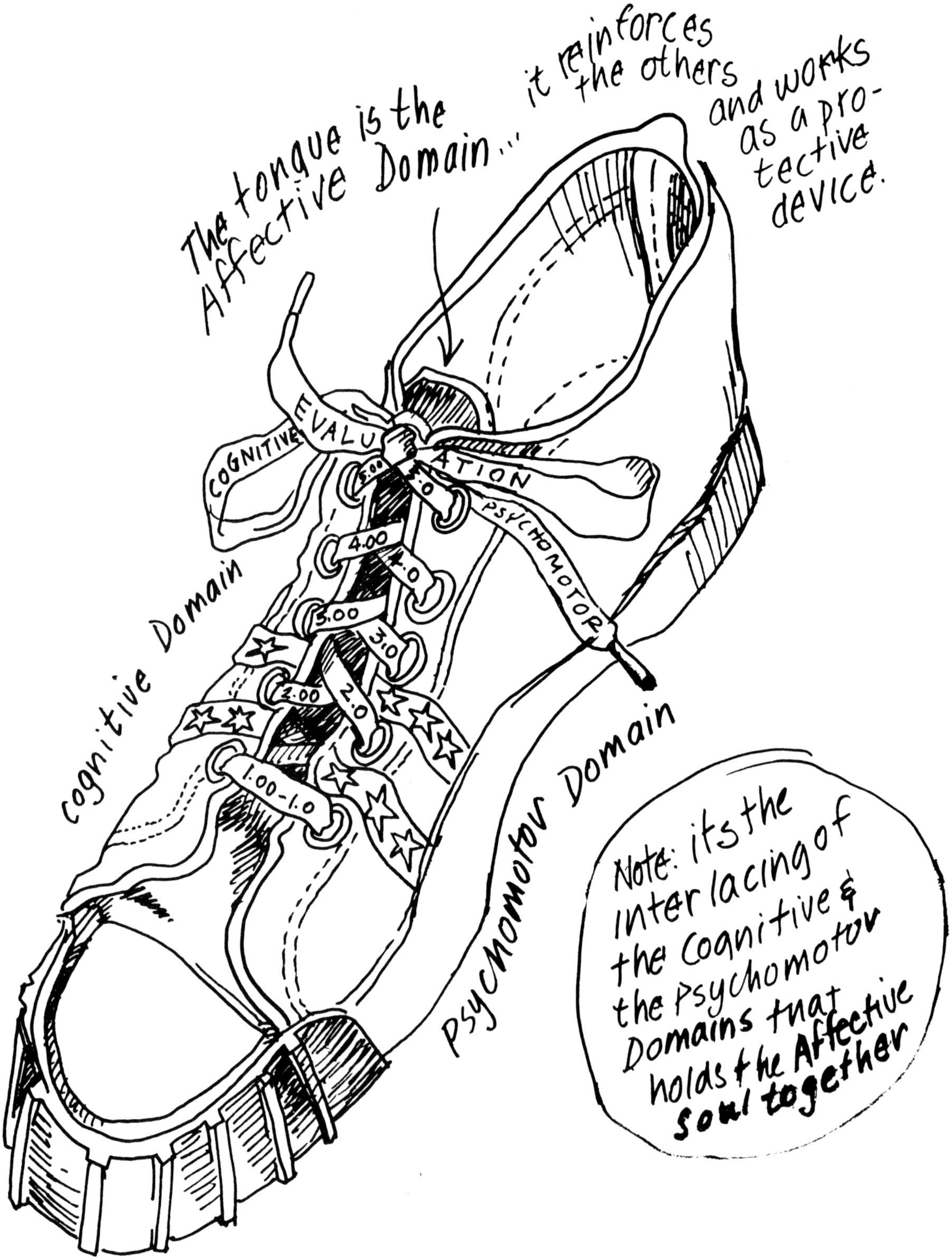

Figure 9.2 The taxonomical tennis shoe.

education? (Estimate each according to the time you spend during the school week.)
_____ waiting for someone who is late?

c. At what price level will you refuse to pay to
_____ see a first-run movie?
_____ get a hardcover book, and wait for the paperback? (which type of books do you prefer to buy in hardcover? in paperback? to borrow from the library?)
_____ visit an art museum (if admission is charged?) attend a concert? attend the theater?
_____ buy a particular pair of shoes? get your hair cut or styled? order certain items on a menu?

What does this tell you about your everyday value system? Has it changed since you entered college, or got a teaching position?

3. While in the teacher's room, compare the amount of time teachers spend talking about problems in the classroom or problem students, successes in a certain lesson, the principal or other teachers not present, their home situations, rising living costs, leisure-time activities (movies, television, art-making, reading, theater, sports, etc.). What does this suggest about the attitudes, values, and commitments of your colleagues? Where do you stand?

References

BELL, QUENTIN. *Virginia Woolf: A Biography.* New York: Harcourt Brace Jovanovich, 1972.

BRAIDER, DONALD. *George Bellows and the Ash Can School of Painting.* Garden City, N. Y.: Doubleday and Co., 1970.

KRATHWOHL, DAVID R.; BLOOM, BENJAMIN S.; and MASIA, BERTRAM P. *Taxonomy of Educational Objectives: The Classification of Educational Goals. Handbook 2: The Affective Domain.* New York: David McKay Co., 1964.

SARTRE, JEAN-PAUL. "The Childhood of a Leader." In *Intimacy and Other Stories.* New York: New Directions, 1948.

SKINNER, B. F. "Creating the Creative Artist." In *On the Future of Art,* sponsored by the Solomon R. Guggenheim Museum. New York: Viking Press, Viking Compass Book, 1970. Copyright 1970 © Solomon R. Guggenheim Foundation.

10

Child growth, art, and me:
a time capsule
from the memory bank

The author speaks:

Before finishing elementary school, I knew, as did George Bellows and the others mentioned in the preceding chapter, that I would be an artist when I grew up. In high school my direction veered: I considered becoming an art teacher, but only (so I thought at the time) until I could establish myself as an artist by painting at night and during weekends. I was trying to conceptualize a value system around both the need for time to become established in art and the necessity for earning a living also. Like so many others in the artist-teacher conflict, I had to make value decisions; either to accept myself as an art teacher or to attend solely to being an artist. Some, particularly those at the college level who never resolve this conflict, remain cultural schizoids, who insist that they are artists, not teachers. Moreover, they by no means consider themselves art educators, who are the lowest on the art instructional status scale. Yet, in spite of everything, they derive the largest part of their professional income from instruction, rather than from the sale of their work! Unfortunately such individuals instill the same unrest in their fine arts students, some of whom go into art teaching, but resent it.

My first thoughts about being an art teacher came (while in high school) when helping a friend in "Introductory Art" design a radio casing. He was getting low grades in art, and had to stay after school in order to finish the design. As great as I thought our teachers (Phyllis Wallen, Anna Grogan, and George Sorenson) were at Herbert Hoover High School, I felt art-talented students such as I was, and non-art-talented students, as my friend George Talbot was, should not be graded on the same basis. I decided to become an art teacher so that I could teach art the way it should be taught, with considerations such as the "talent" situation in mind. Introductory art or introductory music was required of all tenth-grade students. Art majors had semester courses in color and design theory, illustration, advertising art (during which we produced the yearbook), lettering, figure drawing, costume design, and other facets of art. Across the hall was a ceramics, crafts, and sculpture program. On occasion Miss Grogan would send a couple of us to a nearby elementary school to give demonstrations in drawing or painting for their art lessons.

After two years in the U.S. Navy (1944-46)—I had joined immediately upon leaving high school—and directly following World War II, I was admitted to San Diego State College as an art major, even though I had failed the college entrance examinations. At that time they were taking chances on veterans, who were backed by the G.I. Bill—were "more mature"—and I wanted to major in art, my one strong subject. I also took "bonehead English." Throughout college I was still undecided between fine arts, commercial art, stage design, or art education. The decisions and courses kept pointing toward teaching. Yet there still seemed to be something missing about my art education. There must be more to art, but I didn't know what.

Then, one day, I found Viktor Lowenfeld's *Creative and Mental Growth*, first published in 1947, in the college library stacks, and began reading this book. Suddenly, everything opened up; what had seemed missing was there in the visual-haptic continuum, the art therapy and, yes, the grotesques modeled by blind children. He explained "talent" for me, and also what was called "lack of talent," in his visual-haptic theories. Suddenly, art held real importance for people, far more than just the satisfaction derived from looking at it, recognizing famous paintings, or even making it. I was moving from a generalized set, to the characterization level of my value complex. I knew I had to study under this man, and I did.

I worked with Lowenfeld as a student assistant the summer (1952) when he was a guest professor at California State College in Long Beach, and then, after a "wanderjahr" in New York City getting commercial art and stage design out of my system, I went to Pennsylvania State College (later, University) to study under him.

I was beginning to have the feeling that there was not enough service and direct contribution to others in just "producing" art. Teaching art seemed, for me, more important—and as I think of it now—more humanistically oriented. But, we are dealing here, not with the end result, but with those elementary school influences which helped set the pattern. Before dealing with such personal experiences, I want to provide a background for such growth by briefly discussing three popular sets of stages for child growth and development: Lowenfeld's stages of growth in child art, Erikson's "Eight Stages of Man," and Jean Piaget's Stages of Mental Development.

Lowenfeld's Stages of Development in Child Art

In *Creative and Mental Growth* (1947), Viktor Lowenfeld defined the stages of growth in child art as they derived from the German Child Study movement of the 1890s, and touched on briefly in our chapter 2. (By the time his book was written, the phylogenetic law associated with the German orientation and used by Maria Montessori had fallen into a state of disregard.) Refer to figures 10.1 and 10.2 that follow, depicting these stages.

I. *Scribble Stage: First Stage of Self-Expression (2-4 Years)*. Children make their first marks in *uncontrolled* scribbling, getting a kinesthetic reaction and sense of movement, and seeing marks made as a result of their actions as well. As they learn muscle control, they also produce *controlled* scribbling, usually in repetitive longitudinal and circular marks. As their scribbles become refined to single configurations, the children may give them names. Lowenfeld calls this "naming of scribbles" a most important event because for the first time the child is using his or her imagination to give meaning to an abstract symbol.

Rhoda Kellogg (1968, pp. 45-63, 287) has contributed data since Lowenfeld, which breaks down this part of the stage into *shape* and *design* substages (3-4 years). First, the shape substage has simple geometrical configurations, called diagrams. The design stage continues as two diagrams are put together in *combines,* and then three or more as *aggregates.* Lowenfeld's naming of scribbling and Kellogg's design substage coincide, but each author interprets this phase differently.

II. *Preschematic Stage: First Representational Attempts (4-7 Years)*. In this, called by Kellogg the Pictorial Stage, children experiment with drawing people, pets, houses, trees, and other things into visual symbols, frequently changing their approaches. They include only details emotionally important to them at the time, such as the person with only a head, arms and legs, but no body, referred to by Piaget and Inhelder (1969, p. 64) as a "tadpole man." These are part of the child's *active knowledge.* They may know the body exists, but it is not important at the time. It is part of their *passive knowledge.* Proportions, placement of objects on the page (floating), and colors are used subjectively, or emotionally. This is part of children's egocentricism, at what is still a symbolic stage wherein visual configurations are an assimilation of geometrical shapes and lines. Combinations of both visual and haptic (nonvisual, feeling) responses may show up in children's drawings.

III. *Schematic Stage: The Achievement of a Form Concept (7-9 Years)*. The previous stage was characterized by the search for a schema or form concept that goes beyond the geometrical symbols of the child's first representations. It is also a dangerous stage. When children find a satisfying symbol for a person, or one for a tree, or one for a house, flower, car, and so on, they may repeat it over and over again whenever they draw that specific object, thereby making it into a stereotype. When this happens, little further development takes place. One of the dangers of coloring books, stenciled color-ins, and copying is that each provides adult-created

models for the children, who assume them to be correct, though beyond their abilities. The stick figure is such an adult stereotype. The child either imitates it, says "I can't draw," or, having enough other opportunities, can disregard these restricting-type adult influences.

Frequently, when conducting art workshops for teachers, parents at P.T.A. groups, or college students, I find many, who at this adult level, still draw as if they were eight years old. After discussion we arrive at the fact that either they never had art, or did not have the kind that helped them solve growth-type art problems. They became retarded in art at the schematic level. Their visual vocabulary became stereotyped.

Children need opportunities and experiences that will encourage them to draw different kinds of people and animals in various activities and situations, as well as flowers, bushes, trees, cars, and a diversity of other subjects—and to depict their emotional feelings about the subject matter.

As they become more sociocentric, children relate their objects to a *baseline,* a line either at the bottom of the picture or at the bottom of the page. This indicates an awareness of their environment, the world outside themselves, and social growth. When the child draws the people and things all on a baseline, the teacher knows that he or she is ready to begin learning to read. At that point children are able to follow a linear sequence of symbols, and learn words which have no egocentric or organic meaning to them (see fig. 10.2).

Other approaches to depicting three-dimensional space on a two-dimensional plane (or paper) includes the *double baseline,* one above the other, the *X-ray* (in which both the inside and outside are depicted), and *fold-overs* (on which objects, buildings, and people are drawn flat, but when the paper is folded, they stand upright). Other approaches include *overlapping* (figures in front or behind others) and *conceptualizing* (where two different planes are depicted flat, though adjacent, as in the Ancient Egyptian drawings depicting front and profile views of a person shown in the same image).

IV. *The Gang Age: Dawning Realism (9-11 Years)*. Children discover they are members of society. They form groups or gangs, develop peer authorities, and try to establish their independence of adult authority. Their figure concepts take on sexual differentiations through clothes, hair, and activities. Exaggeration is used less to show feeling, color is objectively used, and drawings often become stiff and small. Visually oriented children may do this more than the haptic. They may criticize their earlier attempts at X-ray and fold-over. The sky will, at last, be brought down to the horizon, if that hasn't happened earlier. They will add decorative details to drawings. At this stage, children's visual perception increases faster than their ability to transform it into visual symbols. To heighten their visual and other sensory perceptions, children should be given many opportunities to see and experience their environment, and to delineate and express it through art. Though this

uncontrolled scribbling
Age 2½ years. (wowenfeld)

contro lled scribbling
longitudinal. Age 3 years
(wowenfeld)

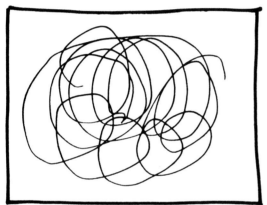

Circular scribbling
Controlled.   Age 3 years
(wowenfeld)

Diagrams. Design Stage
3 years (Kellogg)

Combines. Design Stage
(Kellogg) 3 years
Mandalas & radials.

Aggregates. Design
Stage 3-4 years.
(Kellogg).

Figure 10.1   Scrible stages 2½-4 years (simulated).

is a natural stage for saying "I can't draw," those opportunities to see and experience may keep their abilities for expression through art alive.

V. *Age of Reasoning: The Pseudonaturalistic Stage (12-14 Years).* Children begin making rapid changes into adolescent growth. Childlike actions conflict with their assimilation of adult attitudes, behavior, and criteria. They may be shocked by the realization of the childishness of their drawings. If the art-average youngsters haven't already sloughed off the use of drawing as a natural way of expression and communication (due to neglect in school), they usually do so at about this time. Art-interested children, on the other hand, will continue to draw, explore methods of depicting ideas, and increase their visual vocabulary.

VI. *The Period of Decision: Adolescent Art (14-17 Years).* This is the period of conscious effort and the need for professionalism. In the elementary stages, emphasis was placed on growing and the process of growth, while at the high-school level it can be placed on the quality of the product and technique. Art teachers are expected to be able to do what they teach, and do it well. Students want to learn and perfect their skills and techniques. They want to feel they can do something well by adult professional standards.

These briefly stated descriptions may help elementary teachers identify at what stage children are in their creative and mental development, as is indicated in their drawings and paintings. These stages are based on average and normal growth of the pretelevision child. We used to draw while lying on the floor listening to the radio. I think that now watching television provides children with visual stimulation demanding of their attention, and so takes the place of much of the drawing at home they once did.

Art lessons should be selected to present problems of depicting people, and things, emotions and situations, and spatial representations, the solutions to which will lead children from one stage to the next. Children who are gifted and talented in art may achieve some stages before others in the class. Children retarded in art may be one or more developmental levels below the others. This is particularly possible after the schematic stage, especially where art is considered a frill, and opportunities to grow beyond the schematic stage are not provided often enough. Once a month is not often enough. Once a week helps.

Erikson's Eight Stages of Man

In *Childhood and Society* Erik H. Erikson identified eight stages of man.[1] They are:

1. *Oral-Sensory: Trust vs. Mistrust* (infancy)
2. *Muscular-Anal: Autonomy vs. Shame and Doubt* (early childhood)
3. *Locomotor-Genital: Initiative vs. Guilt* (play age: preprimary)
4. *Latency: Industry vs. Inferiority* (preprimary to primary)
5. *Puberty-Adolescence: Identity vs. Role Diffusion* (later elementary to secondary)
6. *Young Adulthood: Intimacy vs. Isolation*
7. *Adulthood: Generativity vs. Stagnation* (or self-absorption)
8. *Maturity: Integrity vs. Disgust; Dispair*

Erikson describes these stages in terms of normal versus abnormal, positive versus negative growth patterns. In view of my observations in chapter 9 about antisocial learning in affective growth, I think individuals following the abnormal patterns can develop characterizations with an antisocial, or criminal value complex.

We have all gone though Erikson's stages of man, one way or another. Infants who learn to trust themselves and others in the Oral-Sensory (first stage), can enter the Muscular-Anal (second stage) potentially able to realize their autonomy. However, parental pressures in the home can redirect the normal development from autonomy to shame and doubt. Child rearing in the seventeenth and eighteenth centuries, especially under the Puritan Ethic, struggled mightily to subdue the child's autonomy or will and establish a sense of shame. Infants in the Oral-Sensory stage who learn to mistrust themselves and others are liable to enter the Muscular-Anal stage with a proclivity to shame and doubt. Similar comparisons can be made about the transition from one to another of the rest of Erikson's eight stages.

Before the children who have developed a sense of shame and doubt can be brought to a realization of autonomy, any negative effect of the previous stage must be undone. Mistrust must be replaced with trust; shame and doubt replaced with autonomy.

Children entering kindergarten are ready for stage 3, Locomotor-Genital. They are either ready to initiate their own actions, or are conditioned to feel guilt for initiating their own actions. The other two stages relevant to the elementary school are stage 4, Latency: Industry vs. Inferiority (kindergarten to primary or grade 3); and stage 5, Puberty-Adolescence: Identity vs. Role Diffusion (upper-elementary, middle school, and up).

Children entering school following abnormal growth patterns are apt to continue in that vein unless teachers can help them replace their mistrust with trust, and their shame and doubt with a realization of their autonomy. Otherwise mistrustful children struggling with autonomy in the classroom, become disruptive and antisocial. They reinforce their tendency to shame and doubt by encouraging disciplinary action by the teacher or principal.

The teaching of art in terms of Erikson's stages makes possible changes of focus in keeping with the changing needs of children at each of their various stages of growth. For example, at the Muscular-Anal: Autonomy vs. Shame and Doubt (early childhood)

1. Erik H. Erikson, *Childhood and Society*, 2d ed. Copyright © 1963, W. W. Norton & Company, Inc., pp. 247-74.

Emotional placement
Pre-schematic (no baseline)
4-7 years old-egocentric.

Baseline placement-Late
Pre-schematic stage 5-7yrs.
through the schematic stage.
socio-centric orientation

Double base-line to show
distance 7-8 yrs.

Fold-over spatial repre-
sentation. By folding up the
left and right sides of
picture the walls are upright.

Figure 10.2   Spatial representative stages (simulated).

Drawings tend to get tight
and visual from 4th to 6th grades
Dawning realism. More opportunities needed for drawing to develop flexibility.

Overlapping distance by
drawing one object or person
in front of another. Dawning
realism - ages 9-11 years

Conceptualizing - when two different planes are depicted in one
picture. note: up right drawing
of parking lot, and front of factory building on same picture
plane. x-ray view of factory.
Based on mural by 4th graders.
smoke overlaps sun. sidewalk
also drawn up-right or flat.

stage, children are scribbling, drawing design shapes, composites, aggregates, manipulating crayons, clay, or play-dough to establish their own muscular control over the media, and establish their autonomy in making geometrical shapes and visual configurations.

The Locomotor-Genital: Initiative vs. Guilt (play age: preprimary) stage coincides with the late naming of scribble and early preschematic stages of drawing and visual configuration growth. Children begin creating their own visual symbols, and solve drawing, modeling, and construction or building problems in their own way, thus establishing their own initiative. It is at this stage where coloring books impose adult visual symbols and representations upon the child, and thus establish feelings of doubt and guilt instead of confidence in their own initiative.

Children need opportunities at this age to establish their own judgment in working with crayons, paints, modeling clay, or making things. They need adult support and encouragement to trust the differences which they see between their work and that of other children. Praise in their various psychomotor abilities and manipulative skill achievements helps replace doubt while reinforcing their satisfaction of response, and value in their activity.

Erikson's Latency: Industry vs. Inferiority (pre-primary to primary) stage coincides with Lowenfeld's Pre-schematic (4-7) and Schematic stages, or roughly kindergarten through grade 3. Basic learning skills are usually taught during these grades, as children learn new verbal vocabularies, reading, and writing. Their visual vocabularies are too often allowed to deteriorate through neglect. Since the age of 2½ years, children have been developing their own communication symbology and skills, applying their imaginations to their imagery and learning play, only to have their efforts disregarded when the classroom emphasis switches to reading and writing skills instead of using one to learn the other. While classroom activities develop their industry (work habits) around reading and writing skills, they develop inferiority feelings about drawing and other nonacademic skills. This is a delicate and dangerous stage in which children need to feel that *all* their skills are important.

In art, they can be lead to explore various schemata, encouraged to keep flexible in their solutions and to try different approaches to relating three-dimensional space to paper (double-baseline, X-ray, fold-over, and possibly overlapping).

Erikson's Puberty-Adolescence: Identity vs. Role Diffusion (from late elementary up) stage coincides with Lowenfeld's Gang Age (9-11 years) and Age of Reasoning stages (11-13 years) and up. Art can help children explore their world and community at this stage. They can learn cooperation and share territories by making murals, depict themselves playing games in the gym or on the playground, model themselves playing games in Plasticine, on tabletop courts or playing fields drawn on 18-by-24-inch paper. They could draw cognitive maps of their routes from home to school, to the community pool, church, shopping center, police station, library, a friend's house, or other local public places. They might draw themselves in exploratory spatial relationships to develop overlapping, such as, "I am in a crowded elevator," . . . on an escalator, . . . on the school bus, . . . sitting in a movie, . . . or in similar crowded locations. They might follow mural-making, filmmaking, painting stage scenery, and other large group activities, with supplemental discussions regarding the importance of cooperation and sharing in large tasks to recognize the contribution of the individual to the whole. In *Art for Preadolescents*, Angiola R. Churchill tells how she used art to lead a group of upper-elementary students who were destructive of each other through individual projects about themselves, their rooms, their likes, and so on, and through group sharing and discussion to group unity (1970-71, pp. 107-42).

The child's identification with the world at this level includes the role one will play in maintaining the culture and social structure, and earning a living—finding a meaningful place in the world and in the world of work. It is essential that children interested in the arts be taught about the importance of the artist to society and to cultures, and the importance of art in all its forms for potential careers. Teaching them and all children how and why artists, designers, architects, illustrators, dancers, composers, musicians, poets, novelists, actors, and actresses are important community helpers—as important to know about as doctors, lawyers, policemen, and the lady selling cookies in the bakery—can begin at the first and second grades. Such study units in arts careers may help change stereotyped attitudes about artists. Children interested in the arts might study the lives of artists, dancers, and other creative people and about the encouragement or opposition they received from their parents and teachers when they were children. It is important for older children to know about possible careers in the arts, if they are to find their role in society.

At the Puberty-Adolescence: Identity vs. Role Diffusion stage, a healthy sexual identity must be completed before the job-role identity can take place. According to Erikson, both identities must be resolved, instead of diffused, if the young individual is to make a healthy adjustment to the adult world and face the responsibility which goes along with it. Insofar as possible, artists should be presented as hardworking, normal individuals which many or most of them are, rather than as emotionally disturbed, as "sissies," or as irregular, if children who think of themselves as artists are to avoid struggling against social stigmas placed against them.

This is a brief summary of Erikson's stages of man as they apply to the elementary school child who can be aided through arts instruction. They coincide with Lowenfeld's stages of development in child art. Piaget's stages of mental development bear a resemblance to both.

Piaget's Stages of Mental Development

In *The Psychology of the Child,* Jean Piaget identifies six stages of mental development.[2] Stages 1, 2, and 3 are part of the Infancy stage (birth to 1½-2 years), and coincide with Erikson's Oral-Sensory: Trust vs. Mistrust stage. This is a prelanguage stage, and Lowenfeld's stages after it has been completed.

1. *Hereditary* (instinctual) drives and reflexes (nutritional) drives appear for the first time.
2. *Motor habits,* organizational percepts, and differentiated emotions appear for the first time.
3. The *sensorimotor stage* (18 months-2 years) demonstrates practical intelligence, affective emotions, and fixations.
4. *Intuitive intelligence* (2-7 years) demonstrates spontaneous interpersonal feelings and egocentricism. The child subordinates to the adult. This is the beginning of symbolic play. The child's drawing progresses from scribbles and geometrical symbols to intellectual realism (drawing what is known rather than what is seen). The child draws geometrical symbols, imitates signs, and uses intuition to determine realities, semiotic meanings, and so on.

    This coincides with Lowenfeld's Scribble and Preschematic stages, and Erikson's Muscular-Anal (Autonomy vs. Shame) and Locomotor-Genital (Initiative vs. Guilt) stages. Piaget and Erikson both refer to the child's use of imitation at this stage, while Lowenfeld refers to the child's first use of his or her imagination at this stage. Adults who accept their intuitions or imaginations at this stage reinforce their growth and trust in their intuitions and imaginations.

5. *Concrete intellectual operations* (7-11 or 12 years) see the beginning of logic, and moral and social feelings of cooperation. The child's egocentrism gives way to a sociocentric orientation. Children can separate their own points of view from those of the others. They play games (marbles) by the others' rules, identify consistencies and differences in the partial changing and reshaping of clay, and other phenomena. Their affective development is demonstrated through their organization of will (commitment), and new moral feelings prior to establishing values. The child's drawings, as described by Piaget, become more visually realistic, and proportions more correct by adult criteria. Their use of visual detail makes their drawings more representational than symbolic. Drawings that Lowenfeld would identify as X-ray, Piaget calls *intellectual realism* (seeing the inside and outside of a phenomenon simultaneously).

Piaget's stage of Concrete Intellectual Operations coincides with two of Lowenfeld's stages, the Schematic and Gang Age, and perhaps an early phase of the Age of Reasoning. The drawings which become stiff and academic in the fifth and sixth grades become, in Piaget's terms, "visual realism." They have more visual orientation, and show less emotion and affectivity.

These stages of Piaget and Lowenfeld coincide with Erikson's Stages of Latency, and the early phases of Puberty-Adolescence. They are particularly attuned insofar as moral development and abstract thinking are concerned. Pleasure, will, and duty come into conflict within children, who can do abstract thinking and speculating rather than just producing logical solutions or following specific thought patterns. Lowenfeld, Piaget, and Erikson, each in his own terms, describe this last phase, corresponding with the elementary grades, as one in which children begin to develop clarity of thought, increase their abilities to think objectively, and come closer to adult concepts.

The Affective Domain and I in Elementary School

Prologue:

My twin brother, Earl, and I went through Alexander Hamilton Elementary School (San Diego) between 1932 and 1938. Our older brother, George, was already in second grade when we began in kindergarten, walking to school along paths through canyons of sage, scrub oak, manzanita bushes, and across dry creek beds. We played in these canyons, and among the eucalyptus trees along their edges with other children in the neighborhood, built huts with woven branches for prisons, and cut bows and arrows (that were not very good) from the straight western sumac.

Art—Right from the Start!

Our kindergarten teacher was very nice, but old enough to retire the following year. She may have used some of the Froebelian ideas, but not, that I remember, Froebel's gifts. We had easels at which to paint, a woodworking room, and an indoors sandbox. In the woodworking room were straightedge and coping saws, nails, plywood, paints, and patterns. I made a Scottie dog from a pattern on plywood, nailed a wedge to the back and painted it dark green. It was a wobbly doorstop. I also remember painting a house at the easel. It was blue, on a baseline, with a trapezoidal roof. Red smoke came from a chimney in the center. It was a wiggly line that filled the upper rectangular space by repeating the shape and spiraling inside itself. I remember figuring it out as I went, and was very proud of it—even more so when, at open house, I saw it hanging on the wall. Of course, I pointed it out to my parents.

Earl and I also liked to trace pictures on toilet tissues and make flowers from them. We found the tissues at school harder, smoother, already cut, and easier to

2. Excerpted and paraphrased with the permission of Barbel Inhelder from *The Psychology of the Child,* by Jean Piaget and Barbel Inhelder. Translated from the French by Helen Weaver, © 1969 by Basic Books, Inc., Publishers, New York.

see through. One day I was caught with my pockets full of toilet tissues to take home, and was made to sit at the book table incommunicado for the remainder of the day. Earl, who was brighter and got better grades than I did, told me I should have taken the toilet tissues just before leaving school, not at the beginning of the day, sitting there with my pockets bulging. Later, we did make some toilet paper flowers for our teacher.

Grades 1 through 4 were divided into semester units. Children could enter school in September or in February. Each grade level had two parts, low 1 and high 1, low 2 and high 2, and so on. We had a different teacher and room for each. In 1-B (low-1), I remember Mrs. Neighley with affection. She taught us to make oilcloth pillows using geometrical patterns which we drew around on the back of the oilcloth. Then we cut out the material, sewed it with a loop stitch in yarn, and stuffed it with cotton. I finished mine first, so she gave me another and a more difficult one to do—a round scalloped design in black oilcloth; and then she showed me the blanket stitch. On Valentine's Day we made cards; mine was a folded card with large and small red and pink hearts hanging out of the inside on long thin strips of paper. It must have been a mess to carry home. There were no doubt other activities, but these are the ones I remember. In thinking back, I find that I tend to identify the art project by where I happened to be sitting in the room when I was working on it—unless there had been a related event which has helped keep it near the top of my memory bank and which is recalled from time to time.

In grade 1-A (high 1), Mrs. Sutter read us the story of the Big Rock Candy Mountain and we were to illustrate it. Mine had a diagonal road leading up to the right, with two children on it. Trees were lollipops, there were ice-cream cones, candy canes, and chocolate creams. Right out of a Silly Symphony cartoon, I am sure. I remember it because we had to put our names on the back. Earl could spell our last name, but I couldn't. So I started with an "S" and mixed in every letter of the alphabet, thinking that a few might come out in the right order.

That was the year we went into second grade and Miss McMullen told me I was being passed on trial to keep up with my brother. If I didn't do well enough, she told me, I would be sent back. After that I became quite conscious of being compared with Earl, or being told by teachers who had previously taught George, and later Earl and me, that we should be as good as George, who skipped a grade, but we never did. (The most bothersome was our sixth-grade teacher who would at times address me as George.)

I do remember in the second grade making a drawing in which the sky came to the horizon. It was such a surprising reality that I looked around at everyone else's drawings to see if anyone had discovered what I had finally realized. Then I covered my drawing with my arms to make sure that they did not.

Most classes in our elementary school put on a play at least once a semester. In some classes, such as Mrs. Stocklinger's (3-B) the same plays were put on semester after semester depending on the study units; the Hopi Indians and Japan or China. In 1-A we did nursery rhymes. We painted flowers on a long sheet of kraft paper thumbtacked to laths at each end for support. Earl and I, because we looked alike, were asked to carry it onstage. We did "Mary, Mary, quite contrary." We got new white pants and yellow shirts to wear, and walked onstage carrying the scenery between us. "Mary," whoever she was, carried a watering can. Other classmates, in crepe paper ruffles, were flowers. Mary recited her rhyme, dipped the can at each flower-child, and said a few words. The flower then said a few words back, after which we all left the stage. I had a feeling nobody even knew that we, Earl and I, were behind the scenery. So much for the new pants.

In 3-B, Mrs. Stocklinger's class, it was our turn to study Japan and the Hopi Indians. In the play on Japan, Earl and I got to be extras because our mother had real Japanese kimono's, but we didn't speak any lines. At least, we felt, we were almost authentic. In the play on the Hopi Indians we wore burlap bags painted with Indian designs, and nobody was authentic. We also built a model Hopi Indian village or cliff-dwelling pueblo out of large brown cardboard boxes stacked one on top of the other and painted with smoke holes, kiva, and posts supporting the roofs. At that time Earl and I took a streetcar from our home in East San Diego to Balboa Park, alone for the first time, I think, on a Sunday afternoon to attend a lecture on Indian art at the Fine Arts Gallery in Balboa Park. I remember the ride, sitting on the left side, and a table of real Indian pottery, but not much else. It was also while in Mrs. Stocklinger's class that I frequently had to stay after school to do my addition and subtraction.

In 3-A, Mrs. Abrams gave us specific art lessons. We were told about the "center of interest" and made designs on one-inch quadrille paper (nine-by-twelve-inch manila) demonstrating the concept. Mine was a square inside a small circle which itself was inside a larger circle, with zigzag lines at each corner of the square connecting the small circle to the large one, like a radio microphone during the 1930s. She also told us never to start an object, such as a tree, on the side of the picture but to make sure each object was complete within our picture. I remembered this, even in college, when I was shown a slide of Henri de Toulouse-Lautrec's *At Moulin Rouge* with its green mask-like face looking in from the right picture edge. I also associate with this class the rule that blue and green do not go together. But the sky and grass seemed to go together in real landscapes, and they are related colors.

It was in this same class that I realized one day, when drawing a house, that we cannot see both ends and a side at the same time, but only one end and a side. When I erased one end, I had to change my trapezoid roof to what later became a parallelogram. For me, it was a discovery important enough to remember to this day. These are the memories of the perennial memory bank. We do not dig deeply, they are there. Sigmund Freud would place them on the top level of the unconscious, along with our sense of humor.

Mrs. Abrams taught us music, and was music teacher for other classes. When she taught them, their teachers came to our class to teach reading and other subjects. She also sponsored a *choric verse* club, which Earl and I joined. We memorized poems and song lyrics, and recited them in a group, which was easier than music when you couldn't sight-read—and I couldn't. We performed for assemblies and P.T.A. nights. It was good for public relations, but out of it we also learned about words—their rhythm and sounds—and about poetry.

In 4-B, Mrs. Hardecker's class, I drew, as a special project, a mural in colored chalk of a farmhouse on a hill with evergreen trees behind the hill and a water pump on the right side of the hill. I am not sure why— we may have been studying farms, or my teacher may have wanted to keep me busy in art since that was my only strong subject. In her class the left half of the room read Charles Kingsley's *The Water Babies*, but I do not remember what we read on the right side, my side of the room. She was also the teacher who read us, *Alice in Wonderland*. Either she or Mrs. Abrams had Olive Perry, the art supervisor for San Diego, come to our class to give a demonstration on watercolors. We felt that it was an honor, but by that time, I remember, I (or we) already knew how to use watercolors. We had never seen her before, or since, but later on her name became familiar. Later, she was replaced by Margaret Erdt, who wrote *Teaching Art in the Elementary School* (1953). I never saw Miss Erdt until, after graduating from college, I substituted as an art teacher, and she evaluated me. At the time, all art instruction was done by classroom teachers who, very much like now in those school districts without art teachers, had varying degrees of interest in and abilities for teaching art. As an art teacher, I have never known whether or not I might not have done better to think of myself, and to be secure as an artist, if we had had an art teacher at Alexander Hamilton. I did not discover that special art teachers existed until junior high, and did not think of becoming one until senior high. So much for an early career orientation to art education.

Somewhere about the fourth grade we learned to draw repeat patterns for borders, and repeat designs in one-inch quadrille paper for the inside end sheets of books we bound for project reports. I think now, they were reminiscent of Arthur Dow's *Composition* and the arts and crafts movement of the 1910s and 1920s. It was about this time, I think, that I began using one-inch, and one-fourth-inch quadrille paper for designs. I filled in each color on a diagonal basis first, in order to establish the square in the rectangle (nine-by-twelve-inch paper), and then tried to overcome the square and make a total rectangular design. I continued this personal involvement during classtime until the sixth

grade when I was accused of not paying attention to a student report on the Children's Crusades.

Essentially, I believe we had progressive education in our school, or aspects of it. While in grade 2-A, under Mrs. Landis, we took field trips to the Qualitee Dairy farm, after which we made butter and cheese in sugar sacks hanging in the cloakroom and dripping into pans. Then we wrote invitations to our parents to a tea with our butter spread on soda crackers. We also put on a play about the discovery of gold in California. Mrs. Landis also took a yo-yo away from me, and wouldn't let me play a new harmonica (which I really couldn't play anyway) in music class. We also took a field trip to the Museum of Man in Balboa Park and saw models and dioramas of how the Eskimos lived, and some cutaway igloos. We had a school literary publication hexographed in purple ink, but the cover was mimeographed on colored paper. Once I drew a tree and birds for the cover, and on occasion Earl and I each had a poem or short piece printed in it. In one of the upper grades we studied Persia and made "Persian rugs" on jiffy looms, learning how to loop the yarn, tie the knots, cut the top even, and recognize the design on the bottom. I think they were used at home under a vase, or for hot pads. Once at Thanksgiving we put on a play about Pilgrims, and dipped candles in colonial fashion. We melted down yellow crayons in beeswax in two tall fruit-juice cans, each on one of two kerosene stoves— one in the front, the other in the back of the room. We walked in a line from can to can dipping a string as we went. With each dip it got wider. At home we used them for Thanksgiving table decoration, but after a while they began to break crossways, and the wax chipped off layer by layer. One Christmas we made calendars with colored paper wrapped around rectangles of cardboard, with fitted corners, and a picture above a small dimestore calendar. Shellacking was done before the calendar was added. When finished, we wrapped them and placed them under a small tree in front of the room, before taking them home. Whenever I have smelled shellac since that time, I remember Christmas in elementary school.

Once in 5-B, we had instruction in, I believe, linear perspective. We used nine-by-twelve-inch manila paper and charcoal. I drew a desert scene and had trouble with the road that went over the top of the mountains on the horizon. Our teacher, Mr. Churchill, sent it to the San Diego Union for the Sunday School News page, and it was reproduced. I was very proud. Several years ago, when we were selling the family house, Earl found a copy among our childhood memorabilia.

In the sixth grade another boy and I drew a window-sized *Sistine Madonna* enlarged from a small reproduction of Raphael's painting on brown paper (made translucent with linseed oil), using colored chalk. It was installed in the classroom window with spotlights behind it, to look like a stained glass window. When we took it down, I paid twenty-two cents to the other boy for his half and took it home. I also liked to draw (during class time) rocket ships and cities of the future, based on ideas from Alex Raymond's "Flash Gordon," and the Saturday morning movie serials about him. I also enjoyed drawing Maggie and Jiggs from George McManus's "Bringing up Father," "Jane Arden" (girl reporter), Popeye, and Mickey Mouse. Once I sent a drawing of Mickey Mouse to Walt Disney. His studio sent back two printed outlines of Mickey and Minnie Mouse, painted with watercolors and the official Walt Disney signature. This was where, in terms of the affective domain, I tried to communicate with and compare my ability with the adult professional world.

On Saturdays, when we didn't go to the movies, Earl and I visited our grandmother Saunders, Aunt Ethel, and Uncle Jimmie. He was a floorwalker in a department store, and collected slip-sheets of white paper which came in the ladies' hosiery boxes, for us to draw on. When at their house, I liked to sit on their front curb and draw the house across the street. It was Spanish in style, with a red tile roof, arched windows and awnings. It was at their house, curled up in a chair, that I struggled with the problem of drawing mountains, waterfalls, and rivers. As I erased and redrew, I realized that rivers do not go over the tops of hills and mountains, but cut through, go around, and come out between them, often disappearing from view as they go behind slopes, but come out between the foothills. Sometimes we sat quietly listening to Admiral Richard E. Byrd broadcast shortwave from Antarctica.

One Saturday afternoon, following Thanksgiving I remember lying in bed, ill, with a mustard plaster, and listening to the Saturday afternoon Metropolitan Opera broadcast of *Madame Butterfly* for the first time. Now, almost forty years later, listening to them is still an important part of my Saturday afternoon schedule during their radio season. That particular afternoon, must also have been during my Gang Age, because I had an idea for a club and spent it designing a secret code of various symbols. Earl, others in the neighborhood, and I had our first (and I think our last) meeting using a chicken coop in our backyard as a clubhouse.

Interlude:

At home Earl and I liked to draw a lot, lying on the floor listening to Orphan Annie, Jack Armstrong, and the Lone Ranger on the radio. Our mother and father both worked. It was during the depths of the depression. Our father had been a designer of electrical lighting fixtures for movie theaters, hotels, and so on. But his partner ran off with the funds, so father began doing covered buttons, pleating, hemstitching—the manufacturing half of mother's dressmaking shop. Our grandfather, on mother's side, had been an architect in Chicago. We grew up with a large framed architect's drawing of the Des Moines, Iowa, courthouse which he had designed, making us very proud of him. We liked looking at our father's designs for lighting fixtures, and when mother brought home her pattern books and fash-

ion plates, Earl and I liked to use them to copy from, or to adapt their contents to ideas of our own. Among other things, they helped me solve the problem of drawing feet, and folds in fabrics. George showed interest in architecture in high school, and is now a civil engineer.

All three of us were encouraged to follow our own interests. We were not discouraged from drawing or thinking of careers in the arts in our early years. I do not recall any pressures from our parents, but do remember that we were always considered as three entirely different individuals, Earl and I even fighting our twinship by not dressing alike. However, we have been startled by spontaneous evidence of psychical affinity over the years, which we no longer shy away from. Our father died when we were fifteen. By then World War II had started and we were already working after school to help support ourselves.

"Bobby Is Strong in Art"

My report cards usually indicated that I needed to improve in something, but most important was the extra phrase, "Bobby is strong in art." It was the only subject in which I did not feel inferior to my brothers, or the boys good at sports, or those who read better than I did. Now, as an adult, an art teacher, and art educator, I remember how important that extra phrase was for me. When reading art education texts that question grading art, or hearing elementary art teachers say art should not be on the report card, I wonder where I would be now if art had not been on the report card. I wonder where those children are who were strong in art but were in a class where every child got the same art grade, an "A" or "B" or an "E," and so never really knew if they were better than the others in the class. I wonder about children, strong in art, who were lead to feel that the only subject they were good at was not important enough to be on the report card. Because of this, I have a personal commitment (3.3 Affective Domain) to grading art, and organized my elementary art program to include (4.2) Organizing a Value System. (See chapter 13 on grading art.)

I think I had reading and arithmetic problems. I know I had other problems, because I was on the principal's lineup. This was like the police lineup. There were certain boys in the school, who, whenever there was something done wrong (but the office did not know who did it), were called down to the principal's office for questioning. By the sixth grade I learned to feel nausea everytime I was called to the office.

I am not sure what my problems were in reading and spelling. Our classes were divided into two sections for reading, and I don't know which section I was in. I know the books were different for each. Except for Carlo Lorenzini's *Pinocchio* (read in the sixth grade), I don't remember any of them. I consider myself a slow reader, but I enjoy reading nevertheless. My father took Earl and me to the public library with him evenings. We had our own cards. I preferred fairy tales and short stories until about the seventh grade. After seeing Charles Laughton's movie portrayal of the *Hunchback of Notre Dame*, I read Victor Hugo's novel in two days of continuous reading. I preferred to see the movie and then read the book, as I did with Daphne duMaurier's *Rebecca*, Emily Brontë's *Wuthering Heights*, and so on. My mind was more often in these areas and in art, than with my other studies. Most of my nonfiction was in the form of biographies and history, but always dealing with people.

When, in 1939, we were all promoted to Woodrow Wilson Junior High School, I knew I wanted to be an artist. In seventh grade, boys took mechanical drawing, woodshop, and art. In eighth grade they took metal shop, electrical shop, and print shop. Because I had told my guidance counselor I wanted to be an artist, and would rather take eighth-grade art, even though it was for girls, she let me do it. In so doing, I was organizing my value system. It was then that I met John Osgood and Marcia Chamberlain, two other art students. John and I were also on the stage crew together. John and Marcia had a puppet theater and gave puppet shows for children's birthday parties. The three of us, with Earl, took Saturday morning art classes at the Fine Arts Gallery. We continued through high school as a group of four, working on the school papers, and the yearbooks. Marcia took more crafts than we did. We had by then a generalized set in terms of what our careers were going to be. After the war, Earl, Marcia, and I went to San Diego State College for fine arts and art education. John went to the Art Center in Los Angeles and into the commercial art field. He does freelance work in New York City and in eastern Long Island, where he lives. Marcia is coordinator of crafts at California State College in San Jose, and Earl is teaching art at Abraham Lincoln High School, a mostly black, Mexican, and racially-mixed school in San Diego, involved in the arts, leagues, and does some mural painting and exhibiting. And, me? I am writing this book, such as it is. We all began our art careers in elementary school, and we had classroom teachers and parents who encouraged us.

Reinforcing Activities

Note: This chapter was written to provide a brief comparison between the stages of development described by Lowenfeld, Erikson, and Piaget, and to relate my own elementary growth in part to them but mostly to the affective domain. It was also meant to serve as an example for the activities suggested below which are planned to give readers new insight into their own elementary school experiences.

1. Write an autobiographical sketch of your own elementary art experiences in terms of your present value judgments about art or art education. These might be positive experiences leading to a commitment to the arts, or they might be negative experiences leading to a rejection or low stage on the affective domain hierarchy.

2. Think back to a period of time when, as a child, you may have drawn the same picture over and over again, making minor changes or thinking through a drawing problem. It may be a person, house, horse, landscape, airplane, car, rocket ship, or a group of things. Use similar materials and try to draw it now the same way you did then. Capture, if you can, the location, and the situation associated with that activity. As memories of that time come back to you during this process let them come freely. Take the drawings to class and share what happened with others of your group.

3. Trace your current career orientation, or other major interests and enthusiasms, as far back as possible. Can you pick out activities, events, attitudes, or particular teachers or other persons in the elementary school which may have set your direction?

References

CHURCHILL, ANGIOLA R. *Art for Preadolescents.* New York: McGraw-Hill Book Co., 1970-71.

ERDT, MARGARET. *Teaching Art in the Elementary School.* New York: Rinehart & Co., 1953.

KELLOGG, RHODA. *Analyzing Children's Art.* Palo Alto, Calif.: National Press Books, 1969.

LOWENFELD, VIKTOR. *Creative and Mental Growth.* New York: Macmillan Co., 1947.

———, and BRITTAIN, WM. LAMBERT. *Creative and Mental Growth.* 5th ed. New York: Macmillan Co., 1970.

PIAGET, JEAN. *Six Psychological Studies.* New York: Random House, 1967.

11

Toward a structure
of aesthetic education

Aesthetic education is the process of organizing and structuring values around our sensory perceptions as they are developed by participating in and observing the arts, thus to give each of us our personal sense of order. There are two different concepts of what aesthetic education should be which may confuse art and classroom teachers. One follows the Renaissance traditions, while the other follows the sense realists traditions. A brief historical background may help to understand how these traditions differ, and how they interrelate.

Time Capsule: Aesthetic Education

The modern origins for the sensory perceptual approach to aesthetic education derive from the realist educational philosophers of the sixteenth and seventeenth centuries. The basic origins derive from the concept of "aesthetikos," defined by the ancient Greeks, as "of or pertaining to things perceptible by the senses."[1] As described in chapter 2, it meant a way of learning through the senses.

The Realists were reacting against Renaissance humanism, which stressed style and form, analyzing and judging works of art, dance, literature, and music according to specifically related aesthetic criteria. The sense realists concentrated on learning through the senses according to prescribed laws of perception. The movement grew from the inquiries of sixteenth- and seventeenth-century scientists into natural phenomena, and its discoveries were organized into natural laws of order governed by mathematical and scientific principles.

Today's science education, mathematics, music, physical education, art, and industrial arts come from the same fountainhead, which may explain the frequent overlapping of their subject matter within our school curriculums. The realist tradition might be likened to a lake at the top of a mountain whose waters, overflowing its banks, course their diverse routes down the slopes and crags, across the alluvial plains and erosions, and finally gather again in a new lake at the bottom— to become the open classroom as portrayed in figure 11.1.

The realist movement had three different submovements, each with its own leaders and philosophies: (1) the *verbal realists* (François Rabelais, Juan Luis Vives, and John Milton) emphasized literature but insisted that content and meaning are more important than style and form; (2) the *social realists* (Michael de Montaigne) insisted that education should be practical and prepare the gentleman for a world of interaction with society and social institutions; and (3) the *sense realists* (John Amos Comenius, Wolfgang Ratke, Francis Bacon, and Richard Mulcaster), with their cousins the *sense philosophers* (René Descartes, Gottfried von Leibnitz), insisted that nothing exists in the intellect that had not either previously existed in it or reached it through the senses.

The sense realists established new theories of perceptual learning along the Cartesian line of reasoning and Leibnitz's laws of perception. Leibnitz identified three grades of perception: (1) the lowest in the inanimate world below the levels of consciousness perception; (2) the middle level, in the animal world, includes the animal nature of man, where minute perceptions take place; and (3) the highest level, the rational, spiritual, and intellectual, wherein the self is simple substance and God the infinite substance.

These theories helped reinforce the Doric dichotomy discussed in chapter 2 between learning through the intellect (*arte liberales*) and the senses (*aesthetikos*, and associated with *artes serviles*). Because perceptions change according to the changes in sensory stimulus, they were considered inferior and less reliable or true than the intellect which could establish additional truths of some consistency. This attitude persists to the present day. It is found in the popular predisposition that the cognitive domain is more important to learning than the affective and psychomotor domains.

When, during the Renaissance, painting and sculpture received liberal (fine) arts status, it was partly as a result of geometrical rules of the golden mean, linear perspective, and other mathematical formulas to govern their organization and production having been established. Music achieved this status through the mathematical ordering of sounds, and poetry through the ordering of the rhythms and sounds of words. In song the rules governing music and poetry were combined. Dance established rules governing the movement of the human body through space, usually in relation to the music.

Sense perceptions which were more body-oriented, such as touch, taste, and smell, did not lend themselves to such intellectualized order and were considered animalistic and of the lower levels of cultural interest. Nevertheless they had been considered part of the Greek

1. *Oxford English Dictionary,* 1933 edition (Oxford: Oxford University Press), s.v. "Aesthetics."

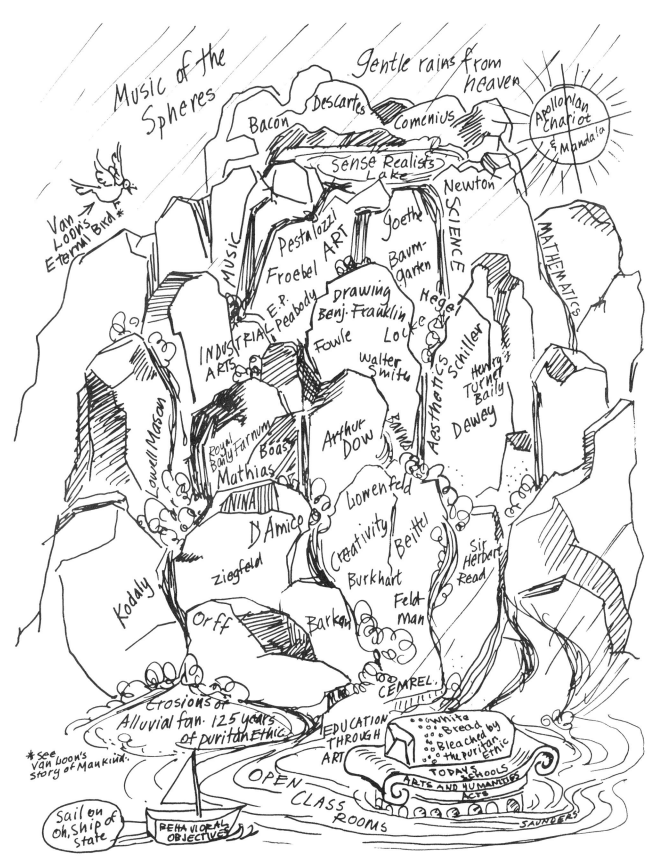

Figure 11.1 "The Sense Realist Mountain."

concept of *aesthetikos.* Thus, when Alexander G. Baumgarten published his book, *Aesthetiks,* in the 1750s, he was roundly criticized by various philosophers and art critics, among them Immanuel Kant, who sustained the ancient traditions of aesthetics as the science treating "of the conditions of sensuous perception."[2]

Baumgarten identified the aesthetic study of works of art as a new science and recognized sensuous perception as worthy of intellectual consideration. He related Leibnitz's laws of perception to the arts in the following stages: (1) the *obscure*—attributed to sensory perception; (2) the *confused*—assigned to art; and (3) the *distinct*—produced by pure reason. By 1798, so the *Oxford English Dictionary* states, "aesthetics" was used to mean sense or sensuous gratifications, but was considered by at least one critic as "not delicate."[3]

The English, after some criticism, began to follow Baumgarten's distinctions as a philosophy of taste and study of the beautiful. Thomas Carlyle used the term "aesthetic tea" in *Sartor Resartus* (1858) to imply a weak or watery substance instead of a "solid pudding."[4] Herbert Spencer in *Psychology* (2d ed., 1872) suggested that "aesthetic sentiments originate from the play-impulse," and later stated that "the aesthetic character of a feeling is habitually associated with separateness from life-serving function."[5]

By the time the Victorians, during the aesthetic movement of the 1860s and 1870s, got finished with "aesthetics"—and with it John Ruskin's art criticisms, William Morris's and Charles Eastlake's interiors, Pre-Raphaelite paintings and poems, Oscar Wilde's plays, fairy tales, and *Picture of Dorian Grey,* or James McNeil Whistler's caped carpings about art-for-art's-sake; and upper-middle-class children had finished with books illustrated by Walter Crane, Arthur Rackham, and Kate Greenaway, and nurseries covered with wallpaper of Walter Crane illustrations—the English were ready to treat "aesthetics" satirically. This they did through cartoons in *Punch,* and in 1880, Gilbert and Sullivan moved it from the sublime to the ridiculous with patter songs in *Patience,* through such lyrics as, "I am a broken hearted troubadour, whose mind's aesthetic and whose tastes are pure." Popular family literature referred to a relationship between a young man and woman as "aesthetic" or "platonic" when it meant "free of sensory responses and sensuously related interactions with one another."

The *Oxford English Dictionary* states "recent extravagances in the adoption of a sentimental archaism as the ideal of beauty have still further removed *aesthetic* and its derivatives from their etymological and purely philosophical meaning."[6] It would seem that the extravagances of the aesthetic movement have placed aesthetics in the public's eye at the upper-middle-class level. The popular attitude about aesthetic education has reflected the Herbert Spencerian point of view, as something separated from the life-serving functions. But, we are now (in the late twentieth century) discovering that the functions of the right side of the brain govern affective, emotional, aesthetic sensory, and expressive learning, while the left side of the brain governs cognitive, intellectual learning. In overemphasizing, by education, the development of the left side of the brain and sacrificing the development of the right side, we have been educating only half of the human being. Aesthetics, sensory, affective, and expressive factors, contrary to being separated from the life-serving functions, are essential to them if we are to fulfill the promise of being human beings instead of just surviving.

Sir William Hamilton, an art collector of note (whose most noted object d'art was Emma, Lady Hamilton) mocked Baumgarten's use of the word "aesthetic" by suggesting "apolaustic" instead,[7] which—ugly as it may sound—means devoted to enjoyment. General education is returning to this aspect of aesthetics. One of the earlier considerations of the Educational Policies Commission identified the *joy principle* as one rationale for the arts and aesthetic education in the schools. This is considerably more important than just educating the *whole person* as thought of by Elizabeth Peabody in the mid-nineteenth century, and the Progressive Education movement. The concept of educating the *whole person* has moved beyond the point of having the individual culturally informed about the arts and humanities, towards the idea of using the entire human organism, the "whole person," to help the child or individual to learn. It now means to develop the entire human organism as a potential for learning, not just the cognitive sections of the brain, but the body itself.

This growing concern for the quality of life and the richness of the curriculum is somewhat like the loaf of white bread. After decades of bleaching the flour, changing the texture and color, and so removing the nutrients from white bread, American corporate bakeries put back the nutrients, called their product "enriched bread," and raised the price. Now, after decades of bleaching American public education of anything related to the arts—imagination, aesthetics, or those nutrients which give the learning experience its savor—these are now being federally injected into what is called the "enriched" curriculum.

The term Aesthetic Education has, thus, come to mean two different aspects of the aesthetic response: one, the sensory perceptual response which can be used on works of art and natural phenomena alike; the other, the sensory analysis of works of art according to aesthetic criteria and emotional response of a transcending nature. Similarly the term "art appreciation" changed in connotation from reference to the monetary appreciation of value in a work of art to meaning the intellectual appreciation of its form and style. Historically

2. Ibid.
3. Ibid.
4. Ibid.
5. Ibid.
6. Ibid.
7. Ibid.

interlocked as these interpretations are, they cannot be totally separated from one another in our educational programs if either approach is to be fully realized.

Sense Organs and Modes

Sensory perception means receiving information and giving meaning to stimuli through all of our sense receptors, organs, and body. It is a total perceptual-cognitive system. To teach one but not the other neglects the education of the whole child, just as the traditional emphasis on the cognitive domain has deprived us of more successful learning in the affective and psychomotor (including sensory perception) domains. Sensory perception includes all the sensory modes. Besides visual perception, it includes auditory, olfactory, tactual, gustatory, and kinesthetic perceptions. Some terms related to sensory perception are confusing. The following brief outline may help clarify them.

Sense Organs are not the eyeballs, ears, nose, mouth, fingers, or body, which are but the cartilage and the outer appendages that protect the retina, rods, and cones, the organ of Corti in the cochlea, the olfactory bulb, and the taste buds on the tongue. The eyeballs, nose, mouth, ears, and the fingers are also the conventional avenues by which the sensory stimuli is directed toward the appropriate receptor or sense organ before being transmitted to the brain.

Sensory Mode is the covering name given to the particular perceptual process in terms of the specific sense receptor, such as the vision mode, aural mode, olfactory mode, gustatory mode, and tactual mode. The kinesthetic mode refers to the total body sense of balance and movement.

Sensory Responses are seeing, hearing, smelling, tasting, and touching the stimuli, which can be anything causing a response of one or more sense organs. Although these terms define how we gather sensory data, other terms define the *conscious act* of gathering sensory data, such as looking, listening, sniffing, tasting and/or savoring, and feeling.

Art Forms have been created for each sensory mode, such as the visual arts, music, perfumery (for lack of a better word), gastronomy, tactile arts (for lack of a better classifying term for making things related to touch), and dance.

Each art form has its own aesthetic criteria for producing and judging works within its confines. Such new multimedia (multisensory) art forms as light-sound shows, kinetic sculpture, and happenings require a combination of the aesthetic criteria from the visual, oral, and kinesthetic art forms. Other art forms, such as gastronomy, opera, cinematography, involve more complex criteria dealing with the visual, aural, kinesthetic (taste and olfactory in gastronomy), and time-sequencing.

Creative artists who explore new ways of working in their art form or combination of art forms, make it necessary to redefine the aesthetic criteria related to it.

The establishment of aesthetic criteria is more often done by the aestheticians, critics, arts philosophers, and gourmets than by the artists, composers, and chefs themselves. As cultures change, so do the aesthetic standards and notions of what is acceptable, or of value, within the terms of the arts themselves. Some cultures call for the return to historical standards of classical origin, while others, more romantic, create their own. In these cases, the creative artists, composers, dancers, and so on serve as the advanced guard. They reflect the radical cultural changes through the arts, while protecting society by making these changes more familiar, understandable, and less formidable.

Claudio Naranjo, in *The One Quest*, describes such changes, not so much as revolutions and rebellion, as the "questioning and taking leave from cultural forms, institutions, and sources of authority." He goes on to say, "today the broad cultural divisions of religion, art, reason, standards of morality, and political institutions are 'dead.'" He likens this to the leaving behind of the old skin by the snake, "unchanged and still beautiful perhaps, but too tight and therefore not functional."[8] While aesthetic education helps us find our way through cultural changes, a history of the arts helps us see changes as a part of a process in which the past remains still beautiful, without binding ourselves to it in too small a skin.

An Aesthetic Structure

The similarities in aesthetic criteria between the different art forms presents a problem to teachers in aesthetic education and the related or unified arts. Does "style" and "form" mean the same in painting, sculpture, dance, theater, music, poetry, or the novel? Can they be taught on the same arts vocabulary-spelling list? Which works of art, music, theater, or literature are the best vehicles for teaching a particular humanistic theme or aesthetic concept? In attempting to solve these problems in aesthetic education, CEMREL, Inc., a research and discovery center for aesthetic education produced *Guidelines: Curriculum Development for Aesthetic Education* (Barkan, Chapman, and Kern 1970). The authors surveyed the arts and those involved in them to describe a taxonomy of aesthetic education terminology, and the indexing, cross-referencing, and organizing of traditional aesthetic phraseology, and examples in each art form to help relate the arts to each other.

To unify within his own mind the interaction of the sensory modes with their art forms, and the three learning domains (cognitive, affective, and psychomotor) the author devised a set of cubes, fashioned somewhat after J. P. Guilford's "structure of intellect" (1967). This aesthetic structure consists of 150 cubes (see fig. 11.2) with a front surface of six layers representing the sensory modes. The left surfaces (not visible) represent the

---

8. Claudio Naranjo, *The One Quest* (Copyright © 1972, The Viking Press, Inc.), pp. 1-2.

cognitive hierarchies stacked vertically, front (1.0-knowledge to 5.0-synthesis). The right surfaces stacked vertically represent the affective hierarchies (1.0-receiving to 5.0-characterizing). The underneath (bottom) surfaces represent the psychomotor hierarchies laid out front to back (1.0 imitation to 5.0 naturalization). The top surfaces, extending from right to left (forward to back) represent the Areas of Aesthetic Response. The rear surfaces of the structure, and of each cube within the structure represents evaluation (6.0-cognitive domain) as it touches upon each of the three domains, the Areas of Aesthetic Response, and the related sensory mode. Each cube within the structure has its individual relationship to these same parts as they relate to each other and to their sequence within the total structure. The coding for evaluation is 6.0, but in examples given below, I use "Evaluation: Cognitive (6.1)" to indicate evaluation of the Cognitive domain, first level, "Knowledge Evaluation: Psychomotor (6.2)" means evaluation at the manipulation level of the Psychomotor domain (see fig. 11.3, open view).

Aesthetic Response Areas

People have aesthetic responses to all matter of man-made and natural phenomena. We may respond to the texture of driftwood affected only by water and sun contacts, or the texture of fabric woven by hand—by a real sunset, or by a painting or slide of one. The one made or changed by human hands may be an art work. The other, untouched by human hands, may be equally beautiful and judged by aesthetic and personal criteria, but it is not a work of art, so much as a work of nature.

To call a sunset a "work of art" is to give it, in Hegelian terms, a status above a work of nature, by comparing it with a work of man. How you accept that statement depends on the status or relative value you place on the works of nature and the works of man. Hegel spoke from the point of view of the eighteenth century, while we speak from the point of view of the late twentieth century. Hegel was more proud of what man hath wrought than many of the present generation are.

The aesthetic response to both natural and man-made phenomena may be the same. Similar aesthetic (and emotional) criteria might be used to evaluate each. Although aesthetic criteria have been defined for the cognitive domain, and in terms of skills and techniques of the artist for the psychomotor domain, they have not as yet been identified for the affective domain.

To make my aesthetic structure a workable set of cubes, I have identified five areas of aesthetic responses. Categories 1-3 deal with sensory perceptual areas. The individual can have an aesthetic response to (1) natural objects and phenomena, (2) to man-made objects and phenomena, and (3) to communication symbology in each of the sensory modes (usually made for nonaesthetic purposes). Where areas 1-3 follow the sense realist tradition, areas 4-5 follow the Renaissance humanist tradition. In area 4, the individual uses aesthetic

criteria to make, design, plan, or choreograph a man-made object or phenomenon. In area 5, the individual uses aesthetic criteria, rather than morality, personal tastes, cost, or other criteria, for evaluating works of art and establishing likes and dislikes. These later phases require specific cognitive information about principles, rules, techniques, and so on.

(1) *Natural objects and phenomena* are those untouched or unaltered by human hands, in any of the sensory modes (rainbow: vision, bird song: aural, scent of a rose: olfactory, etc.). Most natural phenomena cannot be isolated to a single mode, and in units on sensory perception all possible modes should be considered.

(2) *Man-made objects and phenomena:* those articles made by hand or machine for nonaesthetic purposes (functional) or aesthetic purposes (arts). Most man-made objects, art forms, and phenomena can be perceived by more than one sensory mode and elicit responses from different sense organs.

(3) *Communication symbology* is essentially man-made, unless in the aural mode we are listening to birds' mating calls, but then they aren't communicating with us. Communication takes place in each of the sensory modes—a traffic sign, a hand gesture, the smell of fresh soup when the lid is lifted up to indicate dinner is ready. An aesthetic response to communication symbols goes beyond the communication level to the quality of the communication itself.

(4) *Use of aesthetic criteria when designing or producing a man-made object or phenomena* presupposes knowledge of aesthetic criteria, of style and form, repetition, contrast, balance, harmony, melodic line, and so on in making a picture, throwing a pot, creating a dance, or composing a piece of music, for example (including objects serving functional rather than aesthetic purposes).

(5) *Use of aesthetic criteria when judging, evaluating man-made objects and phenomena,* or determining likes and dislikes, and differences in taste. The individual uses them to judge man-made objects, art, and natural phenomena rather than using monetary, moral, historical, or other criteria.

Example: Vision Mode—The Rainbow

We have seen above how the top surface of our aesthetic cube can be read down through each sensory mode and how a particular study area or cluster of areas be identified. For an example of how this can then be applied to a single study unit, the upper-left category in the vision mode of the natural phenomenon aesthetic response area has been singled out as our first example. (See fig. 11.4, the vision mode.) Natural phenomena rarely elicit only one sensory response; however, the rainbow is singularly visual. (See chapter 6 for discussion on the rainbow as a core monument.) In using the cube to plan a study unit, each surface identifies an aspect of study, as you will note. This particular example, and the first of several, deals essentially with the first levels of each domain's hierarchies, but may extend to the 2.0 and 3.0 levels in some aspects.

Figure 11.2 "The Aesthetic Structure." Visible surfaces: Front, sensory modes; top, areas of aesthetic responses; side, the affective domain. Surfaces not visible: Left side, the cognitive domain; bottom, the psychomotor domain; back, evaluation. (Photo credit: Hank Londoner, Photographer.)

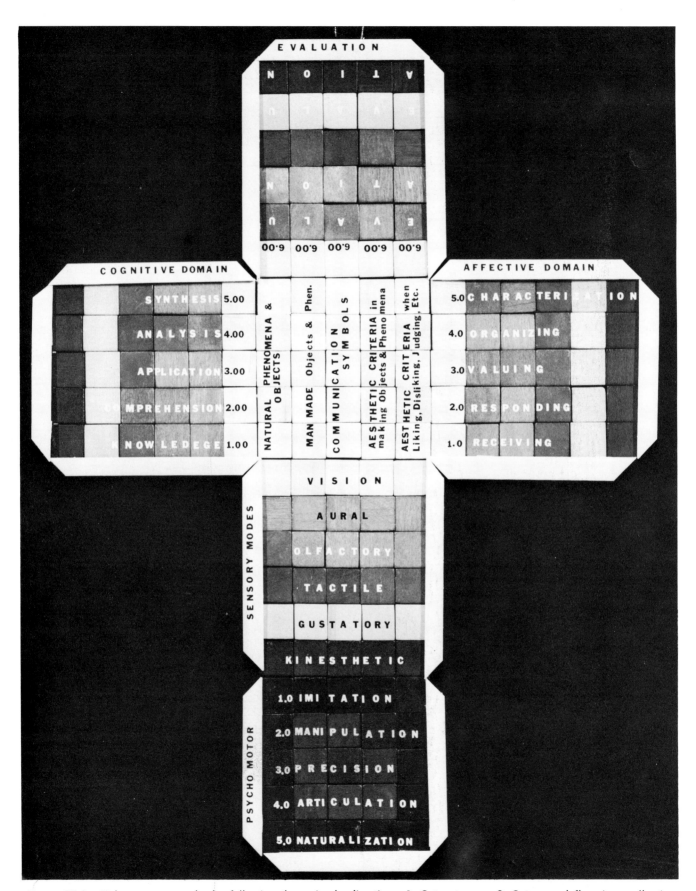

Figure 11.3 Make your own cube by following these simple directions: 1. Cut out page. 2. Cut around flaps/tags, allowing 1/4 inch extra around all borders. 3. Score corner areas/edges of each side of cube. 4. Fold corners and tabs inward. 5. Glue or paste with tabs inside. 6. Press corners together and hold until set. Now you have your own aesthetic cube!

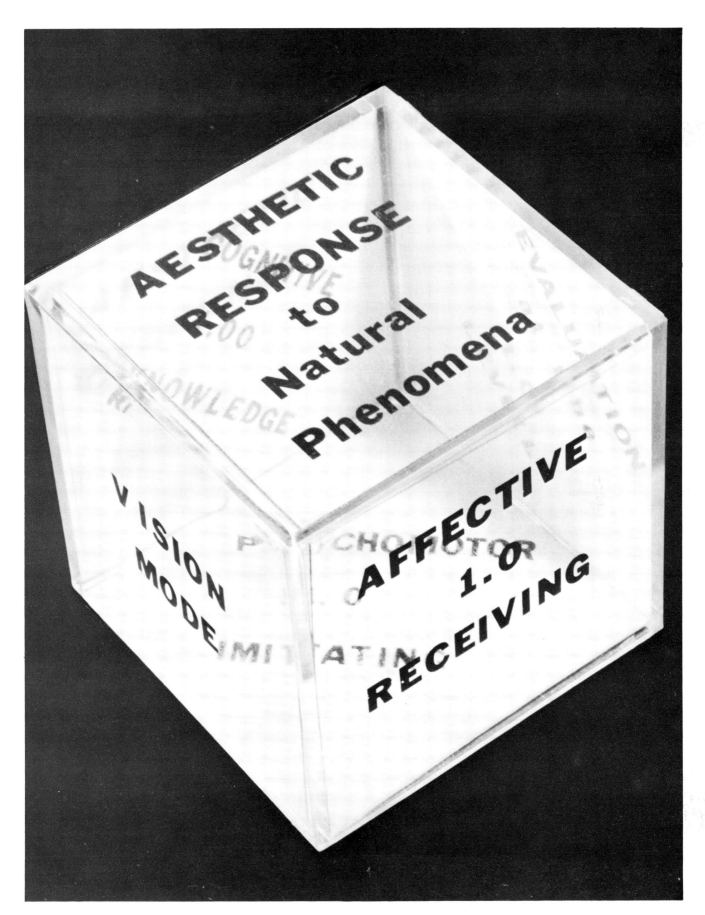

Figure 11.4 Example of one cube from the total aesthetic block. (Photo credit: Hank Londoner, Photograhper.)

INSTRUCTIONAL SCORE

I. *Aesthetic Response Area:* Natural phenomenon: The rainbow.

II. *Sensory Mode (or Modes):* Vision (only).

III. *Cognitive level* (**1.0**) *Knowledge:* Teach

(1) the sequence of colors in the rainbow—outer arc to inner arc—red, orange, yellow, green, blue, violet (Note: if two rainbows appear, the inner one has its colors in reverse, violet to red.),

(2) the relative positions between sun, rain, and observer for rainbow to be seen, (low sun, opposite the rain, the observer to one side but in between).

IV. *Psychomotor level* (**1.0**) *Imitation*, (**2.0**) *Manipulative:* Save unit for rainy day when rainbow is seen. Alternatives: Have students make rainbow in school yard with garden hose and spray on a sunny day, blow soap bubbles for prismatic effect, or use soap suds in the sink. Show students a picture of a rainbow. Have students draw a crayon-resist rainbow in a watercolor landscape.

V. *Affective level* (**1.0**) *Receiving:* Students will receive information about rainbow (color sequence, rules for observation), ask questions for clarification. (**2.0**) *Responding*—students will look at rainbow, or make alternatives, and draw a crayon-resist picture of one.

VI. *Evaluation* (**6.0**) *Cognitive*, (**6.1**) *Knowledge:* Use written test for correct spelling, sequence of colors, and conditions under which rainbows are observed. *Cognitive* (**6.3**) *Application:* Apply knowledge of color sequence in crayon-resist drawing. Optional or extra credit: inclusion of sun and observer in correct relationship to the rainbow. (Optional if it has been taught but not asked for in the art motivation or assignment). *Psychomotor* (**6.1**) *Imitation* (**6.2**) *Manipulation:* Look for ability of students to create rainbow with garden hose after simple instruction. In crayon-resist look for control of crayons in making parallel arcs, freedom of brush in watercolor landscape, consistency of paint in not washing out crayons, evidence of previous learning about watercolor techniques (if any) carried over to present picture, evidence of flexibility or stereotypes of clouds, trees, foliage, flowers, houses, persons, etc. Did new schemas for clouds, rain, etc., result because of new awareness of rainy days? Is there evidence of feelings, emotions, or expressive aspects related to a rainy day and the rainbow? *Affective* (**6.1**) *Receiving:* Look for students who are paying attention, listening, or asking questions (selected attention), (**6.2**) *Responding:* Look for nature of students response, willingness, spontaneity, and so on when asked to look out window at rainbow, make rainbow with garden hose or other alternatives, and draw a crayon-resist or take written test (if any).

Note: Core monument on rainbow (chapter 6) can be related to this activity as a humanistic theme on myths explaining natural phenomena.

Example: Gustatory Mode—Peanut Butter

Peanut butter was selected for use in this example in developing aesthetic criteria because it is already a popular food item with children, and receives considerable advertising that affects children's taste preference.

INSTRUCTIONAL SCORE

I. *Aesthetic Response Area (Purpose):* To develop aesthetic criteria for judging a man-made phenomenon—peanut butter.

II. *Sensory Modes (s):* Gustatory, olfactory, tactual, and visual.

III. *Cognitive* (**1.0**) *Knowledge:* Teacher provides historical data about invention and development of peanut butter (George Washington Carver), uses of peanut butter by American Indians, and modern uses through industry. Discuss with students the ways and means of eating peanut butter (sandwiches, crackers, on salads and bananas, with finger, etc.) Identify terms used by advertisers to sell their brands of peanut butter; add others for aesthetic criteria. Translate quantity in jar from ounces to metric weight.

IV. *Psychomotor:* (**2.0**) *Manipulative:* During snack time, children taste different brands of peanut butter (supplied by teacher, or by students from home). Compare smells, tastes, texture, consistency, and so forth according to criteria decided upon earlier. Alternatives: Compare differences of same brand when used on bread, crackers, toasts, fruits; or with butter, margarine, mayonnaise, jellies, honey, and so on. Stir and spread for consistency, and oilness. Keep milk, juices, Kool-Aids available for clearing taste buds between samples. When making comparisons of peanut butter brands restrict bread or crackers used with them to one brand.

V. *Affective* (**3.0**) *Valuing:* Have each student identify his or her favorite brand of peanut butter and tell why. If any students do not like peanut butter, have them explain why (written or oral). Discuss television commercials as influences on taste preferences and selection of peanut butter. Identify other influences on preference (parents, peers, brother or sister). Have students identify the combinations of peanut butter with other tastes which they like best (or do not like) and explain why. Compare difference of price of brands with favorite.

VI. *Evaluation* (**6.0**) *Cognitive* (**6.1**) *Knowledge:* Written tests on historical development and invention of peanut butter, different uses and products made from peanuts, spelling of aesthetic criteria, and so on. (**6.4**) *Analysis:* Observe abilities of students to identify tastes, textures, consistencies according to terms listed as aesthetic criteria, or use terms in discussing qualities. *Psychomotor* (**6.2**) *Manipulative:* Ability to taste, smell, differentiate texture, observe color, and identify or describe them is a sensory perceptive technique. Evaluation criteria compares student's response with evidence within the testing sample. Students might try to identify peanut butters by the brand, with jars hidden from view. Students are analyzing and using gustatory memory to identify brand names. *Affective* (**6.3**) *Valuing:* Do students use aesthetic criteria defined by the class for explaining their favorite peanut butter (oral or written statement)? Do they equate superior and inferior brands with their own taste preferences and rejections? Wait two or more weeks. Then ask students which brand of peanut butter they are presently using. Is it the same as their previously stated favorite? Did the lesson affect their choice of a favorite brand? Did any students apply the same comparing techniques to other brands of consumer items, such as chewing gum, breakfast cereals, TV dinners, and so on?

Example: Aesthetic Analysis: **Wedding in the Thirties** *by Edward Lamson Henry*

The following example was one of the author's most successful units in having children look at an art reproduction in the elementary school, not so much because they remained actively interested in the picture and discussion, but because it was the only art lesson in two years of working with this particular classroom teacher during the course of which he remained for the entire period without finding an excuse to leave the

room. Afterward, he said, "I was surprised that you could keep children interested in a single picture for forty-five minutes." Actually, for forty-five minutes, he, the teacher, remained interested in art.

Setting: A fifth-grade class studying the Federalist period. The instructor asked the author to give an art lesson relating art to their study. He decided on history through art, rather than a mural, or other type of project.

Selection: Wedding in the Thirties by Edward Lamson Henry (see fig. 11.5), which depicts a narrative of the period, the antebellum South, including architecture, fashions, mode of transportation, and evidence of social customs of the period.

Procedure: After setting the reproduction up on the chalk tray in front of the room, and gathering the class closer so they could see it better, the picture was discussed from three points of view: (1) history through art, (2) aesthetic analysis, and (3) an object in American art history. Each phase was announced to separate it from the others and to let the students know which point of view was going to be used. The students were asked what they saw, rather than told what to look for. Before the presentation, the author had done some research on the painting, the period, and the artist so as to be able to feed back knowledgeable information to the students. It was most important to elaborate upon and explain what they saw.

Figure 11.5 Edward Lamson Henry: "Wedding in the Thirties." (Courtesy: Shorewood Reproductions, Inc.)

Phase 1. History through art: opening question: "What does this picture tell you about the Federalist period which you have been reading about in social studies?" They identified, and we discussed Georgian architecture, the under-structure of women's skirts (blackboard diagram), formal gardens (blackboard diagram), social customs such as bride kissing mother last before going on honeymoon, status differences between house slaves and field hands, roof in back which may be carriage house, smokehouse, or kitchen. Blackboard diagrams were also used to provide information clarifying evidence found in painting as it was pointed up by students.

Phase 2. Aesthetic analysis: Students' point of view was shifted by saying, "We have been looking at this painting for what it tells us about how people lived during the Federalist (antebellum) period. Now, let's look at it as a design. Why do you think the artist painted the house, people, horses, garden, and colors where he did?" Before the discussion was finished we had dealt with symmetrical balance (vertical porch columns on the left with vertical trees and arbor on right), linear perspective (converging lines of porch, windows, hedges, trees, horses) leading to center of interest (bride, groom and parents), accompanied by diagrammed analysis (blackboard) for clarification. The repetition of blues in the men's clothes, and the use of the white horse between the dappled grey and the hedges were also discussed. Then the topic switched to the third point of view.

Phase 3. The painting in the history of U.S. art. This phase did not depend on what the students knew, but on what the teacher could provide. It required teacher knowledge rather than student perception. "Genre" painting (new word), as a type of subject matter, was introduced. The author briefly presented information about Edward Lamson Henry (1841-1919) as an American genre painter who painted pictures of the nineteenth-century upper classes. He was born in Charleston, South Carolina, studied at Philadelphia Academy of Fine Arts, went to Paris in 1860 to study painting, returned in 1863, and sketched and painted battle scenes during the Civil War like Winslow Homer. After the war he set up a studio in New York, where he was popularly successful for his paintings of early nineteenth-century upper-class life in New York, Philadelphia, and the South. The author also discussed the possibility that the couple getting married in *Wedding in the Thirties* could have been his parents, since he was born in 1841.

Unexpected follow-up: After a lesson with an art reproduction, the author would leave it in the classroom so the students could have further reference to reinforce their familiarity with it. One or two weeks later when he went to the same class, the students were whispering about something. Finally, a boy held up his hand, and on inquiry showed me an illustration in a book he was reading about Francis Marion, Swamp Fox. It depicted Marion's arrival home during the American Revolution, and had been based on *Wedding in the Thirties*. In the children's book illustration, a brush line drawing,

Swamp Fox was also shaking hands with his father, and a part of the same carriage was in view. The porch, architecture, children, adults, and women's fashions were the same. A dog had been added.

The starting of the day's planned art lesson was delayed to discuss the illustration in comparison to the painting, and the relative differences of time in cultural change. The students felt that fashion in clothes changed more rapidly than style in transportation vehicles, and architecture. Therefore, the porch and architecture might have been appropriate for the time of Swamp Fox, but not the clothes. Before we could verify the carriage, we would need to know when the "caleche" was first imported from France. As a result, it was decided that for reliability's sake it would be better to use a painting closely related to a period of time in question for historical research, than to depend on an illustration by a contemporary illustrator in a children's book.

In these same art classes, the author also fostered discussions pertaining to the illustrations in history books, social studies books, and even encyclopedias when they were used in the classroom. The artists were identified, and when possible larger sized reproductions of the same pictures as those in their classroom resources were shown.

Brief Example: Mixed Sensory Modes and Learning Domains

Drawing to music is a combined art and music activity which elicits sensory responses in three different modes: visual, aural, and kinesthetic. The *purpose* of such a lesson is to help the student realize the concepts of rhythm, melodic line, and counterpoint in music, as related to visual repetition, dominance, and subordination, along with both visual and aural movement. Students are *given* wax crayons (they can be used without replacing or refilling, and colors can be changed quickly), 18- by 24-inch paper (it allows large freedom of movement), and music selected in terms of presenting a good example of the type of musical concept to which the children are to listen, respond, and express in visual form; among these: Offenbach's "Barcarolle," Ravel's *Bolero,* Mozart's *Toy Symphony,* or Dohnáni's *Variations on a Nursery Theme,* (both of the latter suggest "Twinkle, twinkle, little star"). *Methods:* Children are asked to listen to music, move their hands along with the music, choose crayons, the colors of which seemed to express the musical sound or instrument, and follow the melodic line of the music on the paper with the crayons. (See figs. 11.6-11.10.)

In the course of the lesson referred to in the previous illustrations, students were using the aural mode while listening, the visual mode in the linear and color associations they related to, and the kinesthetic mode in coordinating their hand movement to the music, lines, colors, or shapes on the paper, as well as eye-ear-hand coordination, also in the kinesthetic mode. Learning in the cognitive domain includes terms used in art such as

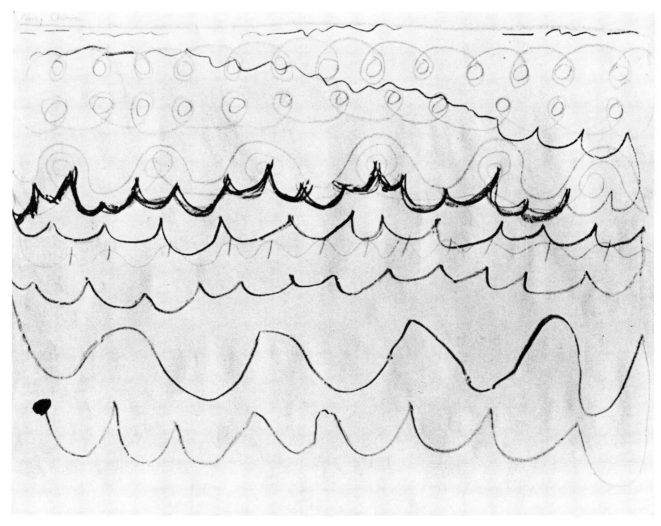

Figure 11.6 "Barcarolle" (Offenbach) by Nancy Chimini, elementary teacher. (Photo: J. Richard McGinnis)

"rhythm," "dominance," and "subordination," related to music with such terms as "rhythm," "melody," and "counterpoint." In the psychomotor domain, learning might be at any of the levels, as the hand responds to the music in its movement. In the affective domain, the students' participation in the drawing action demonstrates their willingness to respond, and the results might be satisfaction of response. This example demonstrates how a single art-music activity can deal with three sensory modes, at different stages in each of the three learning domains. The resulting art product represents the child's expressive response to music (an aural art form) through drawing with crayons (a visual art form). Sometimes in this art activity, the same music has been played twice (Offenbach's "Barcarolle") with instructions to first listen and draw the dominating theme or melodic line, and then to the subordinate theme, or counterpoint. This is a lightly evaluated activity, to determine the variety of visual interpretations to the same musical composition. Such drawings make excellent bulletin board exhibits of abstract or nonobjective visual statements.

Sensory Imagery

Each sensory mode has some degree of recall imagery. The imagination draws it forth when the stimulus is no longer present. Some sensory modes have more elusive imagery than others. Through our visual memory we remember how a particular person, painting, building, flower, or other object looks in order to describe it or recognize it again. The chef needs good gustatory imagery or memory to compare a particular sauce with an ideal example when tasting it. The olfactory sense lends itself to memory associations. We use our aural or auditory imagery in recalling a musical piece, when whistling it, or when comparing one recorded version with another. Memorizing poetry is a part of our verbal memory, but remembering a particular inflection or interpretation by a great actor is also auditory memory inasmuch as it draws forth aural imagery.

Marshall McLuhan (1973) has suggested that wheels are the extension of our feet—tools and weapons the extension of our hands—television the extension of our eyes—the telephone the extension of our ears. In these terms, hallucinogenic drugs might be considered an extension of our sensory imagery, and the various art forms the extensions of our sensory modes into less illusory and more enduring areas of expression.

Extrasensory perception, and hyperesthesis are extensions of our sensory perceptions beyond their common uses and the limitations usually attributed to them. Individuals trying to move beyond the western European, Judeo-Christian suppression of sensory modes are investigating eastern and oriental religions and practices, Integral Yoga, Transcendental Meditation, and other meditative processes to bring forth from their subconscious selves images of mandalas, yang and yin, and other preternatural symbols of psychic origin. Others try to contact previous existences, or the dead through

intermediaries. Their media is the medium. Still others attempt to feed their sensory imagery through hallucinogenic drugs. More healthily, others turn to the arts. As observed by Colin Wilson:

All human beings share a common craving: to escape the narrowness of their lives, the suffocation of their immediate surroundings. This, as Einstein says, it is why men want to escape from cities, to get into the peace of the mountains at weekends. The narrowness of our lives makes the senses close up, until we feel stifled. This also explains why Ouspensky found a "strange flavour of truth" in books on Atlantis and magic. It is important for us to feel that there is another kind of knowledge, quite different from the everyday existence, strange realities beyond the walls that surround us. Art, music, philosophy, mysticism are all escape routes from the narrowness of everyday reality; but *they all demand a large initial outlay of conscious effort;* you have to sow before you can reap. (italics RJS)

9. Colin Wilson, *The Occult: A History*, copyright © 1971, Random House, Inc., pp. 109-10. Reprinted by permission.

Figure 11.7 "Barcarolle" (Offenbach) by Judy Haddad, elementary art teacher. (Photo: J. Richard McGinnis)

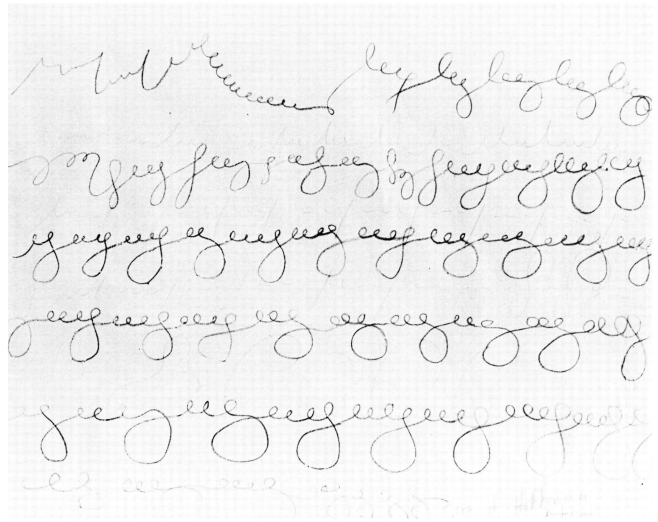

Figure 11.8 "Barcarolle" (Offenbach) by Ruth Hennesy, elementary teacher. (Photo: J. Richard McGinnis)

Wilson makes a distinction between the use of the occult and the uses of the arts for achieving transcendence over the narrowness of everyday existence (identified as a human need in chapter 3).

. . . occultism is a simple direct method of escaping the narrowness of everydayness. Instead of turning outwards toward the world of the great composers or philosophers, the student of the occult turns immediately inward and tries to reach down to his subliminal depths.[10]

Whatever the direction, the need for a transcendence, through the feeding and extending of our sensory imagery is catching up with us all. Through the arts one can take a sociocentric, rather than an egocentric orientation to our culture, society, and environment.

Some Goals of Aesthetic Education

Aesthetic education programs can provide the basis, range, and concepts by which children can grow up to draw on the arts when making personal decisions and selections of an aesthetic nature in their everyday life,

home, community, or in the total man-made environment. To this end, the following goals of aesthetic education are suggested:

(1) to broaden the student's repertoire of choices and associational experiences in the arts from which to select healthy means of satisfying particular aesthetic needs or sensory hungers.

(2) to develop the student's ability to focus or concentrate each sensory receptor on related stimuli in order to extract a deeper wealth of fulfillment from one or more repeated encounters with those stimuli.

(3) to raise (or lower) the student's thresholds of perception as needed for greater receptivity to healthy stimuli, rather than using drugs or increasing intensity of stimuli to overcome sensory fatigue—as playing rock music at high intensity levels.

(4) to help the student develop a generalized set of aesthetic criteria for making personal value judgments and selections concerning the satisfaction of personal

10. Ibid.

Figure 11.9 "Bolero" (Ravel) by Paul Dworak, elementary teacher. (Photo: J. Richard McGinnis)

needs and dealing with the home and man-made or the built environment.

Reinforcing Activities

1. In different art forms, identify those types you like as a group, such as western movies, horror films, love stories, novels of a certain kind or by a certain author, specific performing groups, authors, types of dishes (egg plant parmigiana, omelettes, hamburgers, veal scallopini, etc.). Describe the criteria by which you judge good examples of their type, from less good examples. Once achieved, this identifies your own aesthetic taste criteria.

2. Draw a line continuum with five degrees of taste preference and rejection. Use your own terms if those used below do not apply:

loves/cannot get enough	likes accepts	neutral tolerates	dislikes avoids	hates emotional rejection

As a class group or individual, list examples in categories, such as art (artists, styles, periods), music (types, composers, styles), reading matter (authors, novels, poems, etc.), movies/television shows (types, actors, actresses, directors), foods (kinds of food or beverage, types of cuisines, sauces, franchised eateries—McDonald's, Hardee's, etc.). Choose a category and list under taste preference levels. What does this tell you about your special generalized set? To what extent does it agree or disagree with others in the class? Try this out with your best friend or spouse.

References

Aslin, Elizabeth. *The Aesthetic Movement.* New York: Frederick A. Praeger, 1969.

Barkan, Manual; Chapman, Laura; and Kern, Evan J. *Guidelines: Curriculum Development for Aesthetic Education.* St. Louis: CEMREL, Inc., 1970.

Boring, Edwin G. *A History of Experimental Psychology.* 2d ed. New York: Appleton-Century-Crofts, 1950.

Butts, Freeman R., and Cremin, Lawrence A. *A History*

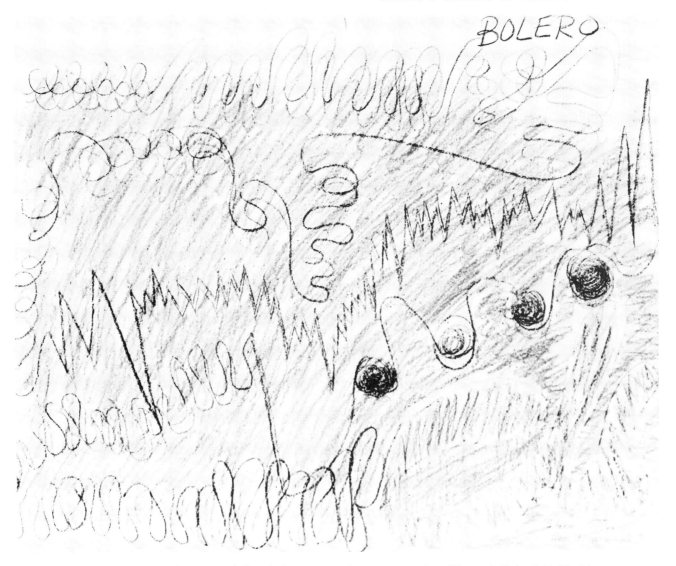

Figure 11.10 "Bolero" (Ravel) by Shelia Troppe, elementary teacher. (Photo: J. Richard McGinnis)

of Education in American Culture. New York: Henry Holt and Co., 1953.

ELLIS, HAVELOCK. "Introduction." In J. K. HUYSMAN's *Against the Grain (A Rebours).* New York: Dover Publications, 1969.

GUILFORD, J. P. *Nature of Human Intelligence.* New York: McGraw-Hill Book Co., 1967.

HARROW, ANITA. *Taxonomy of the Psychomotor Domain.* New York: David McKay Co., 1972.

LINDERMAN, EARL W., and HERBERHOLZ, DONALD W. *Developing Artistic and Perceptual Awareness.* 3d ed. Dubuque, Iowa: Wm. C. Brown Company Publishers, 1974.

LOWENBERG, JACOB. *Hegel Selections.* New York: Charles Scribner's Sons, 1957.

McLUHAN, MARSHALL. *Understanding Media: The Extension of Man.* New York: McGraw-Hill Book Co., 1973.

RIETZ, CARL R. *A Guide to the Selection, Combination and Cooking of Foods.* 2 vols. Westport, Conn.: AVI Pub. Co., 1961-1965. Note: excellent for charting and categorizing tastes, odors, and flavor continuums.

STRAUS, EDWIN W. "Aesthesiology and Hallucinations." In *Existence: A New Dimension in Psychiatry and Psychology.* Edited by Rollo May, Ernest Angel, and Henri F. Ellenberger. New York: Basic Books, 1958, pp. 139-169.

VENTURI, LIONELLO. *History of Art Criticism.* New York: E. P. Dutton & Co., 1964.

WILDS, ELMER HARRISON. *The Foundation of Modern Education.* New York: Rinehart & Co., 1948.

12

Writing student performance objectives
in art and the humanities

School districts throughout the country are rewriting their curriculum guides as related to behavioral objectives, which are being taught in some college teacher preparation courses. More than another educational bandwagon, however, they are part of a very serious effort by the federal and state governments, and educators, to assess the quality of education in the public schools. The vehicle for achieving this was the National Assessment Program, which resulted from a program under the Exploration Committee on Assessing the Progress of Education (ECAPE), sponsored by the Carnegie Corporation, in 1963-64. The committee's main objective was to survey school administrators, teachers, board members, and laymen involved in education for the purpose of obtaining information that would be helpful in the designing of a useful assessment and evaluative tool for constructively keeping and supporting the schools. After ECAPE's final report, the committee began operating as the Committee on Assessing the Progress of Education (CAPE). Forty-three states and territories adopted the plan under the aegis of the Education Commission for the States. From this, National Assessment grew, and a system for evaluating schools according to observable outcomes was deemed necessary. National Assessment standards were set for educational programs, and children were tested at ages nine, thirteen, and seventeen. The testing results were identified and described for art, music, mathematics, science, and other subjects. The National Assessment objectives for art at the elementary level were discussed in chapter 3.

Observable outcomes, as such, were identified as the behavior or the performance of children (or the learner). A structure was designed to fit them, which included the Taxononomy of Educational Objectives. Several authors, Mager (1962), French (1957), Gronlund (1964), Popham (1970), Shutz (1971), and Sullivan (1971), have written popular instructional and behavioral objectives handbooks, or guides for writing them. Like Bloom, Krathwohl and the taxonomical committee, they deal more with the cognitive domain than with the affective domain, and even less so with the psychomotor domain.

Florida was one of the states involved in the National Assessment Program. The Florida State Department of Education (Neil Mooney, art consultant) through the art department of Palm Beach County School system with Jo Kowhalchuk, supervisor of art, made the first comprehensive development of an assessment program on art using behavioral or student performance objectives (1972). *A Guide for Writing*

Performance Objectives in Visual Arts has also been prepared by Weidenheimer and Barr-Johnson, based on national assessment criteria (Weidenheimer, 1971). Another approach, by Virginia M. Brouch, *Art Education: A Matrix System for Writing Behavioral Objectives,* offers a broader and more comprehensive coverage.

The National Art Education Association has published some articles in *Art Education* and *Studies in Art Education.* Laura Chapman and David Ecker (1971) developed a game of art curriculum design. Donald Jack Davis (1971), Mary Rouse, and Guy Hubbard (1970) have added to the growing literature. Eliot W. Eisner (1972) introduced the concept of "expressive objective" as another aspect of the behavioral objective approach. This is his one particularly important contribution to arts education, but it is difficult to write about in behavioral terms and properly assess. In chapter 1 self-expression was dealt with in terms of the Taxonomy of Educational Objectives; later in this chapter ways in which expressive objectives might be written are suggested.

Upon completion of this chapter the reader will have picked up as cognitive knowledge some terminology, and will also have learned ways and means of writing behavioral objectives. You will have analyzed sets of examples and chosen one or the other as correct. In the reinforcing activities you will be asked to apply what you have learned by writing examples of your own, which you might do either at the imitation level of the psychomotor domain by rewording examples found here or elsewhere, or at the manipulative level by experimenting with ideas of your own. As you become more involved and struggle further with the examples, you may have less need for trial and error, and be more precise.

Finally, it is hoped, you will find satisfaction in your responses and in the examples you write, but you are not expected to value them or have a commitment to them just because of this chapter.

Behavioral Terminology

Behavioral (whether student performance or observable) objectives are not difficult to comprehend nor are they to be feared. They represent a technique, not a philosophy, and as such can be learned like any other psychomotor skill. They can, with practice, be conjured up in the mind which is the "psycho" or mental skill aspect of the psychomotor domain. The act of writing or typing the objectives is the motor skill.

Since the terminology is new it is at times confusing, owing largely to the fact that different authors use different terms. An example is the use of "student performance," "observable," or "behavioral" to identify a precise technique of writing an educational objective in terms of what the student will do. "Behavioral" connotes a type of prolonged activity, such as good and bad behavior or behavior modification. They might also confuse its meaning here. Student performance and observable objectives, might, therefore, be more precise. The author will use all three terms interchangeably, since he has no commitment to any one.

Behavioral (*Student Performance, Observable*) *objective:* The description of a learning objective identifying an observable activity by the student (or learner) as evidence of having achieved the objective.

Conditions: The stated elements under which the learner will perform. Popham (1970) uses "conditions" while Mager (1962) uses "givens." Both describe what the learner is provided with in order to achieve the desired objective. They may be demonstrations, experiments, a lecture, art materials, and such like.

Expressive Objective: A term used by Eisner to describe "an encounter the student is to have. From that encounter, hopefully positive consequences will flow."[1]

Goals: The long-range end results (of a global or conceptual nature) upon which an individual or group focuses its efforts, and which may take several years to achieve. Goals may not reach fulfillment until long after the influence of the initiating individual has terminated. Well-stated goals should be directed toward the solution of identified problems confronting the individual or group in relation to society or culture. These are usually set by the school board for the entire district.

Instructional Objectives: A term frequently used as if interchangeable with behavioral objectives, but more appropriately used to identify the objectives of a study unit or what the teacher will do to help the student succeed.

Objectives: Short-ranged end results of a specific nature related to one or more goals or subgoals. They are not always written in behavioral terms, or into that format.

Subgoals: Intermediate goals, or the subdivisions of major goals. Teachers, when they relate subject matter goals to the major goals set by the board of education, are really writing subgoals.

Terminal Objectives: Those objectives expected of a student at the end of a specific lesson or study unit. They may be part of a sequence of objectives taught through several student-learning activities. Most examples in this chapter are terminal objectives.

Ways and Means for Writing Behavioral Objectives

A complete and well-written behavioral objective includes three factors:

1. What the student (learner) does or is expected to do.
2. The conditions (given) under which the student does it.
3. The extent or degree to which the student will achieve (and evaluators can identify) success in doing it.

Although this is a precise set of rules, it does not restrict the teacher or the student as such, any more than the rules governing the meter and rhyme scheme of an Elizabethan sonnet restricts the thoughts of the poet who adopts that particular form. The philosophy of the teacher will show up in the type of objectives and performance activity asked of the student. Those objectives may be quite academic and restrictive, or they can be open, imaginative, and varied.

Students might even work with the teacher in writing their own performance objectives. Indeed, this is what is being done, in some ways, by student-teacher contracting. Although the contracts are not quite so concisely stated as the behavioral objective defined above, they usually contain similar features.

Actually, the examples used in behavioral objective workbooks tend to include all three factors in a single sentence. Nothing the author has found in the literature says this must be so. In fact, doing this sometimes makes awkward phrasing and sentence structure. If necessary, a behavioral objective should take more than one sentence.

A behavioral objective describes the student's performance, but *does not* dictate the teaching methods used to achieve that objective. These are usually left up to the teacher. However, if an art project is to result directly from a demonstration, or specific type of motivation, then this might be included as a part of the conditions or givens.

Behavioral objectives in the arts are especially easy to write for the psychomotor domain, because the very acts of painting, cutting, or drawing are student performances. Art teachers, unaccustomed to teaching cognitive information or data, for fear it will inhibit the child's imagination and creativity, tend also to avoid cognitive verbal (written or oral) tests. However, such data might also be tested when applied to the psychomotor art activity. Taking a written test is at best a meager psychomotor activity, except for the mental process of recall.

Vocabulary is important in writing behavioral objectives. Certain words and terms are considered vague, ambiguous, and nonobservable. They are such terms as, to understand, appreciate, get a better understanding or deeper appreciation of, and such. How does one evaluate the difference between appreciation and a deeper appreciation?

1. Elliott W. Eisner, *Educating Artistic Vision.* Copyright © 1972. The Macmillan Co., p. 156.

Identifying Behavioral Objectives

Of the two following statements in the cognitive domain, which one is written in behavioral terms?

A. Given a demonstration from color charts the student will learn color theory, and take a written test.
B. Following a discussion of the color theory charts, the student will classify and list the primary and secondary colors (correctly spelled) in a written test.

If you said statement B, you were right. Statement A seemingly has the three factors, but it is not clear what the student will learn about color theory, or what will be written on the test. Statement B makes both quite clear, while reminding the teacher that correct spelling should be part of the performance. This objective can also be applied to the psychomotor domain, while still testing cognitive knowledge, as in this variation:

C. Following a discussion of the color theory charts, and given a set of watercolors, water, and 9-by-12-inch manila paper, the student will paint the primary and secondary colors on the paper, correctly labeling and spelling each.

Statement C includes both the cognitive data found in statements A and B, but requires the child to apply this knowledge through a psychomotor activity, at probably the imitation level. Statement C might also become a terminal objective, if subsequent lessons are added to increase the child's knowledge and experience in color theory, such as the following:

D. Following the previous lesson of the color theory chart, and given a fresh piece of 9-by-12-inch manila paper, a set of watercolors and water, the student will mix the primary and secondary colors and paint tertiary colors on the paper, correctly labeling and spelling each.

Since the mixing of colors is more experimental than just applying them to paper as in statement C, the student's activity would be at the (2.0) manipulative level of the psychomotor domain. After some trial and error, the student may get to the precision level, thus obtaining the equal balance of primary and secondary colors to achieve the tertiary quality. That this is a follow-up objective is evident by the open phrase, "Following the previous lesson," the teacher then checks the previous lesson to make sure it was taught, and its objectives achieved.

Here are two objectives from the affective domain, which one is stated behaviorally?

A. Following a presentation of twenty reproductions of paintings by Edward Hopper, Joseph Albers, Charles White, Romare Bearden, and Jackson Pollock (four by each artist), the student will choose one or more that he or she would like to hang in his or her room at home, and explain why (orally or written). If none is preferred, this will also be explained.
B. Following a presentation of twenty slides of works by Edward Hopper, Joseph Albers, Charles White, Romare Bearden, and Jackson Pollock (four works of each artist), the student will demonstrate his or her appreciation of contemporary art in the U.S., by correctly identifying fifteen paintings and the artists.

Statements A and B are both completely written behavioral objectives. B includes the phrase "will demonstrate appreciation of," but students are asked "to identify." They can do this without appreciating. Statement A is an affective objective because students are asked to choose, while B is essentially cognitive, since students are asked "to identify" (rather than choose) fifteen out of twenty examples. Statement B can omit the phrase "will demonstrate appreciation of" and be a well-written cognitive-type behavioral objective. Statement A, therefore, is the behavioral objective written in the affective domain.

The student is asked to make a choice, which allows both satisfaction and dissatisfaction with specific works of art. By being asked to explain why, or justify choices, the student is asked to make an affective statement. Consequently this is an expressive-type objective, the student being asked to explain a reaction between the self and twenty examples of contemporary American art.

Objectives are usually associated with the affective domain if they ask the student to differentiate, separate, combine, respond to, explain, spend leisure time in, select, choose, support, protest, discuss, debate, organize or rate in priority order, or respond similarly. Objectives in the cognitive domain usually ask students to identify, recall, recognize, translate, rephrase, estimate, conclude, interpolate, apply, generalize, classify, analyze, synthesize, judge, assess, and so forth.

Here are two statements in the psychomotor domain. Which one is the most complete?

A. The student will assemble a collage of found materials brought from home, and sew, paste, glue, staple, or otherwise attach them to a 12-by-18-inch piece of oaktag, in a design showing balance, repetition, contrast, movement, dominance, and subordination.
B. Using magazines brought from home, and given paste, scissors, and a 9-by-12-inch piece of colored construction paper, the student will cut out pictures of either fruits or vegetables (but not both) and paste them on the paper in a collage, making sure the paste is smoothly applied, and the pictures cut with smooth edges.

Both are completely expressed behavioral objectives. Selection is a matter of their development. Example B is more appropriate for preprimary or early primary grades where skills and simple classifying and sorting is taught. Example A is more appropriate at the upper elementary level, after students have learned their cutting and pasting skills, and have been taught the principles of design asked for in the written objective.

Art problem-solving objectives might be considered a special category in the psychomotor domain. The student is asked to do a specific thing, but the final product is not identified. Problem solving is also considered a cognitive skill when it deals with arithmetic and "thought problems." Here is an example of an art problem-solving objective:

> Given toothpicks and fast-drying airplane cement, the student will build a three-dimensional structure which will stand up by itself.

The objective is open-ended, since the only criteria for achieving it are that the structure be three-dimensional, and that it can stand up by itself. It may be a house, person, tree, animal, or vague structure. As long as the students solved problems of bracing, supports, and three-dimensional structural concepts, they have achieved the objective. Although problem solving is identified as a cognitive domain activity, such as thought problems in arithmetic, there are also psychomotor problems in art, as in the example above, or in any other situation wherein the problem is specified as part of the objective activity even though a specific end product is not defined except in such terms as to be a solution to the problem.

Objectives in the psychomotor domain usually ask students to: cut, paste, draw, paint, polish, assemble, build, construct, letter, print, solve, weave, wedge, sew, staple, soak, wash, model, and so on.

Evaluating Behavioral Objectives

The degree of success achieved by a student, as stated in the objectives, can be considered the *external criteria*. Read again each example of behavioral objectives for the cognitive, affective, and psychomotor domains. The external criteria as stated in the objective are compared with the internal evidence of the student's behavior or performance to determine the degree of success. Affective statement B depends on internal evidence of a personal, subjective, or self-expressive nature, although the cognitive factors are the correct use of terms, and use of specific knowledge when justifying a preference. The student and teacher may end up with different affective results, but the evaluation is based on terminology and process rather than on agreement with an outside (teacher) point of view.

External criteria should be stated clearly enough for students to know what is expected. One private school headmaster prepared a series of approaches to essays and book reviews for his students to read. The series demonstrated the various possible forms which he wanted, and the students were to analyze each form— the type of terminology, and the precise statements he expected. He did not judge their opinions in the same way, since they represented two different aspects of

expression. He might personally disagree with the student's point of view, but find the techniques or skills of expression to be very good indeed. Accordingly, a teacher might disapprove of a student's subject matter or expressive content, yet recognize the *quality* of the expression itself.

The Nature of Expressive Objectives

Expressive objectives are more complex than straight-forward behavioral (student performance or observable) objectives, since they ask the student for the expression of an inner response rather than for a demonstration of skill, or the recollection of specific data or knowledge. The nature of the expression and its commentary is up to the student.

Writing behavioral objectives is a cognitive-psychomotor technique which can be learned. It includes three factors, previously described. The wording used when writing them can be open, leading to individual expression, or closed, leading to intellectual replication and subjection.

Eisner (1972) introduced the concept of the "expressive objective" to art education literature, and identified it as something other than a behavioral objective. Like the problem-solving objective, expressive objectives are also behaviorally oriented. Valid self-expression is in response to some sort of motivation or stimulus, which may be an emotion, a recent event, an abstract idea, or something similar. Eisner describes the interaction between the individual and the stimulus as an encounter. Expression is usually an attempt to communicate a particular feeling, response, or emotion to known others, to generalized others, or to a concept such as God or the heavens.

The arts help individuals develop their expressive abilities by supplying the media for expression. Art education can supply the stimulus or opportunity for encounter and the materials for communication. Behavioral objectives, written to elicit expressive behavior, are certainly more complex to write than those for cognitive, psychomotor, or affective end results.

Expressive objectives, as interpreted here, involve all three domains, but at the upper hierarchical levels. The student is asked to respond (affective 2.0) to a particular stimulus or motivation, to make a uniquely personal communication (cognitive, 5.0 synthesis), effectively enough to be understood (psychomotor 4.0 articulation). The very process of expressing a feeling, emotion, or concept through the arts may help move it from the satisfaction of response level, toward commitment in the valuing level of the affective domain.

Stating Expressive-Type Behavioral Objectives

Hesitancies about formulating expressive-type behavioral objectives may result from the fear that too much closure or direction may stifle self-expression, free expression, or creative expression. Not only is balance necessary between the three aspects of a well-stated behavioral objective, but it must be open-ended as well. Cognitive and psychomotor objectives tend not to be open-ended. Here are a few examples of how the author thinks expressive objectives might be written.

Example 1: From within the areas of dance, film-making, music, creative writing, sculpture, painting, found art, found sound, combinations of these, and/or other art forms of individual choice, the student will express his or her reactions to the bombing of Hiroshima, so that others recognize or comprehend the student's message.

In this example, the method of expression is left open, the stimulus is stated (the bombing of Hiroshima), the behavior or method of expression is student's choice, and the criterion is that the expression be comprehended by others. Additional evaluation might include the student's control and use of the art form or media, originality of expression, and so forth, but these are subordinate to the external criteria as stated.

Example 2: While Saint-Saëns's *Carnival of Animals* is playing on the phonograph, the student will pretend to be the animals described in the music, and express the movement of the animals while moving around the room.

The music is the given. It describes the animals and provides a stimulus to which the student responds. The external criterion, if one is applied beyond the expressive pleasure, might be to compare knowledge of the animal to the student's expression, or compare the student's movement with the music.

Both examples identify the subject matter to which the student is expected to respond. Example 1 leaves the art form up to the student, while example 2 specifies the mode of expression through body movement. A completely open behavioral objective might be written something like this:

Example 3: Given complete free choice of art forms and necessary materials (either provided by the school or brought from someplace else) the student will express a feeling, emotion, or attitude of personal commitment which will be comprehended by others.

Evaluating this might be difficult. It is free of any specific focus. Finding out the student's own criterion might require some questioning and discussion. The student, in this situation, is being asked to state his or her own external criterion and compare it with the evidence of the product or performance.

Example 4: Following encounters with the work of Käthe Kollwitz and Mahler's *Kindertotenlieder* (Poems on the Death of Children), the student, either individually or with a group, will create dance movements expressing sorrow and grief over the death of children.

Example 5: Given a 1-lb. ball of Plasticine, and after acting out, recalling, or empathizing with a horror film seen in the cinema or on TV, the student will model in Plasticine, "I am watching a horror movie."

Both examples 4 and 5 state the topic and the mode

of expression. The stimulus or motivation was also stated. The students are asked to encounter the situation, empathize, and draw the expressive emotion from within themselves.

Lowenfeld and Behavioral Objectives

It is not difficult for someone who has studied under Lowenfeld and accepted his methods seriously (as has the author) to adapt to behavioral objectives. He taught that if we wish children to express particular emotions, feelings, concepts, or visual configurations, then we must focus our motivation and stimulus on that particular factor. We evaluated our own methods, and the student's performance and growth in terms of the evidence in the final product.

We were taught to involve the students in the motivation by acting out the situation (such as, "I have a stomachache"), while we activated their passive knowledge about the body part (stomach, body-cognitive), how it feels (emotion, pain-affective response to stimulus), before making the drawing (psychomotor). A behavioral objective: to have the child express the feeling of having a stomach pain, might be written as the following example.

Example 6: Following the acting out of having a stomachache, the student will express the visual enactment of pain with crayons on 12-by-18-inch (or 18-by-24-inch) piece of brush manila paper, in the drawing "I am having a stomachache."

Criteria evaluation asks: Is there a feeling of pain in the picture? Has the student included the stomach? Does the student identify with the drawing by including personal details (color of hair, eyes, clothes worn during art lesson, freckles, glasses, and so on).

Other topics leading to expressive feelings, self-image and emotional relationships are: My mother and I (emotional and size relationships), I am brushing my teeth (teeth), I am drinking my milk (mouth), I am picking flowers (hands, arms), I am playing with my doll—or pet (emotional relationship). Others leading to expression: My father (or mother) spanked (or slapped) me. I got in a fight after school. I was sent to the principal's office. I got hit in the back (or other body part) with a ball in gym. Examples 5 and 6 above are essentially a Lowenfeld motivation. Other Lowenfeld motivations can be found in the various editions of *Creative and Mental Growth* (Lowenfeld and Brittain 1970). They can easily be written into behavioral objectives of the expressive type.

Reinforcing Activities

1. Select one of the art activities described in this book and write a behavioral objective for it. Do not use examples already given, but you may refer to them. Compare it with those by others in the class.

2. As a class, decide on a single art, music, or other type of humanities lesson. Each student is to write

his or her own version of a behavioral objective for that lesson. Bearing in mind the three elements of a well-written behavioral objective, check for correctness of form. Compare with one another to get an idea as to how many different ways behavioral objectives can be written to encompass a single objective.

3. Take the course for which you are using this textbook, and write three behavioral objectives for classroom activities of the previous week as if you were the instructor. Of the three, one should be in each of the cognitive, affective, and psychomotor domains. Discuss results in class, in terms of the instructor's actual objectives for those activities.

References

BROUCH, VIRGINIA M. *Art Education: A Matrix System for Writing Behavioral Objectives*. Phoenix, Ariz.: Arbo Publishing Co., 1973.

DAVIS, DONALD JACK. "Human Behavior: Its Implications for Curriculum Development in Art." *Studies in Art Education* 12, no. 3 (1971):4-12.

ECKER, DAVID W. *Defining Behavioral Objectives for Aesthetic Education Issues and Strategies for Their Resolution*. St. Louis, Mo.: CEMREL, Inc.

———. "Playing the Aesthetic Education Curriculum Game." *Studies in Art Education* 13, no. 1 (1971):26-39.

EISNER, ELLIOT W. *Educating Artistic Vision*. New York: Macmillan Co., 1972.

Catalogue of Pre-Objectives in Art K-12 and Revised Performance Objectives 9-12. Assessment Project in Art No. 720-077. Tallahassee, Fla.: Florida State Department of Education, 1972.

FRENCH, W. AND ASSOCIATES. *Behavioral Goals of General Education in Elementary School*. New York: Russell Sage Foundation, 1957.

GRONLUND, NORMAN E. *Stating Behavioral Objectives for Classroom Instruction*. New York: Macmillan Co., 1964.

LOWENFELD, VIKTOR, and BRITTAIN, WM. LAMBERT. *Creative and Mental Growth*. New York: Macmillan Co. 5th ed., 1970.

MAGER, ROBERT F. *Preparing Instructional Objectives*. Belmont, Calif.: Fearon Publishers, 1962.

———. *Developing Attitudes Toward Learning*. Belmont, Calif.: Fearon Publishers, 1968.

———. *Goal Analysis*. Belmont, Calif.: Fearon Publishers, 1972.

POPHAM, W. JAMES. *Educational Criteria Measures*. Instructional Product Development, vol. 5. New York: Van Nostrand Reinhold Co., 1971.

POPHAM, W. JAMES, and BAKER, EVA. *Establishing Instructional Goals*. Englewood Cliffs, N. J.: Prentice-Hall, 1970.

ROUSE, MARY, and HUBBARD, GUY. "Structured Curriculum in Art for the Classroom." *Studies in Art Education* 11, no. 2 (1970):14-26.

SHUTZ, RICHARD E. et al. *Stating Educational Outcomes*. Instructional Product Development, vol. 1. New York: Van Nostrand Reinhold Co., 1971.

SULLIVAN, HOWARD J. et al. *Developing Instructional Specifications*. Instructional Product Development, vol. 3. New York: Van Nostrand Reinhold Co., 1971.

WEIDENHEIMER, RUTH, and BARR-JOHNSON, VIRGINIA. *A Guide for Writing Performance Objectives in Visual Arts*. Oviedo, Fla.: Visual Arts Productions, 1971.

WILSON, BRENT. *Art Objectives*. Denver: National Assessment Office, 1971.

13

Grading art,
and other processes of evaluation

Assessing, evaluating, and grading student art and art programs in the public schools can be neither circumvented nor dismissed. 'Tis true; 'tis pity, but 'tis true! Perhaps less pity, for the author is inclined to agree with Eisner, who observes that teachers have a moral responsibility to evaluate the consequences of the teaching of their students (Eisner 1972, p. 293). Through National Assessment, state assessment, and local concern for the results of the money spent on education, considerably more emphasis is being placed on accountability and evaluation now than in the past. The actual evaluative and testing processes do not seem to have changed nearly as much as the terminology and the sophistication with which it is being applied to every aspect of the total school program.

Let's face it—public education is probably the largest single area of expense in most local budgets. At the state and federal level it is still considerably lower than defense and the space program. But it is, nonetheless, a local industry that has direct contact with most homes, and the teaching staff is usually the largest group of tax-paid employees of the town. Every voting citizen and taxpayer has been to school for part of his or her childhood. This, they feel, gives them the right to inquire into and criticize what is going on in education. They do not feel this way about hospitals, the courts, police stations, or factories.

There are different ways of looking into and evaluating. Hopefully, the objective should be improvement rather than disapproval-based criticism and blame. Today's assessment and evaluative techniques can be applied in such ways as to make art more meaningful for today's children, so that they, in turn, can recognize its importance for their children. The long-range affective fruits of our labor are generational and go far beyond any current disagreements in educational philosophy.

Assessing, Evaluating, and Grading

There are three procedures for measuring learning: assessing, evaluating, and grading.

Assessing is the process of identifying the conditions or state of being of a particular phenomenon. It identifies the *is* rather than the *ought*. Assessments are non-judgmental, although they are conducted with specific questions of inquiry to determine specific facts about the area of concern. Assessments are made by surveys, inventories, reviews, polls, diagnostic tests, questionnaires, canvassing, and census taking. Just as the supplies in a stockroom can be assessed, so can the art knowledge in a student's mind, or the content of an art program. It all depends upon the purpose of the assessment. Essentially, assessments are made to find out what exists.

Evaluating is the process of determining the status of a phenomenon in relation to a specific set of standards or external criteria. The objective is to determine the *ought* based on the *is* of a situation, or phenomenon. Evaluations are based on the data received about a product or performance. Tests are only one method of acquiring such data. Other methods might be similar to those used for assessments, but the difference lies in their ultimate use. Evaluations are judgmental. The internal evidence obtained about a product or performance is compared to a set of standards; assessments are not. Evaluating learning in the cognitive domain has traditionally received more attention than learning in either the affective or psychomotor domains. It is nonetheless valid and still based on either a product or a performance. Teachers who know what they hope to achieve with a particular study unit, lesson, or learning activity can usually find a means to determine whether the learner got something out of it, and the extent of that learning.

Grading is the process of scoring the data gathered by using an evaluation process on a graduated continuum or value scale. There is usually a letter or number symbol established for each main point on such a scale.

Grading student work has two main purposes: (1) to keep a score on a student in a record book for easy reference, and for averaging a total score at the end of a series of scores; and (2) to report to parents and others interested in a student's growth the degree of learning taking place. Unfortunately, grades are usually interpreted as position in class against the competition. Products are graded—eggs, beef, tires, and student work—not people. Children identify with their work, so that an "A" means to a child that he or she is an "A" student—an "F" means he or she is a failure.

Criteria for Grading Art

Grades usually follow a five-point scale continuum, but the use of pluses and minuses extend this to a 12- to 15-degree scale. The letters or numbers used to identify positions are symbols only. The key to their interpretation is only a means of rating the symbol, but not the criterion for establishing them. Statements on a report card, such as: A=Excellent, B=Above average, R=Recommended, N=Needs more work, and so on, are interpretive levels, not criteria. Grading criteria indicate what is necessary to achieve a specific level of success, such as:

(1) In a spelling test: A=95-100-percent correct, B=90-95-percent correct, etc.

(2) Above average: student identifies ten out of fifteen art slides and their artists correctly.

(3) For a "C" complete one coil pot, a slab pot, and a pinch pot in clay, wedged well enough so not to explode in the kiln, and maintain a consistent wall thickness. The "A" and "B" will be determined by quality of design, shape, and form.

(4) For an "A" complete three prints using a two-color process of consistent printing and color quality throughout. Mat one for presentation. B=two prints, (quality work and one matted), C=one print, D=one print (poorly done or unmatted), F=no print completed regardless of time spent on project.

Sometimes, in establishing art criteria, it helps to begin with the "C" grade and proceed in directions above and below for the other grade criterion. Posting or telling the students what the criteria are can help them establish their own objectives. The examples given in chapter 11 on behavioral objectives contain the simple criteria. They could be extended into a five-point scale of success by deciding what is acceptable or expected. Notice that the scale does deal with art talent as much as task completion and performance. Grades above "C" might reflect some of the distinctions in quality, imagination, and so forth.

Some art educators (Schwartz 1970 and Jefferson 1959) feel that art should not be graded or even included on the report card. For personal reasons mentioned in chapter 8, the author does not go along with that. If art is not on the report card, it can too easily be considered as not important enough to be included, which can then lead to the ultimate challenge as to whether or not art is really important enough to be included in the school program at all. Those students whose strength is art need that grade reassurance for comparison with other marks on their report card. If letters and conferences are used instead of report cards as such, then art should be included. If the art teacher is in the building during parent-teacher visits, then he or she might make themselve available to discuss art growth. Art teachers might even send notes to parents of children having special art abilities, or to those whose children need special help in art, suggesting a visit when meeting with the classroom teacher.

Other authors, rather than criticizing the evaluation and grading of children's art progress, make suggestions, such as establishing criteria for evaluating visual perceptual learning; developing art-related behavior and visual organizational learning (Anderson 1965); or attaining attitudes, knowledge, skills, and habits in art (Conrad 1964); or measuring context, input, process, product, and vehicle used by the learner to achieve the objective (Sisner 1972); or checklists for measuring

perceptual awareness and sensitivity (Linderman and Herberholz 1969). One of the most comprehensive is that suggested by McFee (1970) for evaluating students and their work in terms of her perception-delineation theory, and the child in the learning environment. Lansing (1971) shows more concern for reporting to parents and provides a sample of a "student progress report form" related to art knowledge, attitudes, and skills.

Thomas and Crescimbeni deal with evaluating and reporting student progress from a general education point of view in their *Individualizing Instruction in the Elementary School* (1967), but it is applicable to art education. They also express concern over the inadequacy of traditional reporting techniques in dealing with the individual differences of children. Their conclusion is to hold more parent-teacher conferences or letters written to parents, and provide a checklist of ideas and suggested letter forms. They also suggest a dual reporting system—two types of reports based on the same data, one to the parents and the other to the office records. One cause of reporting inefficiency, they feel, stems from the fact that the report card has been expected to serve for both types of reports.

Thomas and Crescimbeni also made recommendations for the "continuous learning progress reports." These reports include a statement telling where the student is, from a progress standpoint. They also inform the parents where the student is going next, and suggest how they can help the child. The reports are usually sent home after a particular workbook or set of tasks has been completed.

This seems like a very workable idea for the art teacher, although trying to keep up with 700-1000 students in this way is certainly impractical. Art and classroom teachers can, however, devise their own specific continuous learning progress reports for such time as a child completes a level of development in art, or achieves a specific learning task (see: example: *Continuous Learning Art Report*).

The Continuous Learning Art Report

Nongraded programs are developing in more and more elementary school systems. Reporting systems are being designed which reflect the continuous learning philosophy. The children progress through each phase or step of the program at their own individual rates of speed and ability. They use machine-actuated self-testing devices and workbooks while the teacher helps the children as they need help. When the student completes a set number of tasks in his or her language skills, mathematics, or other subject areas a report is sent home for that subject only. It indicates where the student is on the progress scale and the workbook or level to which he or she will advance next.

Art teachers in such programs might seriously consider adapting such methods to their own program. Two advantages to such report cards are that they (1) include the criteria for evaluating growth, and (2) they

CONTINUOUS LEARNING ART REPORT
(Name of School and District)

Preschematic Stage (4-7 years)   Date:

This report indicates that (name of student) has completed the Preschematic stage in his/her art development. His/her art work shows evidence that he/she has achieved art competence in the following areas appropriate to his/her age and development:

	Degree of Achievement (Interpretation below)

Making two-dimensional art:
1. represents the human figure in more than one way, includes prominent facial features, hands, fingers, legs, feet, body, neck
2. uses relevant details to add meaning and narrative to his/her pictures
3. expresses self through exaggerations, emphasis through size, intensity, position on picture plane, etc.
4. includes both interior and exterior environmental subject matter to enrich visual concept
5. uses strong, vigorous line and color
6. uses correct spatial relationships for age group (sky above, ground below, baseline)
7. cuts paper of various thicknesses in a predrawn (by self) line
8. pastes and uses adhesives so that items stick together
9. adapts visual symbols used in drawing to painting at the easel

Making three-dimensional art:
1. models human figure in Plasticine, includes major body parts (expressive qualities may not yet appear)
2. models figures and objects to stand upright without additional external supports or braces
3. can fold and construct forms in paper and cardboard which brace themselves
4. builds structures with blocks, boxes, etc., which maintain balance

Aesthetic and/or seeing art skills:
1. arranges objects in drawings, paintings, designs, or structures with an aesthetic sense of order
2. can identify crayons, paints, colors, and other art materials by name most of the time
3. identifies objects, colors, and subject matter in art reproductions and pictures at least 5 percent correctly
4. can distinguish between a real painting, an art reproduction, and other types of pictures from periodicals, etc.

REMARKS: _____

_____

(student's name) achieved these abilities in the Preschematic stage in art, and is now ready to move into the Schematic stage of his/her art development. You are encouraged to compare the earlier work your child brought home with the more recent work to note the evidence of growth indicated above. The letter symbols used for the criteria above represent the following standards:

A—almost always.
B—with some reinforcement from teacher.
C—skill has been learned but needs additional reinforcement through more opportunity at school, and at home, if possible.
D—while other skills have been adequately learned, this ability is still below the standard which might be expected of him/her at this time, when compared with his/her other abilities in art.

Signature (art—or kindergarten teacher)

COMMENTS BY PARENTS: _____

_____ Signature (parents or guardian)

Please sign and return for the next scheduled lesson with the art teacher on (date). When you visit school for a parent-teacher conference feel free to visit me in room _____.

include the level of achievement or growth related to the criteria.

The criteria in the example have been based on those for identifying children at the Preschematic stage, or about kindergarten age. Other reports could be made out for the Schematic and Pseudo-realistic stages. They might also be made out following major projects indicating specific art abilities the child has learned. Notice at the bottom of the report form, the coding device (A, B,C,D) is worded in such a way as to reflect growths in some areas but not others. The criteria are adapted from those used by Lowenfeld in the 1947, 1952, and 1957 editions of *Creative and Mental Growth.* They

were, unfortunately, not included in the revised editions following his death (Lowenfeld and Brittain 1965, 1970, 1975).

At the completion of each level of development, Lowenfeld suggested an evaluation chart of questions which the teacher asked of himself regarding the student's work. In some respects, evaluating a piece of art is maintaining a dialogue with it asking questions to see its response. Lowenfeld devised a series of several questions for seven different areas of creative and mental growth. One example of each area of growth is provided here, from the Schematic stage (ages 7-9) to mental growth. One example of each area of growth is provided here, from the Schematic stage (ages 7-9) to give an idea what they are like. Lowenfeld provided them for each level of development and each area of growth.

Intellectual Growth: "Has the child developed concepts for things familiar to him?"

Emotional Growth: "Does the child vary the sizes according to the significance of the objects represented?"

Social Growth: "Does the child characterize his environment?"

Perceptual Growth: "Does the child differentiate his color objects relationships? (Does he use different greens for different plants and trees?)"

Physical Growth: "Does the child show . . . signs which indicate his sensitivity toward the use of his body (joints, special details)?"

Aesthetic Growth: "Does the child unconsciously utilize his drive for repetition for design purposes?"

Creative Growth: "Does the child frequently change his symbols for eyes, ears, nose, mouth, etc.?"[1]

Following each evaluation chart, Lowenfeld provided a section interpreting the criteria for specific learning factors and how to identify evidence in the child's art work. He also included charts summarizing each stage of development for evidence in the child's interpretation of the human figure, use of color, design, or repetition of space, in terms easily adaptable to evaluative techniques. If these early editions (1947, 1952, 1957) are available in the college library, they are well worth looking into. A similar series of criteria for evaluating growth factors through art is available in Linderman and Herberholz (1974), and in Sawyer and de Francesco (1971).

Art Contests, Competitions, and Self-Competition

Although art teachers occasionally resist the concept of grading art, it is not an uncommon practice to find art critics and judges for a fine arts exhibit doing just that. However, they do not use the symbols A,B,C,D, and F. They might, when reviewing an art exhibit, or judging the entries, think in terms of excellent, above average, average, below average, or failure. Those works which win prizes are considered the most excellent, or at least above average. The average paintings in the show are no doubt better than those which were not accepted. These decisions reflect the judges' tastes and value judgments. Their criteria, although supposedly based on aesthetic standards, sometimes seem confusing or not easily determinable. For an art competition, the judges might also make compromises with each other in order to come to a decision on awards.

Similar processes take place in art and poster contests in the schools. Children should be encouraged to compete with themselves rather than with each other. This is not always possible because we live in a competitive society. When children compete in sports activities, winning is part of the rules of the game. Either you want a higher score than the opponent, as in base-

ball or high jumping, or a lower score as in golf, swimming, or running in a race. As the competitions progress, the participants and observers get a fairly good idea who is winning, and the score; and they can see why one group or individual is doing better than another.

In art contests, neither artist nor onlooker has that advantage. Professional artists, or pianists, might know who the judges are, what their taste preferences are, and the type of thing they look or listen for. Children submitting art or posters to a contest do not know the criteria. They may know the submission rules (size of work, use of specific words, theme, and so forth), but these are not the criteria for either acceptance or winning. Such criteria may include neatness, presentation, idea only, imagination and originality, meaning, or aesthetic standards. Children who do not know what these criteria are, never know why they lost, or why others won.

Other negative factors in art contests include the distorted conclusion a winner may arrive at regarding his or her art talents. Also those who lose tend to think of themselves as failures, especially if they enter many art contests. The fact is, of course, that except for one or two winners, every other entrant in a contest is a loser, or failure. Ninety-seven to ninety-nine percent of all the children who enter a contest fail to win. The odds against winning are obviously quite high.

The contestant who is given a winning ribbon or prize because he or she needs encouragement may be done more harm than good. One year in New Jersey, at North Arlington Junior-Senior High School, the author had a seventh-grade student who always drew the same mountains over and over again. No matter what the assignment, if it called for drawing or painting, he made the same mountains. One day he was asked "What grade were you in when you won a contest for drawing mountains?" He said, "The fifth." The author finally broke through his stereotype by having him draw pictures hanging on a wall with mountains in them, or mountains being seen out a window or on television. Another time, also seventh grade, the author had a student who had won first prize in a fence show in Stonybrook, New York, tell him about it and how good he was. His friends also told the author. But he wasn't producing very well in class or showing much effort. At open house, his parents wanted to know why he got a "C" on his report card, since he had won first prize in a contest. They were shown his portfolio, and what other students were doing that he was not. A discussion took place regarding the harmful effect contests have on some winners. The parents understood. Later, the author asked the art teacher who had sent that student's work to the exhibit more about it. She said, "It was the only thing he ever did in six years that was much good." She entered it to encourage him, but never expected him to win.

At the secondary level serious art students look for

1. Viktor Lowenfeld, *Creative and Mental Growth,* 3d ed. Copyright © 1957, Macmillan Publishing Co., Inc., pp. 168-69.

chances to test themselves against criteria other than their own, to reach out to the professional world, which is a competitive world. At that age and that level of their involvement in art they are better able to accept rejection, understand the odds, or have enough aesthetic criteria of their own to make value judgments.

Teachers being asked to have their students participate in coloring contests, poster or other types of competition would do well to investigate the learning value of the involvement, and perhaps plan alternate activities. For instance, the annual policemen's coloring contest on taking candy from a stranger has very little learning value in itself. Instead, children might improvise plays about what to do if a stranger offers them candy. Who to go to. How to describe them. The teacher might have a stranger enter the room, talk to the teacher and leave, and then have the children describe him afterwards. If the police, or other organizations, want to give awards to encourage involvement in public-spirited activities, they might consider making them for a group of students, or a class activity instead of for only one individual. The criteria for selection, what they are looking for, might be defined before or when the award is given. The awards themselves might be something other than money. A visit to the police station could be reward enough. At the secondary level arts awards should reinforce the art interest of the winner. A ten-dollar gift certificate to an art supply store has more logic than the giving of cash. The award reinforces the interest that won it.

When selection through competition does take place in elementary schools, the children might discuss the aesthetic and content criteria for selection of the art work or poster to represent their class. They become the judges and can vote for two. One is their own, and one other. The winner or winners go on to the finals.

Self-competition is something else again. Instead of competing with others, children compete with their earlier attempts to do the same things. If a child fails a spelling test, the correct spelling can be provided for relearning. If a child adds or subtracts incorrectly on a test, the right answers can be provided and the error found. But in art, children are using their own symbols. If they make a mistake they can erase part of it, and change it as they go (trial and error) or make something new out of the mistake because it gave them a new idea. Sometimes, they can also throw it away and start over.

One problem with evaluating self-competition results from the need for previous examples of a student's work. Children need some reference point, and unless art work is saved at home, they usually have nothing that will enable them to compare present work with past work, nor have they frames of reference from which to make an evaluation. They are given such criteria-referenced points of view in cursive writing with Zaner-Bloser charts, or other learning skills. They can see improvement, but only because the previous example is available. The classroom teacher, or art teacher if the school has one, can help provide these criteria-oriented frames of reference.

Art criteria frames of reference should maintain certain commonalities. Keeping a portfolio, or folder, on all the different art works a child has done may show the range of offerings and activities, but they do not show growth. We cannot compare a collage with a watercolor and come up with a growth evaluation. Nor can we compare a Plasticine figure with a toothpick structure, if the technique of the first is analytical, and that of the second synthetical, except to demonstrate a child's ability to think in two ways. They do not show growth. Growth in art can be revealed by setting aside works resulting from specific creative activities for evaluative and comparative processes. All others can be used for exhibits, taken home, or used for other temporal purposes.

Testing for Growth in Art

After years of experimenting with the grading of art on an individual growth process, the author finally used a very simple technique popular in longitudinal research. It consists of having each student make drawings of a similar subject matter over a long period of time, then comparing those drawings for evidence of individual growth.

In college the author had been taught other methods to use in practice-teaching by his education instructors. Five stacks, graded A, B, C, D, and F, were set up. Then the work in each stack was compared with the others until stack C was the largest, B and D were equal, and A and F were the smallest. Thus, the bell curve was produced. When practice-teaching was over he gave up this method to try other approaches that didn't have a student's art work being compared to that of other students.

After that he tried a method used by one of his high school art teachers. She set up a scale of 1 to 5 for each of a series of components: line quality, technique, neatness, originality, or whatever the particular lesson called for. The scores were added up and averaged out. Somehow, most students' work averaged to C's, so that method was abandoned. He also tried pluses and minuses until he realized that the scale had expanded to 15, which got a bit heavy in averaging out for report cards. Finally, he began having work turned in in clusters of types of projects so that growth, range, and so on could be compared.

At the secondary level, after the first year or so, he began making out report card grades with the student present. Use of that method made possible a discussion on the different study unit and project grades, and why the decisions were made. They also had a chance to defend or justify or remind the instructor of something he might have forgotten, before the grade went down on the report card. It was a combination of these methods that the author used finally in the elementary schools.

The approach was very simple. For the first art lesson of each school year, each class was motivated to draw in crayon on 12-by-18-inch manila paper, "I am jumping for an apple in a tree." (From kindergarten to grade three.) The child could use a pear, peach, or other type of tree, such as a tutti-frutti tree that has different kinds of fruit on it. From grades four through six, they jumped for balloons, balls, kites, or whatever they wanted to use as a subject.

The children put their name at the top of the paper, with the date, their age, and figure 1 in a circle. Later in the semester, when the lesson was repeated, they put on the figure 2, and at the end of the year the figure 3, with date and any age change. For motivation, the class jumped up to reach the apple several times before drawing. Once to see how our arms stretched and reached, another the pull in the shoulder, again to see how our arms and legs bent or remained straight, and so on. They were asked to look at their clothes, so they could include them in their picture. The author let the children know that their pictures were for him, not for exhibit or to take-home.

When the lesson was to be done the second time, there was some feedback to the effect, "We did that before." So the children were asked if they drew things at home over and over when they liked to. Yes. Do you draw it the same each time? No. Do you think you'll draw this picture the same way as before? No. Why not? They were older. They had learned other ways to draw things. They were wearing different clothes. The second time was just before the midyear report card. The third time was just before the end of the year report.

The reason for selecting this subject matter was that the human figure related to self-image. It can show growth by stiff or bending arms and legs, showing action. The tree was a natural symbol which can either become stereotyped or be changed with growth. The balloons, kites, and so on also bring in the natural environment. The spatial relationships can be shown by the figure. Is it jumping? Arms reaching? Are legs bent? Is the figure in the air or are the feet on the ground and the figure stretched up? What are the changes in the tree, fruit, background, figure, and body parts? Are there features—freckles, glasses, color of hair, clothes worn on the day of the drawing—to identify the figure with the student?

As an art teacher, the author scheduled these drawings two weeks before report cards were due for each class. The following week, during class, the students were asked to draw anything they liked. While they were drawing, the author and their classroom teacher compared the first and second drawings for evidence of growth. These proved revealing to the several classroom teachers involved, some of whom suddenly realized that children can learn something about art and that it can reflect their growth processes. The teachers were helpful to the author, since with 700 students he couldn't hope to remember all of them. The teachers

helped fill in details about their students, about some of the art done between art sessions, some of the three-dimensional work that wasn't saved, or participation in murals and other group art activities. Some subjective adjustments were also made when it was felt that the student needed them.

At the end of the semester the three drawings were given back to the students for them to look over, compare, decide what things they had learned, and choose the one they thought was best. Sometimes it was not the third one; then reasons why the last did not have to be the best were discussed. The drawings were collected and saved for another year. The real surprise for the children came when they saw the six drawings of two consecutive years and the difference between the first and the sixth! Of the six the author retained the first and last for further records, and returned the others. (These two, with an analysis on the back of each, were sent along with the school records when a student transferred from Grace L. Hubbs School to another school.)

Since there were 700 students, this made a 2100 samples collection. The test drawings for each classroom were kept in the cardboard cartons in which 12-by-18-inch paper was shipped, in 18-by-24-inch folders made from 18-by-24-inch oaktag, and each were labeled with the classroom teacher's name.

Although not perfect, this approach made it possible to deal with growth in art, and so to identify changes in concepts. The slower student had, by this system, as much opportunity to get a good grade in terms of individual growth as the student who had greater ability. Neither was compared with the other, even though they were in the same class. Teachers adopting this idea might want to use some topic or object other than jumping for an apple. There are many that can be applied.

Evaluating Art Correlated with Other Subjects

An incident from the memory bank provides an example clarifying the differences between evaluating child art for its expressive factors, and for its cognitive information. A number of years ago the author was visiting a school in which a mural on kraft paper about the Long Island Indians had been taped to one wall of the cafeteria. It was an art project correlated with a third-grade unit on the Long Island Indians. Among the foliage, trees, and various Indian activities were tepees shown as their dwellings.

The art teacher, when asked why the mural had tepees instead of the woven thatch and grass dwellings of woodland Indians, said that he "did not want to frustrate the children in their self-expression." The tepee was a Plains Indian dwelling. Either the students had not been taught the differences between the various types of Indian structures, or they were not encouraged or not permitted to develop the same high standards of authenticity in their art as those they used in their academic subjects. If, for example, the classroom teacher asked in a written test for the name of the Long Island Indian dwellings, and the students wrote, "tepee," it would have been marked as incorrect. Since this was a specific fact and had nothing to do with self-expression, the art teacher could just as well have discussed the woodland Indian dwellings and how they were made without inhibiting the work of any student. Failure to correct this information in art merely reinforced a stereotyped misconception or cliché about Indians, perhaps gathered indiscriminately from television and Western films with Indians. Here was an opportunity to help children realize the differences between the various Indian cultures, and it was missed.

Self-expression through selection could actually have been encouraged in the making of this mural by way of those Indian activities the children chose to illustrate. They could have developed, by research, Indian methods for cooking, building their dwellings, hunting, fishing, making utensils, and so on, and in the doing self-expression would have taken over. Self-expression is not inhibited by helping students learn new concepts and ideas to express, or making selections, but enriched by it.

Psychological and Mental Art Tests

Drawings of human figures are also used by psychologists, psychological testers, and clinicians to assess intelligence and diagnose emotional problems, family relationships, and personality characteristics. The visual data is the same as that used by art educators to determine creative and mental growth.

Sometimes the interpretation of the same data made by the psychologists disagrees with that made by art teachers. For instance, the baseline, which according to Lowenfeld indicates social growth, is interpreted by psychologists Burns and Kaufman (1970 and 1972) among other psychologists, as indicating a sense of insecurity and the need for dependence in the testee.

Mental art tests and intelligence tests using drawings tend to standardize responses in a pattern more rigid than that intended in the evaluation of child growth through art. The most popular are the Harris-Goodenough "Draw a Man" test (Harris 1963), the Koppitz "Human Figure Drawing (HFD)" test (Koppitz 1967), and the Evanston Early Identification Scale (Landsman 1967).

The information obtained from such tests can be useful, but it tends to overlook the aesthetic, creative, and expressive factors in children's drawings. The place that experience and opportunity holds in the development of a child's visual symbolism and schema is not fully taken into account.

Several years ago the children in an elementary school where the author taught were given the Harris-Goodenough "Draw a Man" test as part of a district-wide experiment. The art teachers administered the test for the school psychologists, following the precise wording of the instructor's manual, which included not aiding students by suggesting details. It became evident as the tests progressed that the students were adding buttons, pockets, belts, all fingers, shoes and shoelaces, and such to their drawings. This had become a natural way for them to think of drawing the human figure. The author had been using Lowenfeld motivations with them for several years. He suspected that they might score higher than children of the same age in other buildings. In a brief comparative study, they did rate higher than children at the same grade levels (and in the same building) who had art from a teacher who emphasized cutting and pasting and making things rather than increasing the children's drawing vocabularies. The author's groups rated higher not because they were more intelligent or had a higher mental ability, as the test might indicate, but because their total level of visual communications had gradually increased over the few years through the development of new schema.

Children draw with different degrees of detail from day to day. Rhoda Kellogg (1969) provides illustrative examples of children's human figure drawings within a single week, and of drawings in the Bender-Gestalt tests over a period of time. Each drawing made by the same child within a week's time could receive a different score. She also makes similar observations about the differences in interpretation that may result from the Harris-Goodenough test, the Koppitz test, and Lantz Easel Age Scale.

However, these tests cannot be discussed by art teachers as merely one-sided or uninformed. They do provide important data for clinicians, learning disabilities teachers, and school psychologists. Art teachers should learn about these tests to the extent that they might be able to work in conjunction with school psychologists who use them. Thereby, they can broaden the base of the interpretation. Such cooperation is important at both the elementary and secondary levels. It may also encourage the psychologist to take students out of classes other than art for testing. Also, they can work together with certain children by jointly prescribing specific art activities to help them.

Reinforcing Activities

1. Select an art area, either for a level of development or from one or more of the cognitive, affective, or psychomotor domains, and design a continuous progress report card for the specific phase that deals with art learning. Discuss in class.
2. Write a brief autobiographical sketch of the various types of grading used on you or on your report cards throughout your school years. What were your feelings at times? What interactions with teachers and others about your report card grades do you remember? Discuss in class.

References

ANDERSON, WARREN H. *Art Learning Situations for Elementary Education.* Belmont, Calif.: Wadsworth Publishing Co., 1965.

BURNS, ROBERT C., and KAUFMAN, S. HARVARD. *Kinetic Family Drawings: An Introduction to Understanding Children Through Kinetic Drawings (K-F-D).* New York: Brunner/Mazel, 1970.

———. *Actions, Styles, and Symbolism in Kinetic Family Drawings (K-F-D): An Interpretive Manual.* New York: Brunner/Mazel, 1972.

CONRAD, GEORGE H. *The Process of Art Education in the Elementary School.* Englewood Cliffs, N. J.: Prentice Hall, 1964.

EISNER, ELLIOT W. *Educating Artistic Vision.* New York: Macmillan Company, 1972.

GAITSKELL, CHARLES D., and HURWITZ, AL. *Children and Their Art.* 2d ed. New York: Harcourt Brace & Jovanovich, 1970.

HARRIS, DALE B. *Children's Drawings as Measures of Intellectual Maturity.* New York: Harcourt Brace & Jovanovich, 1963.

JEFFERSON, BLANCHE. *Teaching Art to Children.* Boston: Allyn and Bacon, 1959.

KELLOGG, RHODA. *Analyzing Children's Art.* Palo Alto, Calif.: National Press Books, 1969.

KOPPITZ, ELIZABETH M. *Psychological Evaluations of Children's Human Figure Drawings.* New York: Grune and Stratton, 1968.

LANDSMAN, MYRIL, and DILLARD, HARRY. *Evanston Early Identification Scale Manual.* Field Research Edition. Chicago: Follett Educational Corp., 1967.

LANSING, KENNETH M. *Art, Artists, and Art Education.* New York: McGraw-Hill Book Co., 1969.

LINDERMAN, EARL W., and HERBERHOLZ, DONALD W. *Developing Artistic and Perceptual Awareness.* 3d ed. Dubuque, Iowa: Wm. C. Brown Company Publishers, 1974.

LOWENFELD, VIKTOR. *Creative and Mental Growth.* 3d ed. New York: Macmillan Co., 1957.

McFEE, JUNE KING. *Preparation for Art.* 2d ed. Belmont, Calif.: Wadsworth Publishing Co., 1970.

SAWYER, JOE, and DE FRANCESCO, ITALO. *Elementary School Art for Classroom Teachers.* New York: Harper & Row, Publishers, 1971.

SCHWARTZ, FRED R. *Structure and Potential in Art Education.* Waltham, Mass.: Ginn-Blaisdell, 1970.

THOMAS, GEORGE I., and CRESCIMBENI, JOSEPH. *Individualizing Instruction in the Elementary School.* New York: Random House, 1967.

14

Using creative mental process
in planning art and humanities programs

The fine arts have been a major beneficiary of creativity and a repository of imagination throughout modern history. The word "creativity" is of comparatively recent origin. The word "imagination" has a longer reputation but today it means very much the same thing. In current educational thought, creativity is found to result from a series of interacting mental processes or mental faculties. As such, this approach is a continuation of seventeenth- and eighteenth-century Faculty Psychology.

Throughout most of the Christian era, the imagination was considered metaphysical. It functioned entirely within the mind, or intellect, and resulted in images which seemed visionary. It was often called "inspiration." An artist was considered divinely inspired when he created such sacred works as oratorios, a "Sistine Ceiling," or *Last Supper*. But he was thought to be in league with Satan if he indulged in profane works such as the dissection of corpses for anatomical inquiry, designs for flying machines, alchemy, or the occult.

In the nineteenth century, Elizabeth Peabody considered the imagination a power which could be used for good or evil (Peabody 1886). Around the 1910s and 1920s, art curriculum guides began listing the development of the imagination and creativity as one of the goals and objectives of art instruction. They continue to do so today. Creativeness and the imagination remain sacred, untouchable by teacher's hands, and insufficiently understood. It has been questioned, and is being explored.

Research in Creativity

J. P. Guilford, in his inaugural address (1950) as president of the American Psychological Association, labeled the lack of research on creativity by psychologists as "appalling." He cited that in twenty-three years of published *Psychological Abstracts*, listing 121,000 titles, only 186 were concerned with creativity, originality, and the imagination (Guilford 1962, p. 153).

Guilford was at that time working on his own research program in the Department of Psychology, University of Southern California, to find out what made scientists and engineers more creative than other categories of individuals. He and his research staff used a series of verbal and paper tests. They identified a specific set of factors which their creative subjects possessed that the others did not have.

Over the same period of years, a nucleus of doctoral graduates under Viktor Lowenfeld in the Art Education Department at Pennsylvania State University was working on a series of nonverbal, visual, and manipulative tests. They wanted to find out the differences in the mental processes and problem-solving techniques between art majors and nonart majors. By 1955 they had refined their studies and pooled their results sufficiently to identify eight criteria for creativity.

When those at Penn State found in their literature that Guilford was making similar studies, they made contact in 1955. With considerable surprise each realized they had separately identified the same general criteria for creativity through different testing devices. The Penn State group used nonverbal, manipulative devices, and the USC group used verbal tests and paper work. Some factors had different names but similar descriptive data. Other factors had the same identifying terms. A couple of Guilford's criteria had subcategories drawn from his verbal orientation which could be applied to nonverbal learning.

Both sets of criteria are outlined here, set up in parallel form, and taken from the account by Lowenfeld (posthumously 1962), and Guilford (1959), each reprinted in *A Source Book for Creative Thinking*.[1]

Lowenfeld	*Guilford*
1. Sensitivity to Problems	1. Sensitivity to Problems
2. Fluency	2. Fluency
	Word Fluency
	Ideational Fluency
	Associational Fluency
	Expressional Fluency
3. Flexibility	3. Flexibility
	Spontaneous Flexibility
	Adaptive Flexibility
4. Originality	4. Originality
5. Ability to Redefine and Rearrange	5. Redefinition
	Symbolic Redefinition
	Figural Redefinition
6. Analysis	6-7. Guilford observes that
7. Synthesis	neither analysis nor
	synthesis are unitary
	abilities. They operate
	in degree according
	to the situation and
	subject matter. He

1. Sidney J. Parnes and Harold F. Harding, eds., *A Source Book for Creative Thinking* (New York: Charles Scribner's Sons, 1962), pp. 12-13, 156-59.

8. Coherence of Organization	related them to processes of convergent and/or divergent thinking. 8. Guilford did not, at that time, identify a specific ability which corresponds with coherence of organization.

Guilford extended his theories into a *Structure of Intellect* in which a three-dimensional cube provides the formation of three facets of the intellect: (1) Content, which results from figural, symbolic, semantic, and behavioral data, (2) *Operations* by which the mind uses data such as cognitive, memory, divergent productions, convergent production, and evaluation, and (3) *Products* which result from mental operations dealing with units, classes, relations, systems, transformations, and implications (Guilford 1967).

Mary N. Meeker (1969) describes the interaction of the various components in Guilford's structure with the intellect and other theories of learning, and with reading, mathematics, and psychological tests. Her suggestions are oriented to paperwork activities. Her methods are usually verbal.

The arts and nonverbal learning lend themselves to more factors in the structure of the intellect than were recognized by either Guilford or Meeker in their publications. In fact, even programmers of educational creativity as E. Paul Torrence (1962), Jacob Getzells and Phillip Jackson (1962), John Gowan (1972) and others seem to neglect the entire area of nonverbal creativity.

Their work is generally with *educational* or *functional creativity*. It deals with breaking through academic limitations, but does not get into depth or creativity in the arts. Nor does it deal with the artistically creative youngster who wants a career in the arts, on the stage, or in composing. Their strategies are not designed to deal with an Isadora Duncan, a Virginia Woolf, the Brontë children, or even a George Bellows. Indeed, it is questionable whether our public schools would even be capable of dealing with any like them, or teachers prepared to feel anything but insecure if confronted by child geniuses.

Research in Creativity in Art Education

The research in art education dealing with creativity has focused on drawing and painting strategies. That which was begun by Kenneth R. Beittel and Robert C. Burkhart was defined in *Spontaneous and Deliberate Ways of Learning* (Burkhart 1962). Since then Beittel has expanded his research with more sophisticated techniques, and presented it in *Mind and Context in the Art of Drawing* (1972).

Very simply explained, the *spontaneous* individual may draw or paint with a sketchy broken line, work on different parts of a picture and develop each in relation to the other, and erase or paint over. The *deliberate* individual may draw in continuous unbroken lines, plan ahead, complete one area before going on to the next and make few or no changes after the statement is made. Trial and error for the spontaneous person may be overt and observable, but for the deliberate person it is covert, and not outwardly observable. Both of these types can be creative, since creativeness is not predicated on either spontaneity or deliberation, but on a willingness to reinterpret the subject matter—make variations on the still life or whatever—for the aesthetic or expressive qualities of the finished work.

Beittel found that the noncreative, or academic mind, gave a literal journalistic report of the subject matter; such a student felt insecure if close contact with the still life was not maintained, therefore tended to be the copyist. The academic student also was inclined to work in greyed middle tones, avoiding the risks of using strong darks and lights.

In a joint article, Beittel and Burkhart (1963) related their observations to music. They identified Bach as deliberate and Beethoven as spontaneous. An analogy in poetry might be drawn between the deliberate structure, that of the sonnet, and the spontaneous approaches, as free and blank verse. In dance, many contemporary dances are developed by the dancers as they design their own choreography in a spontaneous way, while the classical ballet with a master choreographer is infinitely more deliberate. The cultural shifts from the Classical to the Romantic styles in the arts are related to deliberate and spontaneous orientations. Each orientation represents an individual style and strategy for approaching the product or performance in the arts.

One significant discovery in their research: creativity was enhanced rather than threatened when students with an orientation to one strategy was put in a situation requiring the use of the other. It became possible for them to express their ideas in both spontaneous and deliberate ways, rather than in only one. The noncreative students, it is true, could not make the transfer from their natural orientation to the other with as much ease as did their opposite numbers.

June King McFee (1968) reported on a study, "Creative Problem Solving Abilities in Art of Academically Superior Adolescents," which has relevance for elementary arts and humanities programs. McFee wanted to find out if students who scored extremely high on the academic scale, but extremely low on the creativity scales, could be made more creative through specific problem-solving techniques in art. They were pretested to identify their high academic and low creativity scores, and given posttests to compare for growth. The students, who were ninth graders, were divided into a control group and an experimental group. The control group had a regular ninth-grade art program. The experimental group had the same curriculum, but the instructional methods and discussions in the classroom dealt with being flexible, and fluent, and with attitudes about creativity. Since academic barriers to thinking were broken down, the verbalizing was necessary. Creativity began to take place at the conscious level, rather than being assumed to take place at the unconscious level as in most art activities. The results of the posttests indicated that the high academic students in the control group (regular art) made no significant increase on the creativity scale. However, the high academic students in the experimental (creative problem-solving) art class made enough of an increase in creativity to indicate that they grew in flexibility, fluency, originality, divergent production, and that they changed attitudes, self-concepts, and values concerning failure and nonconformity. Such evidence raises serious questions about traditional ways of teaching art, and suggests that the methods used are the real source of developing creative potential, not making art activities as such.

McFee's evidence indicates that success in teaching creative mental processes through art is most possible when the techniques and methods used focus on the creative process. The *creative mental process approach* to art planning, which will be presented shortly, is an attempt to achieve that type of focus in the arts curriculum.

Traditional Approaches to Art Curriculum

There are five approaches which are used traditionally when art or classroom teachers plan an art lesson, or write a curriculum. Within the course of a year (or the covers of an art curriculum) each approach is used to some extent, depending upon both the orientation of the teacher and the circumstances. For a well-balanced curriculum each has its place and should be used as the most direct means of achieving a particular art behavior, performance, or end result. The teacher's instructional focus in presenting the lesson determines which approach is being used, since the art product may be the same using any one of several approaches. The five traditional approaches to art lessons are:

(1) *Art concepts,* which focus on art knowledge in such areas as principles and elements of design, art history, color theory, rules of linear perspective, art criticism, aesthetic analysis; or on such art-oriented humanistic themes as art for propaganda, art for visual symbols, war and peace in art, art and the love image, and so on. It has a cognitive and affective orientation and does not need to result in the making of an art product.

(2) *Art subject matter,* which focuses on still lifes, human figures, portraits, landscapes, seascapes, cityscapes, environmental design, abstract or nonobjective art, and the like. It has a cognitive and psychomotor orientation, but does not depend on having the students produce art, although they might do so by painting, drawing, photography, or sculpture.

(3) *Art media* focuses on the materials used: crayons, ink, watercolors, oils, acrylics, clay, glazes, fabrics, film, and so on. It is usually psychomotor in orientation, and results in an art product. It also requires

that cognitive information about the conventions and properties of the media be taught along with the process of using it.

(4) *Art techniques,* which focus on the techniques used in each of the various art media to produce an art product—such as those for teaching drawing, painting, printmaking, carving, modeling, filmmaking, weaving, throwing or wedging clay, and so on. The teacher might decide to teach drawing, and then determine which of the appropriate materials—crayons, pen and ink, pencils, or some other—will be used. Techniques can be taught cognitively, but the best test of a student's knowledge of an art technique is through his or her application of that technique to the making of a product.

(5) *Art projects* focus on such articles as take-home gifts: making greeting cards or piggy banks from Clorox bottles or murals, masks, clay bowls or ash trays, and so on. The instruction is directed to the making of a product, and usually something for an exhibit, or to take home.

In selecting one or the other of the above approaches for an art lesson, the teacher might be considering: (1) "What is the information my students need to know about art before leaving my class (art concepts)?" "What kinds of paintings or sculpture have my students not done yet? It is spring, we'll go outdoors and do a landscape (art subject matter)." "Let's see, now, we used crayons last week, what shall we use this week (art media)?" "We haven't taught printmaking yet. But what materials shall we use—ink, paint, found art (art techniques)?" And, "What can we do for an art lesson? A week from Sunday is Mother's Day. I'll have them make a crepe paper flower on a card (art project)."

Very often the rationale is based not so much on what the teacher feels the children should know or learn about art before the year is over, as on a solution to a problem of expediency. Art from scrap, found art, or crayons and other available materials determine the art curriculum from the opening of school until the art supplies arrive. The tendency is to let the art budget exert more control over what the children are to learn than the curriculum describing what they should learn. A holiday becomes a motivation for a product; the techniques or skill being learned becomes a secondary issue. Sometimes the skill required is minimal in order to assure the successful completion of the project for each child. Thus teachers, in order to make sure that the children will have success in making something, rely on their using old skills rather than attempting to teach them new techniques in which success may not be assured at the outset. Some art lessons may be academic, others may have creative potential, but the mental process of the child while engaged in the act of "arting" (Beittel's term for "making art") is often minimal or left unconsidered. The following approach is designed to give art and classroom teachers, when selecting their art lessons, an orientation which deals more directly with the creative processes.

The Creative Mental Process Approach

In this approach, the teacher selects an art activity based on the predominant mental process used by the child in doing a particular learning task, performing, or arting. The teacher's instruction is based on the solution of problems, whether dealing with art concepts, confronting art subject matter, using art materials, applying an art technique, or making an art project. Certain arts activities lend themselves more to one mental process than another. The governing factor, in selecting from among them, is the predominant mental process or combined processes used by the arts activity. Examples of these, based on the Lowenfeld-Guilford criteria for creativity, are as follows:

(1) *Sensitivity to problems* is the ability to identify a potential problem either before it becomes actual, before something dangerous occurs, or prior to a time when repair is no longer possible. Doctors, laboratory technicians, clinicians, architects and contractors, and politicians are very much in need of this ability. It is the ability to forecast, prophesy, or predict, and to empathize with others.

The evidence of a child's sensitivity to problems may be found in his or her ability to empathize with others on the subject matter; to know when paint is too thick or too thin before applying it, to feel clay getting too dry for easily manipulation (or detecting early bits of cracking), to see that a block structure will fall with the addition of one more block or that it needs another support, and so on.

Teachers might ask questions during a demonstration rather than making a prediction themselves, such as: What will happen if the paint is too thick? How can you tell by the paint on the brush if it's too thick or too thin? What if the clay is worked too long, or bent too fast? What if the paste gets too dry? What if the paper is folded so as to be too thick for cutting? When a student asks to sharpen a crayon, he's saying that it is too thick for a small detail or a fine line. If the student has a problem which developed unnoticed, the teacher can help the student by asking him or her to describe those early symptoms that might have enabled him to predict what would happen. (They might have happened just below the student's level of conscious perception.)

(2) *Fluency* is the ability to think of many solutions to a problem, many uses for a particular material or thing, and to provide alternative solutions in a short span of time. At first their quantity may surpass their quality, but as fluency develops, stereotyped answers diminish and the child's answers become more original. Teachers who ask children to think of various solutions or ideas before selecting one to work with are helping them become more fluent and more original. *Verbal fluency* can be developed through synonyms and finding other words for certain colors to describe a picture. But children also need to be taught a vocabulary for the arts if they are to have use for it. *Ideational*

fluency might be developed by having children think of additional titles for an art reproduction or other phenomena, draw or paint many types of flowers, trees, houses, cars, or draw a map of the school and their home with several different routes for getting from one to the other. *Associational fluency* may be developed by having the students identify or make up different symbols for single concepts. For instance, they might draw or name examples demonstrating "Go" in terms of pedestrian traffic (color "green," word "go," policeman beckoning on, raising a flag at a race, blowing a whistle). They might categorize pictures, postal card art reproductions, or other phenomena under headings of their choice, and then make up other headings and reclassify them, as by subject matter, dominant colors, shape of picture, and the like. "Happy accident" watercolors, letting colors flow, making "Rorschachs" in art, or scribbles and looking for objects in them to outline are other ways of exercising associational fluency. So is the study of color symbolism as used by different cultures. *Expressional fluency* is the ability to express feelings in different ways. In art work it may show up through different uses of line or color to show intense anger, happiness, sadness, grief, and so on. The behavioral objectives in chapter 12, suggesting dance, art, poetry, or other art forms to express reactions to the bombing of Hiroshima, or the death of children, would also apply here to expressive fluency. The students might also select emotion impact words, design an alphabet expressing the word and lay it out expressively on the page. They might study the Expressionists, painters, dancers, or acting techniques.

Art teachers who ask children to make several designs before choosing the one they want are encouraging fluency. Collage making, in which the student is asked to arrange the pieces several ways before pasting them down, also exercises fluency. Such techniques also help delay decision making until the alternatives have been recognized and considered.

(3) *Flexibility* is the ability to change directions in midstream; to be able to restructure a planned outcome when events predict a failure in the original plan; to use a mistake or accident in the making of an art work as a possible avenue to a new idea, rather than to throw away what was started as being a failure. After art lessons our wastebaskets are full of semifailures and unfulfilled art potential discarded by children who were allowed to accept failure instead of being encouraged to adapt—to be flexible. Art activities which encourage flexibility are those which allow arranging and rearranging before deciding on a final form, such as collage, assemblage, and using Plasticine which can be shaped and reshaped rather than clay which hardens while it is being worked. Given a series of geometrical shapes on a sheet of paper (either from cut pieces of paper, or mimeographed), students might be asked to draw them into as many different ideas as they are reminded of by the shapes. Responses which are similar, such as a circle made into 5-cent, 10-cent, and 25-cent pieces,

are examples of *adaptive flexibility*. The coin concept is the constant; only the denomination changes. Responses which are different, such as glasses, a coin, the sun, a button, and so forth are examples of *spontaneous flexibility*. Each is a different concept. To exercise adaptive flexibility, students might choose a letter of the alphabet, draw it a certain way (tall-thin, short-broad, left side fat, or some other way) and then design the remainder of the alphabet in keeping with their idea for the first letter. They might design their initials into a monogram. They might model a figure in Plasticine and have it bend, walk, or do other things to exercise spontaneous flexibility; or they might use found objects for doing printmaking, but print several different arrangements; or study the history of inventors and discoverers who made errors in judgment but ended up with something better than expected, such as Columbus sailing to a new world instead of Cathay, or Charles Goodyear vulcanizing rubber when it accidentally overflowed on the stove, or Alexander Graham Bell knocking over the acid, and so on—all examples of spontaneous flexibility.

(4) *Originality* is the ability to think of ideas other than those presented by the teacher or copied from other students. Arthur Koestler suggests, "The prerequisite of originality is the art of forgetting, at the proper moment, what we know."[2] The most reasonable method of identifying originality is in those students who most consistently think of something not thought of by the teacher, who ask if they can do something just a little differently than assigned. Their ideas are usually extensions of the teacher's idea.

It is difficult to ascertain originality in children, or anybody, since we do not know what ideas they had access to before the activity. The author, for instance, believes that Paul Cézanne was not as original as art historians and other artists at the time thought him to be as regards his concepts relative to Cubism; that is, that all of nature consisted of geometrical shapes, volumes, and solids. This was the essential basis of all manual drawing lessons of the nineteenth century, and the drawing guides which were used, whether for picture making or manual drawing. Having learned it as a child, he adapted it to his perception of nature and the conceptualization of his theories of painting as an adult. It was his adaptation of this approach to the fine arts that was original and creative. After all, the seeds of Cubism were in the nineteenth-century drawing guides used in the schools of France, yet other painters, growing up with the same traditional lessons, failed to adapt their adult perceptions to nature as Cézanne had done.

To develop originality, art activities might follow some of the suggestions that have already been made under "fluency" and "flexibility," seeking out more than one solution or idea, in order to go beyond the stereotyped (if first ideas are stereotypes or clichés) to unusual ideas, and to so expand the student's abilities for originating ideas. Andy Warhol made giant Campbell's soup cans and Brillo boxes. Roy Lichenstein made giant comic strip units. These ideas were original at the time.

The teacher's approach can do more for the development of originality than the lessons themselves can do. During classroom discussions open-ended divergent questions may bring forth more original and expressive responses than closed-ended convergent questions for which only one right answer is possible. When asked for examples or a list of ideas, children often repeat what someone else said. The teacher's response might be, "So-and-so already said that, can you think of another example?" Students might try making variations on other peoples ideas, or make combinations of examples into a new synthesis.

(5) *Ability to redefine and rearrange* is the ability to find other words or ways to define a problem or to rearrange factors and elements in order to achieve a workable solution or a new entity. The composer who writes variations on a theme from another composer's music is restating and rearranging. When Picasso put the bicycle handlebars on the bicycle seat to make a symbolic bull's head, he had redefined and rearranged. When a student does the same thing in an art class it is called art from scrap, or found art, more often arrived at as a result of budgetary restrictions than as a result of inspiration. Some of Salvador Dali's paintings set up optical illusions which intrigue us because the configuration is redefined as we look at them. A similar visual transformation takes place when looking at Pavel Tchelitchew's *Hide-and-Seek*, in which children's faces are found in the branches and leaves of a tree. These visual transformations are referred to by Guilford as figural redefinitions.

Ellen Raskin, a most delightful children's author, used equally imaginative techniques in her book *Spectacles* (1968) in which drawings are made to look like the forms a small girl imagines seeing when looking at objects without her glasses; then other drawings show those same objects as she sees them when she wears her glasses. In *Franklin Stein* (1972) Raskin tells of a boy who won a hobby contest by making a monster from mops and domestic objects. The transformation in the boy, and the changes of attitude of the neighbors when he was making it and after he had won the award, provide an excellent discussion piece about biases and attitudes. In *The Mysterious Disappearance of Leon (I Mean Noel)* (1971), she is dealing with the rearrangement of letters and sounds of words.

(6) *Analysis* is not completely discrete, but includes other mental processes discussed here, and has been previously discussed as part of the cognitive domain. It is the ability to notice details, to separate parts from the whole, to identify evidence inside of contour outlines, and to extract meaning from symbols, in contrast to merely identifying objects and phenomena. Each

2. Arthur Koestler, *The Act of Creation.* Copyright © Arthur Koestler, 1964, 1969 (New York: Macmillan Publishing Co., Inc.), p. 190.

sensory mode has its own type of analytical process. Visual analysis is the ability to interpret and give meaning to visual symbols and stimuli, and make comparisons about visual data. Aural analysis is the ability to interpret natural and man-made sounds, and give them meaning. Similar statements can be made about the olfactory, gustatory, factual, and kinesthetic modes.

Art activities for visual analysis include three types: (1) looking at an object and drawing, painting, or making a sculpture of it; (2) the analytical or subtractive (carving away) approaches to sculpture, and the relief (linoleum and wood cutting) approaches to printmaking; and (3) looking at art, art reproductions, sculpture, and reductions (sculpture reproductions) for gathering visual data and making aesthetic analysis (art criticism).

Taking the class outdoors to draw trees, houses, or the buildings across the street or the school building, drawing their own houses or setting up still lifes, drawing from animals, pets, bouquets, or people as models are all processes using visual analysis for making an art product.

Contour drawing is a technique of sketching the outline of a figure while following that outline with your eye—coordinating a hand movement to the outline by drawing a line—a form of both visual analysis and eye-hand coordination. It is more appropriate at the middle-school and secondary level than at the primary or early elementary levels.

Methods of carving from a block, soap, vermiculite, and plaster of paris are analytical processes. Making linoleum, or woodcut blocks that require planning, positive-negative space considerations, and carving out are also analytical printmaking processes. Children who model in Plasticine or clay by pulling out arms or legs from a ball of clay are using an analytical mental orientation.

(7) *Synthesis* is the ability to put divergent parts together to make a meaningful whole. In the terms of the cognitive domain, it results in a unique communication. In art, it is a mental process exercised by making mosaics, collages, jigsaw puzzles (which are also visually analytical), assemblages, and art from scrap. Although planning a film may involve considerable analytical processes, the sequence of visual images to make a narrative is a synthesizing process. Children who first pull a ball of clay apart, roll it into smaller balls and small snakes and reassemble it in the form of a human figure are thinking synthetically rather than analytically. Photomontage and prints from found objects are also synthesizing techniques. All mixed-media techniques require some synthesis, but crayon-resist, which uses crayon first and the addition of a thin tempera, ink, or watercolor over the top is analytical, as is graffito—crayon colors, covered over with black india ink which is then scratched away to reveal the underneath color. Teachers having students making greeting cards can help verbal synthesis by putting

various words of greeting on the blackboard and letting the children choose their own combination.

(8) *Coherence of organization* is the end result of the ability to give unity, order, and design to a product, performance, or assigned task, and to recognize aesthetic order in the organization or planning of a man-made object or phenomenon. Principles of design provide the basis for a sense of order, if the child has not developed one through other processes of growth. Children might learn *balance* by making mobiles, paper sculpture, and toothpick structures, playing on the see-saw, or rubbing ink blots from the crease of a folded piece of paper. They might rearrange the classroom furniture themselves, and then analyze how it works in terms of use, space, traffic patterns, and fire codes. Children might learn about repetition and contrast by looking for examples in paintings, listening for them in musical examples, reading poems for meter and rhyme scheme, or categorizing and classifying fairy tales according to repeated or contrasting events, and themes, or other similar processes.

Whatever the art activity, process, or expected product, the mental process approach concentrates instruction and student help on the specific mental process for which it was selected, rather than on the use of a particular medium, art concept, subject matter, technique, or product. When the teacher uses this approach, then the emphasis is on the process rather than the product.

Art Reproductions and Mental Processes

The use of art reproductions in the classroom offers advantages that the showing of slides and filmstrips cannot match. Each unit can be looked at for a greater length of time—at close range—and used spontaneously. Unless the audiovisual equipment is always available, then spontaneous use of such equipment for art history or aesthetic analysis is virtually impossible. For these reasons art reproductions seem more flexible and longer lasting in their viewing by children than films, slides and filmstrips. Besides using them for units or lessons in art history and art criticism, art reproductions can also be used to develop visual-perceptual skills on a prescriptive basis for children with related learning disabilities and need for exercise in scanning, tracking, making figure-ground differentiation, and visual closure (Saunders 1972, pp. 90-91). With the help of special education teachers or school psychologists, art and classroom teachers could select appropriate art reproductions from those available for prescriptive work with special children.

Jigsaw Puzzles and Mental Processes

Jigsaw puzzles provide rich opportunities for the exercise of visual perceptual and other mental processes such as visual acuity, scanning, visual memory, figure-ground differentiation, negative-positive space differentiation. They require both visual analysis and visual synthesis. Individuals working jigsaw puzzles are also sorting and classifying according to shape cues at one time (straightedge for border), and to color or detail surface cues at another time, and to both overt and covert trial-and-error methods.

In the elementary schools the author had wooden boards (plywood) with edges around them for jigsaw puzzles. Each side was eight to twelve inches larger than the puzzle. The wooden edge, raised, around the outside kept pieces from falling off. A smaller wooden frame, on the inside just large enough for the puzzle itself, kept the edges together. The subject matter consisted of selected reproductions of famous paintings. Information about the painting was included with the puzzle board. After an initial introduction to the work, which was reproduced on the box top as well as on the puzzle, it was left for the class to work. This medium helped revitalize those visual perceptual, visual analytical, and synthesizing processes which had been left dormant since the early primary grades, before the children had been taught reading and writing.

Scoring Creative Interaction into the Classroom

Lawrence Halprin, an environmental designer and architect, has devised a system of planning and interaction which he described in his book *RSVP Cycles: Creative Processes in the Human Environment*. Although he does not discuss the system in terms of school curriculum and instruction, it is easily adaptable to creative lesson planning, and provides a structure on which lesson plans, study units, and curriculum guides can be designed. The following description is an attempt to adapt Halprin's theory to the educational process.

R—*Resources* are what the teacher works with: materials, inventories, guidelines, reference materials, visual aides, the abilities of the students, background experiences of both teacher and students.

S—*Score* is the process leading to the performance or activity. It can be designed beforehand, like a musical score, choreography, a football play, a lesson plan or behavioral objective, or a tabulation, such as notches on a gun butt, or marks in a record book. It can also be a student-teacher contract. It either suggests future actions, or records past actions and results.

V—*Valuaction* was coined by Halprin to suggest the action-oriented and decision-oriented aspects of the process. Valuaction is not the teaching of values, so much as the action taken by an individual in terms of his or her values and decisions. What one decides to do reflects that individual's priorities and values at that particular point in time.

P—*Performance* is the result of the individual's response to the score in terms of his or her own valuaction. The teacher and the student have different performances in terms of the resources, score, and their valuaction.

For example, the score or lesson plan suggest certain lessons, learning activities, or concepts. The re-

sources do not provide the right equipment, student ability, or teacher ability for all of them. Therefore, the teacher takes a valuaction based on the available resources and performs before the students by giving a demonstration, assignment, or instruction. The teacher's performance becomes part of the score for the students, from which they make their own valuaction and decide (from their own knowledge of the resources) what they will do in terms of the score or assignment presented to them.

The student's performance, when evaluated in terms of the total study unit, or behavioral objectives and goals for the class, becomes part of the resources, thus influencing the score for the next phase, as well as the teacher's valuaction.

Scores and Improvisations

Halprin identifies two types of scores, the *controlling score* which limits action, and the *energizing score* which opens up action.[3] His description is consistent with current educational thought, such as convergent questioning and divergent questioning, or closed- and open-ended programming.

Controlled, or closed- and open-ended, scores include CPM and PERT charts, zoning restrictions in cities, football plays, classical notation in music, ballet choreography, writing out plays and following directions, working from patterns, step-by-step instructions in making art projects, and learning to write by copying a writing chart. Variations are possible but only within a limited range and constitute a replacement of part of the score.

Energizing, or open-ended, scores are open to individual interpretation, and would include *I Ching*, Tarot cards, paintings and poems, music based on chance and non-notational symbols, expressive dancing, improvisational theater techniques, and opportunities to experiment with materials. Each allows and encourages individualized personal interpretation. Freedom of action is provided with a loose-scoring framework.

Conferences are usually energizing scores. The program is the score, but most of it consists of alternate choices. In-service workshops and conferences which do not allow alternate choices are controlled scores. Students' and teachers' schedules are usually controlled scores, but what happens in the classroom during the scheduled time is left up to a different score—the lesson plan, or behavioral objective—which can itself be controlled or energizing, close-ended or open-ended.

Scoring Field Trips to Museums

In *RSVP Cycles*, Halprin presents a score used for a one-day field trip to San Francisco. The group con-

3. George Braziller, Inc., from *The RSVP Cycles: Creative Processes in the Human Environment* by Lawrence Halprin, reprinted with the permission of the publisher. Copyright 1969, George Braziller, Inc. Page 9.

sisted of architects, dancers, and artists. They received a time score from 11:00 A.M. to 5:00 P.M., with the name and number of each participant. What they did at each place depended upon the individual's response to the score, but the time for being at a particular location was determined by the score, and varied with each individual, such as:

1. The Cable Car Barn—Imagine yourself in a place of fantasies and act accordingly.
2. Woolworth's—Buy a present for yourself and bring it to the birthday party which will take place after dinner.
3. Union Square—(a) Share your lunch with someone, at the sound of the 3 o'clock chimes stand and face the sun.

and so on up to seven activities.[4]

Planning a field trip to a museum, or to other places might be scored for energizing action, rather than applying the controlled score of a museum tour with everyone following along in a group. Such a plan requires considerable preplanning with the museum education staff, and preparation with the students. Moreover, the teacher should visit the museum collection in advance to get ideas for the score in terms of the types of things he or she considers desirable for the students to learn, or of encounters they should have with works of art. Many art museums already have games and looking activities, and their own types of score for seeing their collection, the behind-the-scene activities, and the museum's procedures. Art museum field trips might have a score on the order of the following:

(1) Stop in the museum bookstore and buy a postal card reproduction of a work of art in the museum collection, checking first to make sure that specific work is on exhibit (some may be out on loan or in storage). Seek it out and compare the original and the postal card for fidelity of color, for texture, for comparative size, and so on. Be prepared to discuss the differences with the group or back in class.

(2) With at least one other person, find two or more paintings by the same artist, or having the same subject matter. Discuss their similarities and differences with your partner.

(3) Find a sculpture, and assume a position or stance similar to it. Remember what you learned in movement education or expressive dance, and interpret the sculpture in movement, bearing in mind that others will be in the sculpture gallery with you.

(4) In Gallery 3 on the first floor, find the painting with the goldfinch; recall and discuss with the other students there our conversation about Christian symbolism in paintings.

(5) At 10:00 A.M. go to the second floor, in Gallery 5; find a group portrait with seven people in it. Join the six other students who will be there. Each of you choose one person in the portrait, give that person a name and improvise a small play involving these people

in the picture. Begin by assuming their positions. Be prepared to do your play when we get back to the class.

(6) At 10:45 A.M. you will have ten minutes before joining the class for the bus. Use that time to go back to the art work you liked most, look at it so that you can describe and identify it by title and artist back in the classroom.

On a score such as this, some activities are written for the entire group, others for specific individuals because of their specific interests, and still others for a selected small group for interaction. Each student gets his or her own individual copy of the field trip score.

Reinforcing Activities

1. Work a jigsaw puzzle and identify your mental process, visual and nonvisual perceptual skills, during the activity.
2. Play your favorite game of solitaire. While so doing identify your mental processes, and decide how the game can be used for exercising mental processes and numbers skills.
3. Select an art reproduction of a famous painting about 20 by 28 inches in size. Identify those visual perceptual skills mentioned in this chapter and determine how the painting could be used in the classroom. Consider it an energizing score for student response.
4. Draw two columns on a sheet of paper. Label one side "Energizing Score" and the other "Controlled Score." Under each, list evidence in your life, college, school situation, home and cultural beliefs which reflect either type of scoring by which your actions and behavior have been directed. Compare and discuss in class.

References

BEITTEL, KENNETH R. *Mind and Context in the Art of Drawing.* New York: Holt, Rinehart & Winston, 1972.

BEITTEL, KENNETH R., and BURKHART, ROBERT C. "Strategies of Spontaneous, Divergent, and Academic Art Students." *Studies in Art Education* 5, no. 1 (1963):20-41.

BURKHART, ROBERT C. *Spontaneous and Deliberate Ways of Learning.* Scranton, Pa.: International Textbook Co., 1962.

GETZELLS, JACOB W., and JACKSON, PHILLIP W. *Creativity and Intelligence: Exploration with Gifted Children.* New York: John Wiley and Sons, 1962.

GOWAN, JOHN C. *Development of the Creative Individual.* San Diego, Calif.: Robert R. Knapp Pub., 1972.

GUILFORD, J. P. "Introductory Portion of 'Creativity,' Presidential Address in 1950," and "Creativity: Its Measurement and Development." In *A Source Book for Creative Thinking*, edited by Sidney J. Parnes, and Harold F. Harding. New York: Charles Scribner's Sons, 1962.

———. *The Nature of Human Intelligence.* New York: McGraw-Hill Book Co., 1967.

LOWENFELD, VIKTOR. "Creativity: Education's Stepchild." In *A Source Book for Creative Thinking*, edited by Sid-

4. Ibid., pp. 79-81.

ney J. Parnes, and Harold F. Harding. New York: Charles Scribner's Sons, 1962.

McFEE, JUNE KING. *Creative Problem Solving Abilities in Art of Academically Superior Adolescents.* Reston, Va.: National Art Educational Assoc., March 1968.

MEEKER, MARY NACOL. *The Structure of Intellect: Its Interpretation and Uses.* Columbus, Ohio: Charles E. Merrill, 1969.

PARNES, SIDNEY J., and HARDING, HAROLD F. *A Source Book for Creative Thinking.* New York: Charles Scribner's Sons, 1962.

PEABODY, ELIZABETH P. "Hawthorne's Marble Faun." In *Last Evening with Allston and Other Papers.* Boston: D. Lothrop and Co., 1886.

RASKIN, ELLEN. *Spectacles.* New York: Atheneum Publishers, 1968.

———. *The Mysterious Disappearance of Leon, (I Mean Noel).* New York: Atheneum Publishers, 1971.

———. *Franklin Stein.* New York: Atheneum Publishers, 1972.

SAUNDERS, ROBERT J. *Teaching Through Art, Abrams School Art-Print Program.* Series C. Grades 4-6. New York: American Book Co., 1972.

TORRENCE, E. PAUL. *Guiding Creative Talent.* Englewood Cliffs, N. J.: Prentice-Hall, 1962.

15

Classrooms
and the interacting arts

The open classroom, one result of the various changes in educational attitudes about how children learn, has been an extremely influential factor in changing traditional methods used for teaching academic skills and subject matter. Being less restrictive and more child oriented, the open classroom engendered a tolerance in attitude towards the different ways in which children learn. The "British Primary School," a result of the Plowden Committee report, "Children and their Primary Schools" (1966-67), was also strongly influential in furthering this trend. Some, though not all, British primary schools began making changes which were adapted in this country.

The Plowden Report was an extensive study of practices, problems, and philosophies during the mid-sixties. About one-third of the schools were found to be good, others were overcrowded, teachers underpaid, and the buildings were "smelly, antiquated monstrosities" (Featherstone 1971, p. 3). The second part of the study, the growth of the child, repeatedly emphasized the different paces at which children grow and learn. This resulted in vertical or family grouping, in which children are grouped according to levels of skills and abilities rather than age differences. The concept itself was not new. It had been recommended by Pestalozzi, Froebel, and Dewey when they discussed school organization. The vertical organization of students provides several groups in an age range of 4+ to 7+ years (infant stage) and 7+ to 11+ years (junior stage). Then they go to the secondary level. Age determines the group range, but factors dealing with reading, writing, mathematics, and manipulative and other learning skills determine placement with the subgroups.

The design and structure of the classroom changed to become larger with more open space, movable walls, and furniture. Different activities could be taught simultaneously, as the teacher worked alongside the child instead of from a central position in front of regimented rows of seats. For many teachers entering the open classroom for the first time, this adaptation was not easy to make. A brief explanation of how space is used may help teachers develop some degree of readiness for the open classroom if they do not already have it.

Voice-Space Relationship in the Open Classroom

In *The Hidden Dimension*, Edward T. Hall, an anthropologist, identified four distances related to social situations and human interaction: (1) *Intimate distance*, (2) *Personal distance*, (3) *Social distance*, and (4) *Public distance*.[1] Each has a close and far phase. Each has its own dynamics which vary because of sight, sound, smell, touch, or other sensory and environmental factors. These factors operate as much in the classroom as in the cafeteria, at small meetings and large conferences, in theaters, public conveyances, the home, social, and business gatherings, or any areas where people interact and communicate. Distance also controls speech patterns and visual and other sensory perceptions.

Vocalization of speech patterns at these distances are of particular importance in both traditional and open classrooms. At the *Intimate distance: close phase* (actual or potential physical contact) vocalization is of minor importance when physical contact is maximum and other sensory modes are operating effectively. Vocalization may expand psychological distance. At the *Intimate distance: far phase* (6 to 18 inches) vocalization keeps voice low or at an even whisper. Some physical contact is possible, but usually within a conventional or publically accepted fashion.

At the *Personal distance: close phase* (1½ to 2½ feet), physical contact is still possible, but closeness is mostly a kinesthetic sense. It is a close social relationship, possible between a teacher alongside a student during an art project, science experiment, or other activity during which the teacher may look closely over the student's shoulder. Vocalization: speech is moderate and can remain casual. At the *Personal distance: far phase* (2½ to 4 feet) individuals are kept at arm's length of each other. Speech remains at a moderate level and can be heard by others, but they are not a part of the conversation. It may be the distance between a teacher and students painting a mural on the floor or on the wall.

At the *Social distance: close phase* (4 to 7 feet) speech is normal and can be overheard at a distance of twenty feet, even though not directed to everyone within the hearing range. Communication is impersonal. Two people standing and talking at this distance would maintain eye contact to sustain an attitude of listening to one another. At the *Social distance: far phase* (7 to 12 feet) the voice is projected. It is loud without being full volume. Spoken words and phrases are chosen

1. Edward T. Hall, *The Hidden Dimension*. Copyright © 1966, Doubleday and Company and Edward T. Hall, pp. 115-29.

carefully at a formal style. It may receive some advance planning. A teacher talking to part of a classroom, or several groups at once, might use this speech. Student response might be spontaneous and informal.

At the *Public distance: close phase* (12 to 25 feet) speech patterns extend the formal style, and usually require advance planning. Teachers in front of a traditional classroom (about 22 feet long) speak at this level of projection to the students in the back rows. Students in front only require the normal speech of the social distance: close phase, and those in the middle, social distance: far phase. Such differences can affect classroom dialogue. Students in the front may sense part of the teacher's discourse and respond spontaneously. Those in the rear of the room may need specific recognition, such as the raised hand, before responding. Slides and filmstrips require formal speech by the teacher to reach the four corners of a darkened room. Student response cannot depend on raised hands in the dark, but must be projected in formal speech patterns, if questions are asked. For this, among other reasons, the author prefers the use of large art reproductions, with students gathered around them at a social distance, rather than using slides and filmstrips. At the public distance: far phase (25 feet or more), speech patterns are characterized by a frozen style for those remaining at a distance from their audience, as might be the case at school assemblies, or in the cafeteria as used by principals in making announcements, or by teachers on cafeteria duty.[2]

The traditional classroom functions more or less at the public close phase, while the open classroom functions at the social distance far and close phases. The use of space in the traditional classroom also differs from its use in the open classroom.

Organizing Space in the Classroom

Hall identifies three types of organizational models of space: (1) *fixed feature space*, (2) *semi-fixed feature space*, and (3) *informal space*. He deals with the use of space from the anthropological cultural point of view.[3] As in the section above, the references to the classroom are the author's own extrapolations of Hall's theory.

Fixed feature space in the schools is exemplified in the stereotyped concept of the traditional; rows of desks and seats with the seat of one desk part of the desk of the student behind. The students sit in five or six rows, one behind the other. Desks, fastened to the floor, do not move. Bookshelves and storage spaces are located around the walls of the room. The blackboard is in front, with bulletin boards and blackboards on the side and rear walls. The teacher's desk can be moved, but usually is not.

Semi-fixed feature space still has bookshelves around the walls of the room, but the desks are not screwed to the floor. Students have individual desks with a place for books beneath the seat and a surface to write on

which is connected to the back of the desk. Sometimes the seat-desks are arranged in rows; at other times, in one large circle, or in small groups. Students may sit listening to the teacher all at the same time, or rearrange their seat-desks for group interaction.

Informal space, in a school setting such as the open classroom, has walls that move, cabinets on wheels, screens, tables, chairs, and a group of seat-desks. Kindergartens have operated on informal space patterns for some years. Now the open classroom has brought their spatial arrangements into the upper elementary grades. The flexibility of informal spatial organizations lends itself to application of the principle of intimate-personal-social-public distances between students, teachers, and aides.

The design of a classroom has a considerable bearing on the speech patterns of the teacher and on the range of diverse learning activities possible at any given period of time. Diverse simultaneous learning activities require teachers who can so organize their teaching as to properly relate to the informal settings called for by the open classroom.

Monochronic and Polychronic Uses of Time

In *The Silent Language* (1959) Edward T. Hall identifies two types of time, and the ways in which people use them. In *The Hidden Dimension*, he relates them to space and the way it is used, referring then to *monochronic* and *polychronic* uses of time.[4] Individuals and cultures are oriented to one or the other, or degrees in between. Monochronic individuals have a low involvement with others. They become disoriented when forced to deal with several things simultaneously. Polychronic individuals have high involvement with others. They can keep several activities or operations going at the same time. When these two types of individuals must interact, they may have conflicts.

The traditional, fixed feature classroom was designed for a monochronic teacher. All children did the same assignment at the same time. If the class was divided into groups at all, the children merely changed positions in the room if they were not already seated according to a group classification on a permanent basis. The teacher taught only one group, while the others had specific assignments.

The semi-fixed feature classroom allowed for polychronic teachers, but could also be used by monochronic teachers. For instance, the desk-seats could be arranged in smaller groups, or into a large circle. The teacher might range four groups at a single time and set up teams. Simultaneous group activities with the teacher overseeing the situation is still monochronic. A large circle of desk-seats is more flexible than five rows of screwed-down desks, but even if the teacher sits with

2. Ibid.
3. Ibid., pp. 103-12.
4. Ibid., pp. 173-74.

the students for free discussion, it is still monochronic in nature.

The informal space of the open classroom with some students using individual teaching machines, others using workbooks, still others doing arts activities or preparing a project while the teacher works with a reading group is a polychronic teaching situation in a polychronic space. Difficulties arise when monochronically oriented teachers are assigned to polychronically designed classrooms. It is also a misuse of the open classroom to put it in the charge of a monochronically or traditionally oriented teacher unless that teacher is able to meet the challenge of the open space classroom. The arts and non-academic subject areas are generally polychronic by nature. Monochronic teachers assigned to polychronic clusters or school units may need paraprofessionals and teacher aides, but they may tend to misuse the space and not ask for help, since they do not use their space in any way other than having all students operating in teacher-focused learning situations. Polychronic teachers, because they think in terms of diverse simultaneous learning activities, may actually be the ones who ask for paraprofessionals and teacher aides.

Other school spaces designed with polychronic potential are multipurpose rooms, media centers, service centers, art rooms, and the playground. Subject areas which interact with the interdisciplinary factors of a neighboring group may also lead to polychronic scheduling, since different groups may be practicing, preparing, or painting for an activity, while other students are working on academic assignments, or using teaching machines.

The So-called "Interdisciplinary Approach"

The term "interdisciplinary" is not synonymous with humanities, although it is sometimes so used. It is synonymous with such terms as "multidisciplinary" and "cross-disciplinary." The concepts and practices are not too far removed from the integrated and correlated educational practices of the 1930s and 1940s. "Humanities" is often a blanket term covering diverse activities in the arts, but a teacher can focus on art history, English literature, fairy tales, and such, and still teach the humanities without relating to or using the other disciplines. When teachers are oriented and experienced in limited areas only, then team teaching is necessary to make them interdisciplinary. One teacher, working alone, may not have a background broad enough to enable him or her to synthesize the different disciplines to the point of effectively teaching such a program as a singleton.

The purpose of an interdisciplinary approach is to enrich the curriculum by bringing the strengths and concepts of other disciplines and learning skills to focus on a single topic, theme, or activity. By so doing, the subject matter is covered in a broader way, so that students who have interests in disciplines other than those emphasizing textbook reading are able to relate to the topic. On the other hand, students who do not learn well through one discipline have better opportunities available to them through the others.

Vertical and Horizontal Programming

The interdisciplinary approach is usually horizontal in its programming. That is, the diverse activities related to a specific study unit take place during the same school year and generally as a unified total group of lessons centering around a single concept or theme. Vertical programming is generally thought of as being a series of related learning activities of a sequential nature. Each more advanced lesson or unit is based on skills or knowledge learned at an earlier period of time, either within the same school year or during previous school years.

Interdisciplinary and humanistic study areas can also be designed as either vertical or horizontal learning programs. An example of the vertical programming of an interdisciplinary study unit, such as "the rainbow," has been suggested in chapter 6, on core monuments. Another example, based on "Jack and the Beanstalk," is provided in Appendix A.

Art, music, or physical education specialists, when assigned to a single school only, are then in an excellent position for articulating vertical K-6 programs. But they have not been used as effectively as they could be. Consider that in textbook and workbook programs, the child moves from one to the other, each more advanced than the previous one. However, the teacher may change from grade to grade or cluster to cluster, in fact generally does, therefore the following teacher must, in such instances, depend on the school record and the sequential position of the book to know what the student is capable of doing. In the nonacademic areas, such as music, art, and physical education, however, the teacher specialist remains constant and can watch the child grow from stage to stage, grade to grade. If they are allowed to see a student often enough, they can then develop a broad range of vertical learning skills and establish a K-6 program based on needs of that student instead of on the textbook-workbook sequence.

Schools using art, music, and physical education teachers only as coffee-break student-sitters, or as relief for team meetings on I.G.E. programs, are depriving the classroom teacher of necessary information about their students' other learning skills, abilities, and expressive strengths. Current studies of children with learning disabilities are teaching us that problems with academic areas; they also affect skills used in reading, psychomotor skills are by no means limited to non-writing, cognitive processes, and various other communication systems.

Horizontal articulation between elementary schools is also important in the arts, as well as in other subject areas. If two or more schools are to act as feeder schools to a single more advanced school, then those students from each of the feeder schools should have specific skills and abilities in common with the children from the other feeder schools, so that all of them will be on the same level. And it is as important for all students to have specific art skills and knowledge as it is for them to have any of the academic courses, otherwise some will need remediation. In the instance cited here, the horizontal articulation between separate elementary schools would be coordinating the vertical programming of each to a K-12 program rather than to just a K-6 program.

Interdisciplinary Strategies Related to Art

Art and Music

Music and art are usually associated with one another in the public schools because they represent the "fine arts." They may share certain terms, but they are different disciplines. For instance, music has an aesthetic criterion based on time sequence, which neither painting and nor sculpture has. Both music and art use terms like, texture, style, subject matter, and theme, but interpret them differently. Combined art and music lessons might use common terms, but demonstrate their interpretations very differently. Music books are being published (such as *New Dimensions in Music*, American Book Co.) which incorporate fine arts reproductions with musical subject matter. And from time to time, there are art and music histories published which demonstrate sporadic interrelatedness of styles.

The simplest approach to spelling out a relationship between music and art in a single lesson consists of playing a record or tape of a specific selection and having the students listen to its different aspects and then paint or draw its rhythm, harmonies, and counterpoint, or its narrative intent. Suggestions on how this procedure can relate to different terms, thematic variations, or narrative were mentioned in chapter 11.

The author's experiences in such attempts stem from his own practice-teaching in art. Such experiences include using the finale from Rossini's *William Tell Overture* and getting pictures of cowboys on horses, such as the "Lone Ranger" rather than what was intended to be gotten from the lesson simply because the associative affect of the music was greater than expected. Nevertheless, the motivation and musical concepts should be clearly enough expressed by the music as to be recognizable to the students.

Crayons are more appropriate to ear-hand coordination than paints, because they do not require the student to interrupt the kinesthetic movement of the hand for refilling the brush. Finger paints are not suitable for painting to music. (One fifth-grade class, trying to use them, started out well, but as the music progressed the paint dried, and the students kept working in it. Their hands stuck. It was a mess. The following week what was salvageable was used to cover cardboards for bookbinding.) Paper should be at least 18-by-24 inches. Newsprint is smoother than brush manila paper, and the crayon can glide over it easily. (Being thinner, however, it may tear if jabbed.) But it is cheaper than manila paper, and several sheets may be used during a single class session. (Incidentally, be sure to have the students put the title of the music and the composer's name on the finished design or picture.)

The author has successfully used the following music, for the reasons stated. Ravel's *Boléro* comes first to mind because of its regular beat and clearly stated counterpoint. One ninth-grade student (who played saxophone in the school band), using black, thinned tempera paint, drew the major theme with a brush in his right hand, and by dipping his *left* fingers in the paint simultaneously beat out a rat-a-tat-tat with his *left* hand.

Ferde Grofé's "On the Trail" and "Cloudburst," from his *Grand Canyon Suite,* were used for a sixth-grade study unit on the Grand Canyon. The difference between narrative music and abstract music was discussed first. Then, while listening, the class tried to locate in the music those aspects which described erosion, the trail, the donkeys, the cloudburst, rain, the calm, and so on, while drawing pictures of the Canyon. They were encouraged to use other things they had learned about the Grand Canyon in the course of their study unit.

The author brings to mind a beautiful example of music associated with art that he once saw. Beverly Wallace, then art teacher at Winnicomac Elementary School (Commack, New York) had been to Switzerland during the previous summer. There, from a hotel balcony, she took a series of slides of a storm over a lake. They showed the dark sky, the approaching storm, the storm passing over the lake and going beyond, and the sunny calm that followed. While showing the slides to her class (a combination of two classes of fifth-grade boys), she played the fourth movement, the "Storm Allegro," from Beethoven's *Pastoral Symphony.* Then, while the record was being played again, the students painted their storms in watercolors on 9-by-12-inch and 12-by-18-inch brush manila paper.

For the kindergarten, the author prepared streamers —2-inch-wide strips of crepe paper, each 11 feet (half a package) in length, which were stapled to handles of cardboard strips (1 inch wide and 12 inches long). The idea was to play the music, have the children move the streamers to the music, and see the visual rhythm and movements—then, to apply the resulting effect with crayons, to their papers. They had so much fun with the streamers and the music, their teacher and the author decided to forego the art portion of the lesson.

Another time, "Cuckoo, Where Are You" from Carl Orff's *Music for Children* Along with a reproduction of Paul Klee's *Landscape With Yellow Birds* were used for the same class (see fig. 15.1). The drawing materials were Cray-pas and 9-by-12-inch black or purple paper. The objective was to use the picture for discussing imaginary ideas in art, as found in ways of

Figure 15.1 "Landscape with Yellow Birds" by Paul Klee. (Courtesy ARTEXT PRINTS, INC. Photo: J. Richard McGinnis)

drawing flowers, clouds, trees, and birds (a few of which Klee had hung upside down from the bottom of clouds). From the song, the group discussed the meaning of the words, and where birds could fly to. They might even get hidden or lost in a landscape. The children then drew their own birds in an imaginary landscape (see figs. 15.2 and 15.3). While they were drawing, the rest of the record was played. Later, their teacher, Mrs. Cross, used the students' names and adapted other songs from the record to the class.

Sometimes program or narrative music suggests ideas other than those envisioned by the composer. For instance, *Winter's Past*, by Wayne Barlow, has summoned forth drawings of early spring, western landscapes, the sunrise after a dark, cold night, and views of the antebellum South. After hearing the music, one can reasonably give it any or all of these interpretations. The record is played once and sometimes twice. Paper and materials are passed out first. Students are asked to listen to the music (with eyes closed if they wish) and envision what the music might suggest. They are

reminded to wait until they feel a response to the music before starting to draw.
(See also: Appendix A: From the Author's Memory Bank: Moussorgsky's *Night on The Bare Mountain*.)

Teachers Might Like to Refer to:

—Janson, H. W., and Kerman, Joseph. *A History of Art and Music*.
—Karel, Leon C. *Avenue to the Arts*.
—Rich, Alan. *Music: Mirror of the Arts*.
—Wold, Mito, and Cykler, Edmund. *An Introduction to Music and Art in the Western World*.

Children Might Like to Read:

—Calendar, Donald. *Musical Instruments in Art*.
—Smith, P. *First Book of the Orchestra*.

Art and "Theater"

The performing arts provide the most comprehensive platform for interdisciplinary activities in the arts.

Figure 15.2 Drawing by Mark, a kindergarten child, following lessons with "Landscape witht Yellow Birds" and "Cuckoo, Where Are You?" from Carl Orff's **Music for Children.** Drawing on 9" x 12" black construction paper, oil-based pastels. Description: left bird—blue; top bird—green body, yellow head, red and yellow tail; tree—pale blue with red outline and trunk; flowers (left to right)—yellow with blue center; white, pink, and yellow; and yellow green; stones (?)—white outlined in red, pink outlined in brown; smaller birds—yellow and white. Teacher: Beatrice Cross, Kindergarten, Grace L. Hubbs School, Commack, N. Y. (Photo: J. Richard McGinnis)

"Plays" or staged presentations can take place in front of the class group, a cluster of student groups, or the entire school and parents. They can be improvised and spontaneous, or well prepared with written parts and memorized lines. Each method implements different types of learning skills and abilities.

The standard role of art in the putting on of a performance is usually the making of the scenery and the stage decorations—"props" and costumes. Such things can be improvised, even though the play may be a set piece.

Versatile Stage Scenery

The problem of scenery, background, and setting was often more difficult than the costumes. While at the Junior-Senior High School, in North Arlington, New Jersey, the author tried two solutions, both of which seemed to work. Every year a musical and a senior play was produced; there was also a fashion show on occasion; and student assemblies of one-act plays were put on by the English lit students. The music teacher always rented a cyclorama, so that the stage would have a sky-blue background. But one year that rental money was needed for other things, so the custodians were asked to paint the back-stage wall a cerulean blue. It worked for sky, and with lighting changes was used for other backgrounds for several years afteward.

The author also designed a set of frames, hinged together like a folding screen without panels. It was built in the industrial arts shop. Each frame was seven feet high and four feet wide. It was built of two-by-fours. The hinges had removable pegs, so that the rela-

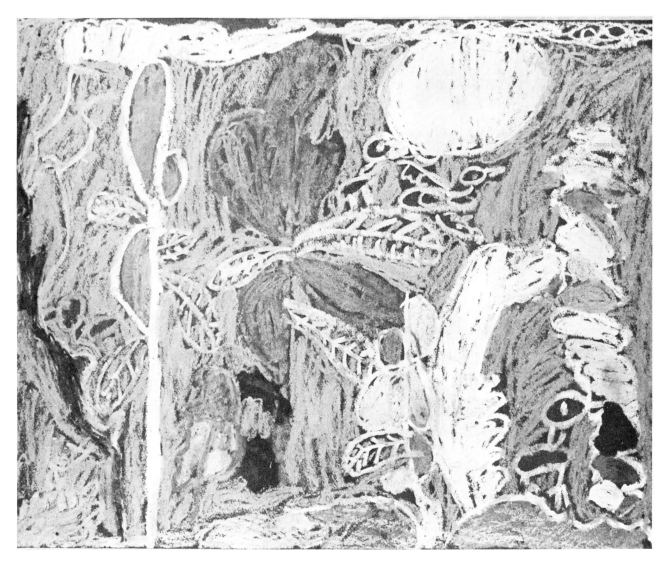

Figure 15.3 Drawing by second grade boy, Craig Penn, following similar lesson adapted to second grade. Black construction paper, 9" x 12", oil-based pastels. Description: background—red-brown; cloud—grey; top cloud—peach; central flower—red outlined in blue; leaves—green; left flower—dark blue outlined in peach; smaller flowers on right—yellow-green, red blossoms; leaf shape—peach; smaller birds (left to right)—dark blue, yellow, orange, and yellow; growth—mixture of blue, yellow, green, red, and brown. (Photo: J. Richard McGinnis)

tive position of each frame to the others could be changed as the occasion required. The crossbars bracing each frame were located in such positions as to give the illusion of windows and doors (see fig. 15.4).

The frames were painted black, with tempera paint, and were extremely versatile. For one play curtains were hung on the window unit, while a picture hung in the space of its opposite unit, with the door frame separating them. For another—a musical review—the saloon for the "Hernando's Hideaway" scene from *Pajama Game* had doors painted and cut from corrugated cardboard, which were hinged and tacked to the door unit. Still another scene had a ticket window with a sign for a railroad station, luggage, and two other signs, all painted on corrugated cardboard, which was then cut out flat and tacked to the frames.

For the same musical review, a quick change system was worked up. Finishing nails were placed in the frame at strategic places and nail holes put in the cardboard sections for the same places. One group of student stage hands entered stage left, took off the pieces for the scene just completed, and exited stage right. Immediately following them, a second group entered, put up the new pieces on the nails provided, and left. Everything was flat, easily made, and assembled in the art room. The frames were unhinged by removing the hinged pegs, and stacked for the next time.

In one elementary school the author adapted this frame to a smaller size. The frames were only about six feet high, and four feet wide. We used one-by-threes instead of two-by-fours. They were lighter in weight than planned, and a bit wobbly, so the corners were

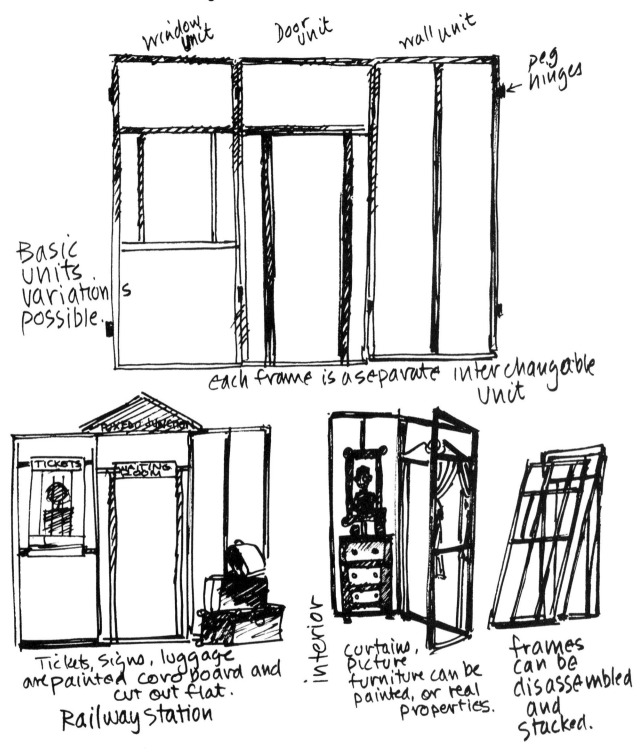

Window unit   Door unit   Wall unit

peg hinges

Basic units. variations possible.

each frame is a separate interchangable unit

Boxed Juncton

TICKETS   WAITING ROOM

Tickets, signs, luggage are painted cardboard and cut out flat.
Railway Station

Interior

curtains, picture, furniture can be painted, or real properties.

frames can be disassembled and stacked.

Figure 15.4   Versatile stage frames.

braced. In the author's estimation the frame idea is quite a usable one for elementary stage productions. Moreover, the skeleton quality of the frames makes them also adaptable to theater in the round, for clusters, and for some of the recently-designed arena-style school cafeterias.

All-School Production, *The Nutcracker*

An "all-school" production does not always need every student onstage. But it is still possible to have wide student involvement in its production. At Grace L. Hubbs Elementary School, Perry Bendickson, the principal, wanted each class to put on some type of production for all the other classes in the school at least once a year. Sometimes this meant only a single class took part in the production. At other times, during a holiday period, several classes might put on a play or program of a historical nature. Virginia Simione, a second-grade teacher, liked to choose one of the children's storybooks and adapt it into an original play with the class.

One example of an "all-school" production was *The Nutcracker*, the Christmas after the school first opened. The stage curtains had been cut from the building budget, so the author's class cut large white and colored snowflakes from 18-by-24-inch and 24-by-36-inch colored poster paper. These were scotch-taped to the back wall of the stage. Long strips of colored crepe paper hung like banners taped to the wall. As the red, blue, and amber stage lights were turned on or off, the color effect of the stage changed.

The music teacher planned the program based on some choral arrangements of Tschaikovsky's *Nutcracker Suite*. The students sang some sections to piano accompaniment, but a recording was used for other sections. Some parts were pantomimed. A fourth-grade girl (who took ballet), danced the Sugar Plum Fairy in solo.

Mrs. Cross's two kindergarten classes fought the battle between the mice and the toy soldiers. The morning class were mice, wearing black crepe paper caps with round black mouse ears stapled to them, and long black strips of crepe paper for tails. The toy soldiers wore caps of colored construction paper tubes with small visors. They wore tabards of crepe paper, full strips with a slice for the head opening, and draped over their shoulders. Their swords were strips of cardboard. Mrs. Cross often had them move and dance to music in her kindergarten, so they needed no real rehearsal. For the first school performance they got some wonderful sword fighting back and forth, showing great (and unexpected) sensitivity for the music.

A fifth-grade girl, who was academically gifted, had been given the special assignment of reading and adapting the narrative account of the *Nutcracker* story by E.T.A. Hoffmann. She was given more than one version, including Warren Chappelle's English translation of the French translation from the German by Alexander Dumas. Before she began the literary adaptations and the making of changes to suit the times and the reading and listening audience were discussed fully with her. All classroom teachers were lent a copy of the book so they could read it to their students before the performance. The music teacher played the record and told about the musical narrative and ballet.

Art classes also got involved. One class told the story in a "movie box," which is a large cardboard box with an open window. It has a series of pictures drawn on 9-by-12-inch brush manila paper, illustrating the story in sequence with brief written narratives told by the student who drew the picture placed under each. The pictures are glued end to end and placed on rollers used as cranks. As the cranks (one on top and one on

the bottom) are rolled the story can be read. Another class made a mural of the part of the story in which Marie throws her shoe at the Mouse King. The fifth-grade class (there was no sixth grade yet) made a giant nutcracker with a cardboard box body. The legs were 24-by-36-inch sheets of oaktag wrapped around 33 ounce size juice cans at top and bottom. The arms were tubes around smaller cans. The face and head was built up of cardboard strips. The whole was taped and laced together, then wrapped in sheets torn into strips and dipped into plaster of paris to which a pint of super-strength mucilage had been added so that it would adhere to the forms. When finished the nutcracker was painted bright colors in tempera paint. It then stood as a mascot alongside the door to the auditorium. Some classes also made decorations for the building, ornaments for the Christmas tree, and wrapped boxes with decorated and folded cut papers for use around the base of the tree.

An exhibit in the hall display case also reflected the theme. A small collection of German nutcracker princes were displayed, together with record covers of fairy stories put to music and ballet and copies of the books with the stories from the school library.

The purpose in recalling this event is to indicate the great variety of activities which are possible with a single core monument in this case, *The Nutcracker of Nuremberg*, for producing a holiday production.

Teachers Might Like to Read:

—Conrad, Edna, and Van Dyke, Mary. *History on the Stage: Children Make Plays from Historical Novels.*
—Diamonstein, Geraldine. *Exploring the Arts with Children.*
—Laban, Rudolf. *Modern Educational Dance.*
—Russell, Joan. *Modern Dance in Education.*
—Spolin, Viola. *Improvisation for the Theater: A Handbook for Teaching and Directing Techniques.*
—Weiner, Jack, and Lidstone, John. *Creative Movement for Children: A Dance Program for the Classroom.*

Children Might Like to Read:

—Baylor, Byrd. *Sometimes I Dance Mountain.*
—Berk, Barbara. *First Book of Stage, Costume and Makeup.*
—Chappell, Warren. *The Nutcracker, Copellia, The Ring.*
—Gasiorowicz, Nina, and Gasiorowicz, Kathy. *The Mime Alphabet Book.*
—Streathfield, Noel. *First Book of the Opera.*
—————. *First Book of Ballet.*

Gertrude Stein in the Sixth Grade

Some unusual school programs can come about spontaneously, particularly when there is encouragement to let things happen and to even help them along. The success of such programs depends on the willingness of teachers, students, and others to get enthusiastic about them. The following story is about such an event.

Barth E. M. Suretsky Jr. was teaching a sixth-grade class at Elmora School 12, in Elizabeth, N. J., several years ago. It was, he recalls, one of those classes in which a teacher feels he or she can do anything. The students were alive with enthusiasm, and "a great bunch of kids." The curriculum was not working right with them, so he began teaching a unit on architecture. At that time he was reading some Gertrude Stein, and ran across a statement that young children understood her poetry more than adults. Suretsky read some of her poetry to them, through parts of the libretto from *Four Saints in Three Acts*. They warmed to her words and humor beautifully, so he played an original cast recording of the opera by Virgil Thomson. They all began memorizing the words and singing them with the record. One of the students suggested they write Virgil Thomson and tell him what they were doing, which they did. Mr. Thomson misunderstood. He wrote back immediately saying he was delighted and would be happy to attend the performance.

Suretsky took the letter to the principal since no performance had been planned. What to do? They decided to have one. The students would sing the parts along with the voices on the record. But how to stage it?

The students contacted Mr. Thomson. He invited a few of them to his apartment in New York City and showed them photographs of the original production designed by Florine Stettheimer and produced in 1934. The scene was a Spanish hillside, with cellophane palm trees, draperies, arches, and costumes of stylized robes, with broad-brimmed hats in bright reds and blues. As accurately as possible the youngsters reproduced the original stage production. Fire laws forbade cellophane, so it was replaced by colored vinyl.

A high school student, John Bressler, "boy genius, put the whole thing together," designed the scenery, stage lighting, spots. Other teachers and administrators helped with the production. The school had no art teacher—mothers sewed costumes copied from sketches and photographs of the original production, but in vinyl instead of cellophane. The total cost was about $700.00. They called the P.T.A. for help. They held "cake sale after cake sale." Admission was free. It was announced in the Newark and local newspapers. They fell short of being totally self-supporting, but it was worth it.

The printed program was also a copy of the original 1934 program with a cover photograph of *The Ecstacy of Saint Theresa*, a sculpture by Bernini.

One of the parents designed a new choreography rather than copying the original. She encouraged the students to interpret the words and music in their own way. One sequence most remembered by Suretsky was the Processional, Act 3, Scene 9. Stein's words go ". . . wet in wed in dead in dead wed led in led dead in dead, in led in wed in said in said led wed dead wed . . .

[and so on]" (Stein 1946, p. 537). For this part, the sixth graders marched from stage, up the aisle of the auditorium to the beat of the words and music, carrying a coffin in a solemn funeral procession. At the end of the aisle, they stopped, set the coffin down, turned, and marched back without losing a beat or phrase as if they were a well-rehearsed wedding procession.

The total evening was the recreation of a historical theatrical event. The audience saw a production of turquoise blue brilliance, red lighting, and palm trees in shining vinyl. They heard their children singing along with the original all-black cast the words of the Gertrude Stein libretto set to music by Virgil Thomson. When it was over, Thomson ran up on stage, kissed all the youngsters, shook hands all around, and hugged everybody. Everybody was elated and happy.

Barth Suretsky left Elmora Elementary School later that year to teach foreign languages in Jefferson High School. He said he still has students from that class come up to him and recite parts of the Stein libretto. Some tell him it was the greatest thing that ever happened to them in elementary school.

Teachers Might Like to Read:

—Mellow, James R. *Charmed Circle, Gertrude Stein & Company.*
—Skinner, B. F. "Has Gertrude Stein a Secret?" from *Cumulative Record: A Selection of Papers.*
—Stein, Gertrude. *Selected Writings of . . .* Edited by Carl Van Vechten. (See references at end of this chapter.)

Children Might Like to Read:

—Burnett, Avis. *Gertrude Stein, A Biography.* Age 12 and up.
—Stein, Gertrude. *The World is Round.* Age 6 and up.

Art and Poetry

Poetry is the aesthetic end of the language arts continuum. The child, instead of learning the grammar, punctuation, spelling, and meaning of words, is dealing with the sound and rhythm of words in relation to surrounding words. The use of words moves from their functional communicative purposes to the quality of the words in terms of their sound and emotive quality.

The pure use of words for their sound qualities in juxtaposition to other word sounds, very much like passages by Gertrude Stein, are at the fully aesthetic end of the continuum. They are used and placed side by side because of the pure sound that speaking or reading them makes on the ear or the mind's ear. This nonobjective, nonfigurative use of words is to poetry what visual arts, or pure music (rather than song, narrative and program music) is to the world of music.

Poetry can be taught on such a continuum. For the young child, poetic awareness begins with the hearing of nursery rhymes, limericks, catchwords from the street, and television commercials. Children often repeat words out of context, or in nonsense combinations, exploring sounds with words at the aural sensory level. These are aesthetic responses. As children learn to read and write, the aesthetic quality of words is forsaken for their functional uses. Their sensory response to words is allowed to atrophy—until such time as a poetry lesson is taught.

Self-expressive poems are finding their way into the schools by way of visiting artists' programs, and special inner-city projects which use poetry-making techniques to develop the verbal expression of children. Free-form poems and free verse tend to be accepted by teachers more readily than those having specific meter and rhyme schemes. They may be considered as related to classroom poetry in the same way that string dipped in tempera and dragged around on a piece of construction paper is related to classroom art. However, these poems should show some evidence of personal expression and understanding of the aesthetic quality of the words used.

On the other hand, if a specific poetic style or form is being taught, then evidence of the required standards should be looked for in the students' work. It is difficult to criticize children's poems, and be helpful, if the teacher feels that any criticism will stifle the child's creativity and expressiveness. There is always that problem and danger. Upper elementary children can handle specific poetic forms more successfully than younger children, but in order to do so, they should have frequent experiences with reading and writing poetry throughout their elementary school days.

Poetry and the expressive use of words can be incorporated into a variety of art activities. Students might make a class poetry book consisting of either their own poems or favorite poems of published poets. The book can be illustrated, and bound. It might also be mimeographed for each student. It might also become a school-wide literary magazine, with the students of one class doing the editorial work.

Chinese and Japanese poetry, done in calligraphy on scrolls, frequently incorporates the poem with the painting. The picture does more than illustrate the poem. It complements it, doing with visual imagery what the poet felt the words alone could not quite do. The poem, on the other hand, expresses in words what the painting does not quite do. A Japanese haiku might be drawn and lettered on a scroll made of oatmeal paper with wooden dowels at each end. An exhibit of small sumi screens made from shirt cardboards folded into panels and painted silver or gold before a Japanese ink painting was put on it can also be very effective. Or the children can make oriental folding books, with each child's picture and poem taped or hinged to the other students' poems (9-by-12-inch paper). These are folded back and forth (accordion-fold), rather than bound at the back as in a book. They may have wooden or cardboard cover pieces, and can be expanded for display.

Because synonyms and homonyms deal with similarities of meaning and sound, they may lead to the aesthetic quality of words. The study of both might lead to the aesthetic quality of their sound, as well as to their functional meaning. When the students study synonyms, have them compare the words and choose the one which seems most expressive, has the nicest sound, beat, timbre, or that rhymes with other words. Besides developing sensitivity to the sensory aspects of words, this may help develop the child's verbal and expressive fluency with prose.

Kenneth Koch in *Wishes, Lies and Dreams* (1970) writes of his experiments in having children write poetry with assignments such as, "I wish," "I used to/but now I . . . ," "I would like/I would not like," or poems in noises and sounds, using comparisons to make metaphors, or in expressing real and imaginary dreams. Sometimes these were individual assignments and tasks. At other times, Koch would provide a theme for a poem, then have a student begin it by giving the first line, and each of the other students add a line until the poem was considered complete.

Art reproductions and original works of art can also inspire poems. William Carlos Williams wrote his poems *Hunters in the Snow* after seeing Brueghel's painting of similar title in the Kunsthistorisches Museum in Vienna (Moore 1968, p. 58). However, Charles Demuth painted his, *I Saw a Figure 5 in Gold* as a visual interpretation of William Carlos William's poem, *The Great Figure* (Geldzahler 1965, pp. 136-137). Kathleen Fraser has written a book of poems for children based Brueghel's painting, *Children's Games* (Fraser 1968).

Carl Orff's methods for teaching music uses the rhythm as well as sounds of words in isolation and with other words. Children work up songs and rounds using their own names. His methods are open enough to be used for children with Puerto Rican, Chicano, and various other language backgrounds.

Teachers Might Like to Read:

- Baron, Virginia Olsen. *Here I Am: An Anthology of Poems by Young People in Some American Minority Groups.*
- Beechhold, Henry. *Creativity in the Classroom: Teaching Without Textbooks.*
- Cataldo, John W. *Words and Calligraphy for Children.*
- Hall, Doreen. *Teacher's Manual, Music for Children, Orff-Schulwerk* (Schott Music Corp. Associated Music Pub.).
- Henderson, Harold G. *An Introduction to Haiku.*
- Joseph, Stephen M. *The Me Nobody Knows: Children's Voices from the Ghetto.*
- Nash, Grace C. *Music with Children* Series. Adaptations of Orff methods into Speaking, Singing, Movement, Dance and Play (Swarthout Enterprises, Box 476, Scottsdale, Arizona, 85252).
- Skinner, B. F. "A Lecture on Having a Poem." In *Cumulative Record: A Selection of Papers.* 3d ed.

Children Might Like to Read:

  —Adams, Adrienne. *Poetry of Earth.*
  —Alexander, Arthur. *The Poet's Eye, An Introduction to Poetry for Young People.*
  —Blishen, Edward. *Oxford Book of Poetry for Children.*
  —Fraser, Kathleen. *Stilts, Somersaults, and Headstands, Game Poems Based on a Painting by Peter Breughel.* Ages 7-12.
  —Hughes, Langston. *The First Book of Rhythms.*

Art and Mathematics

The interaction between the visual arts and mathematics has been historically significant, and can be taught with no stretching of the imagination required to make it meaningful. Canons and rules of proportion, whether ancient Egyptian, Greek, or of the Renaissance period, were based on geometrical formulas and ratios. Those of the golden mean, or golden section, developed into the dynamic symmetry of the 1920s. Ancient Greek dance, song, poetry, and music had mathematical structures. Linear perspective, as originated, developed, and traditionally established during the Italian Renaissance was mathematical and geometrical in origin. Paintings and sculpture were based on mathematical formulas which in turn were used for their critical analysis.

Computers used for designing, for making electronic music, writing poetry, and translating books, are extending the mathematical basis of the arts into new areas of exploration keyed to the future. Today's students, not to be at a loss in the world of the future and the arts of the twenty-first century may well need a mathematical base, as well as the historical orientation necessary to understand the past and the future.

Teachers Might Like to Refer to:

  —Franke, H. W. *Computer Graphics-Computer Art.*
  —Hamilton, Edward A. *Graphic Design for the Computer Age.*
  —Irins, William M. Jr. *Art and Geometry, A Study in Space Intuitions.*
  —Kepes, Gyorgy, ed. *Modules, Proportions, Symmetry, Rhythm* (and others in the Vision and Value Series).
  —Reichardt, Jasia, ed. *Cybernetic Serendipity, the Computer and the Arts.*
  —Schillinger, Joseph. *The Mathematical Basis of the Arts.*
  —Thomas, Richard K. *Three-Dimensional Design, A Cellular Approach.*

Children Might Like to Read:

  —Campbell, Ann. *Paintings: How to Look at Great Art.*
  —Gettings, Fred. *The Meaning and Wonder of Art.*

  —Hicksthier, Alfred. *Color Mixing by Numbers.*
  —Moore, Janet Gaylord. *The Many Ways of Seeing.*

Art and Environmental Education

The arts contribution to environmental education lies essentially in the aesthetic quality of the man-made environment. This includes the sounds, smells, and the kinesthetic feeling of space, as well as in visual surroundings. (See fig. 15.5.) The arts can help establish aesthetic criteria in planning, designing, and building the man-made environment. They might lead to affective value commitments toward preserving the natural environment, rather than just dealing with an awareness of the need. Interest in future careers in environmental design, architecture, ekistics, and archeology can originate in the elementary school.

In the elementary grades more opportunities might be provided for helping children to understand and respond to the concept of three-dimensional space, to draw cognitive maps depicting their routes from place to place, and to develop their personal-private, shared, and community space orientations. The child might, for example, explore the different approaches for representing three-dimensional space on a two-dimensional plane (such as drawing paper). Architects, city planner, interior designers, landscape architects, road and highway engineers among others can be included in units dealing with community helpers. The cities and towns of the world and in history can be included in social study units to a greater degree than is currently the practice. Children might build tabletop cities out of small boxes, spools, blocks, or other devices, all the while taking into consideration how people use cities and how cities change. Architects, environmental designers, and the others might also be invited to class as visiting artists.

Teachers Might Like to Read:

  —Bateson, Gregory. *Steps to an Ecology of Mind.*
  —Dondis, Donis A. *A Primer of Visual Literacy.*
  —Halprin, Lawrence. *The R.S.V.P. Cycles: Creative Processes in the Human Environment.*
  —Jencks, Charles, and Baird, George, eds. *Meaning in Architecture.*
  —Kepes, Gyorgy, ed. *Arts of the Environment.*
  —Linderman, E., and Herberholz, D. *Developing Perceptual and Artistic Awareness.*
  —Lynch, Kevin. *The Image of the City.*
  —McHarg, Ian L. *Design with Nature.*
  —Oliver, Paul. *Shelter and Society: Studies in Vernacular Architecture.*
  —Perin, Constance. *With Man in Mind: An Interdisciplinary Prospect for Environmental Design.*
  —Shepard, Paul, and McKinley, Daniel, eds. *The Subversive Science: Essays Toward an Ecology of Man.*
  —Wurman, Richard Saul, ed. *Yellow Pages of Learning Resources.*

Figure 15.5 Author showing boy a potted geranium in response to a question about drawing flowers and asking the student questions about the plant rather than the drawing. Kindergarten, Grace L. Hubbs School, Commack, N. Y. (c. 1965). (Photo: Curtis School Photographers, Inc. Huntington, L. I., New York.

Children Might Like to Read:

—Bardi, P. M. *Architecture*. Grade 6-7 and up.
—Hiller, Carl E. *Babylon to Brasilia*. Upper Elementary.
—Leacroft, Helen, and Leacroft, Richard. *The Buildings of Ancient Man*. Ages 9-11 years.
—Mainbridge, John. *Graphic History of Architecture*.
—Morman, Jean Mary. *Wonder Under Your Feet*.
—Perera, Thomas, and Perera, Gretchen. *Louder and Louder: The Dangers of Noise Pollution*. Grades 4-6.
—Rockwell, Anne. *Filippo's Dome; Glass, Stones & Crown; The Abbe Suger and the Building of St. Denis; Temple on a Hill*. Age 9 and up.
—Scott, John M. *What is Sound?* Grades 2-4.

References

BEECHHOLD, HENRY F. *The Creative Classroom: Teaching Without Textbooks*. New York: Charles Scribner's Sons, 1971.

FEATHERSTONE, JOSEPH. *Schools Where Children Learn*. New York: Liveright Publishing Corp., 1971.
FRASER, KATHLEEN. *Stilts, Somersaults and Headstands: Game Poems Based on a Painting by Peter Breughel*. New York: Atheneum Publishers, 1968.
GELDZAHLER, HENRY. *American Painting in the 20th Century*. New York: Metropolitan Museum of Art, 1965.
HALL, EDWARD T. *The Silent Language*. Garden City, N. Y.: Doubleday and Co., 1959.
———. *The Hidden Dimension*. Garden City, N. Y.: Doubleday and Co., 1966.
KOCH, KENNETH. *Wishes, Lies and Dreams: Teaching Children to Write Poetry*. New York: Random House, 1970.
KOHL, HUBERT R. *The Open Classroom, A Practical Guide to a New Way of Teaching*. New York: New York Review, 1969.
MARSH, LEONARD. *Alongside the Child: Experiences in the English Primary School*. New York: Praeger Publishing, 1970.
MOORE, JANET GAYLORD. *The Many Ways of Seeing*. Cleveland: World Publishing Co., 1968.
STEIN, GERTRUDE. *Selected Writings of . . .* Edited by Carl Van Vechten. New York: Random House, 1946.

From the author's memory bank

The following examples are taken from notes on arts activities with which I have experimented. They contain various ideas for the interaction of art with other subject areas in the elementary classroom. Hopefully, they may cause teachers to think of variations of their own when teaching the humanities through art.

Easter and Passover

At the North Arlington Junior-Senior High School in North Arlington, N. J., between 1956 and 1957, the teachers were required to read five verses from the Old Testament, and have the Pledge of Allegiance to the flag given during each morning's homeroom. In order to give the Bible reading some meaning, I selected narrative sections, such as the Books of Exodus, Ruth, and Jonah, and read the Psalms as poems, and so on. I read them as serials from day to day, and sometimes exceeded the five verses to complete an episode, chapter, or psalm.

One year I decided, for Easter, to continue this into the seventh-grade art classes. My students were asked to choose one of the days of creation according to the Book of Genesis, and interpret it in a drawing. We read Genesis, chapters 1 and 2, and discussed their interpretations. In some classes (but not in others, because they did not go that way), we compared the wording of the King James Version with the Revised Standard Version. Since I was more interested in teaching the students to interpret in visual statements, rather than in teaching them new media techniques, we used materials which they could control—crayons, and 18-by-24-inch, 60 lb. (lightweight) manila paper, since we were on a very low budget.

Each student chose one or more specific days of creation to illustrate. Those who chose the first, second, or third day had the problem of depicting light and dark, day and night without the sun or the moon, which were created on the fourth day. We looked at Michelangelo's *Creation of Adam* from the Sistine Chapel ceiling as one interpretation of God giving life to man, but not the only one, since man was modeled from clay. Some students who illustrated the sixth and seventh days were encouraged to put as large a variety of animals, birds, trees, and flowers as they could think of for the naming episodes. It was an unexpected surprise to find some students putting dinosaurs and other prehistoric animals in the Garden of Eden. They were encouraged to deal with the nudity of Adam and Eve in whatever way seemed suitable within the text. Usually, they drew plants and bushes in strategic places.

Some students had had seventh-grade art twice a week—others, three times a week; and some worked faster than others. Those, and others who finished early could choose another day, or could illustrate all seven days if they wished. Then, something that would better relate this whole project

to the season occurred to me. For extra credit, they could choose one of the two Passover holidays, the first commemorating the liberation from slavery in Exodus, or the second, the anniversary when Jesus went to Jerusalem, and the Crucifixion. They could choose one or the other according to their religious orientation.

The following year, rather than make this extra credit, we concentrated on illustrating the two Passover's for the seventh-grade Spring study unit. I read them the pertinent passages from the Book of Exodus (Chapters 11, 12, 13), and from the four Gospels. We then discussed the relatedness between them, and the reason for Jesus' visit to Jerusalem. We used library materials and our recollections of movie presentations of the events, and did other research as well, in order to be sure of appropriately depicting Egyptian architecture and dress for the Old Testament Passover, and Palestinian and first-century Roman influences on architecture and dress for the New Testament Passover. We also looked at various examples of the Crucifixion in the history of art, and discussed the details. We might also have observed, at the same time, the extent to which artists from the different historical periods utilized the architecture and dress of their own times in their portrayals of the Crucifixion, although I don't recall so doing. We did compare the passive Crucifixion by Perugino with the expression of agony in that by Grünewald. Both were included with others in an educational bulletin board of art history of the Crucifixion and descent from the cross.

Although used with the seventh grade, these art activities might be adapted to the fifth or sixth grades. The Resurrection might also be included with the seasonal celebrations of springtime and renewal discussed in chapter 6 as a core monument theme. Also related to this theme is the legend of the Phoenix rising from the ashes. The art activity for the biblical version of the creation might also be adapted to a humanities unit in which the various myths of creation can be compared with various scientific theories of how the world began. (See Appendix C for teacher bibliography).

Students Might Like to Read:

—Coen, Rena Neumann. *The Old Testament in Art.*
—Fisher, Aileen. *Easter.*
—Shissler, Barbara Johnson. *The New Testament in Art.*
—Simon, Norma. *Passover.*

Moussorgsky's, A Night on the Bare Mountain and Halloween

Sometimes art motivation and experience is heightened by a bit of dramatization. At Halloween time I have used both Saint-Saëns's *Dance Macabre*, and Moussorgsky's, *A Night on the Bare Mountain* as motivation for children's drawings. Of the two, the latter lent itself to a richer experience when dealing with the beliefs that brought about Halloween. This was usually a fourth- and fifth-grade activity, but I have tried it on the second- and third-grade levels with varying degrees of success.

Moussorgsky's *A Night on the Bare Mountain* depicts in music the night of St. John's Eve, June 23rd, when witches, goblins, and demons arise and circle around Bare (or Bald) Mountain awaiting the arrival of Satan. In Walt Disney's, *Fantasia,* Satan arises from the rock outcropping at the top of the mountain unfolding his great wings and reaching down the mountain side to the village graveyard. The demons, ghosts, and grotesques gather and dance wildly around him until the first rays of the sun and the peeling of the chimes of St. John's Day (the birthday of John the Baptist). Frightened and hovering the evil spirits retreat and slither back to the depths of graves, tombs, and ancient castles. The profane music is followed by the sublime strains of the holy day.

Cognitive information about Halloween is given through questions and discussions relating it to Celtic and Druidic origins and the spring and autumn equinoxes, as discussed in chapter 6. Class discussion might center on the origin, in Wales, of "trick or treat," when children went from door to door asking for peat to put on the village bonfire; and on the more recent humanitarian orientations through collections for UNICEF.

Before our drawing activity we also discussed the narrative aspect of Moussorgsky's, *A Night on the Bare Mountain,* but only after distribution of art materials which consisted of drawing paper, 18-by-24-inch brush manilla in 80-lb. weight, and crayons, or paint. (Distributing art materials after the motivation usually interrupts the student's emotional response to the stimulus. In this case the music was the motivation.)

After the discussions about the origins of Halloween, and the music, the assignment was given. The students were asked to interpret the musical narrative of *A Night on the Bare Mountain* (see figs. A.1, and A.2). To add a sense of drama, I turned off the lights in the room and when necessary partially closed the blinds, so that the students heard the music in what was an illusory darkness, even though there was still light enough for the students to draw by. Then I played the recording. In order to add to the drawing or painting time, I would pick up the tone arm at the place near the end of the music when dawn first lightens the sky, and go back to the beginning. Then as the music again got past the heights of the revels, and the dawn started breaking and the demons and ghosts would gradually return to the underworld and darkness, I would slowly turn the lights on, switch by switch. The children were often greatly surprised at what they had been drawing in the semidarkness. Seeing it in the light really got them excited.

There are, of course, other activities for Halloween, such as making masks out of paper bags, or papier-mâché, or with metal foil pressed over the face after painting, decorating, or otherwise making it grotesque and imaginative. Children might also be encouraged to make their own costumes (instead of buying ready-mades at the discount store) which may help develop their imaginations and improvisational abilities.

Instead of having kindergarten and first-grade children parade from room to room looking self-consciously from behind their masks, it might be better to divide them into groups and help them to improvise small plays. The students might name and identify with the characters they each represent, and act out their roles in a play or pantomime of their own devising. If they wish to go from room to room, they could do so as a group of traveling actors. They might even do that on a low wooden platform on wheels which could be built and used for stages. The "props" and suggested scenery could be put on these platforms so that the traveling actors would have a stage.

Teacher's Might Like to Read:

—Frazer, Sir James. *The Golden Bough.*

Children Might Like to Read:

—Borten, Helen. *Halloween.*
—Les Tina, Dorothy. *May Day.*

Jack and the Beanstalk

This story lends itself to *vertical programming,* that is to say, it can be taught at different grade levels, but for a different objective at each level. It acts as a vertical core monument. This requires *vertical team teaching* (K-6) rather than *horizontal team teaching* (by teachers of the same grade or age-group level). For example:

Kindergarten-Grade 1—Teacher might read story to students for its entertainment value. Some questions might be asked for interpretation or listening activities.

Grade 2—(or other level studying beans). The lesson might focus on the beanstalk. One year, in a second-grade class that was studying beans, we looked very carefully at the beanstalks they had growing, noting the shape of the leaf, how they grew from the stalk, and colors of green. Students were given 9-by-24-inch brush manila paper (I had cut 18-by-24-inch sheets of paper lengthwise to make them tall and thin). Rather than reading the entire story, I acted out before the class the dialogue between Jack and his mother concerning the magic beans, and how Jack might have climbed from one leaf to the other. (This part could also be acted out by the students, making believe they were Jack climbing the beanstalk.) Acting it out, I grabbed hold of each leaf stem like ladder rungs, bent my knees in climbing, and pulled myself up. (The students could have been motivated to do the same). Jack climbed through clouds like the fog and looked at birds flying past. Down below, Jack's mother shook her fist, and shouted, "Jack you come down here. Come down before I spank you!" This can all be dramatized, including how dark Jack's room got when the bean stalk grew up in front of his window and blocked out the sun.

The second graders were then asked to draw Jack climbing the beanstalk, using what they knew of the way beans grew from their plants. Some asked for extra sheets of paper so they could staple the second sheet to the top of the first sheet, the third sheet to the top of the second, and so on to make the beanstalk higher. Others added a horizontal piece at the top for the clouds, and then added another vertically for the castle or giant. The drawing got longer and longer.

When finished we talked about the magic of the beanstalk, what they observed about the bean stems and leaves from their plants in the half-pint milk containers, and about drawing the way arms and legs bend.

Figure A.1 "A Night on Bald Mountain" (Moussourgsky) by Mary Hommick, elementary teacher. (Photo: J. Richard McGinnis)

Figure A.2 Students drawing to music, summer session—"Integrating the Arts in the Curriculum," Southern Connecticut State College. Instructor Dr. Phylis Gelineau, Music Education Department. Guest Instructor, Robert J. Saunders. (Photo: J. Richard McGinnis, Public Relations, SCSC)

The drawings were exhibited in the main display case. Some were two feet long, others four, six, eight, and ten feet long. The longest one began at the bottom of the display case, went up the back, and after having been sliced at the glass, continued outside the case up onto the ceiling of the main hall.

Grades 4-6: At this level, a more intellectual, theoretical and philosophical approach can be taken with "Jack and the Beanstalk." It depends on the type of students. They might reread the story themselves, or have it read to them. In either case the teacher would make sure that all students knew what was being discussed. Various points of view might be considered, such as ecology, symbolism, moral and ethical values, which would result in dramatizations, illustrations, and contemporary classroom versions being produced by the students.

Jerome Hausman, then with the JDR-III Fund's, Arts in General Education Program and in the Art Education Department of New York University, speaking at a New York State Art Teachers Association conference several years ago, suggested the *curriculum map.* For an example, he suggested studying Jack's beanstalk from an ecological point of view. How could it grow in a single night, as large as it did, without sunlight and water, or special fertilizers? How

large was each bean? How were they cooked and eaten? What was the market price? Since Jack brought several beans, what would have happened if they had all grown such tall stalks? When the stalk was chopped down, from how far up did the giant hit the earth?

From a symbolic point of view, Jack represents the common man, a trickster, who defeats the monarchy, the establishment, the government, the school administration, or whatever other forces that be. Other folktales of similar nature might be compared, such as "Molly and the Giant," "Zerelda's Ogre," "The Brave Little Tailor," "David and Goliath," and "Jack the Giant Killer." Students might be asked to symbolize Jack today; from minority cultures, in comic strips, in our economic situation, or on television.

On the other hand, Kohlberg's stages of moral growth (see chapter 7) might be considered. What about Jack stealing from the giant? Compare the version in which the giant does the stealing first from Jack's father, and Jack retrieves his heritage (not knowing it is his), with the version which does not include the giant's earlier act. If Jack does not know the giant's wealth was originally his father's, is he any less of a thief? What are the issues of right and wrong? Are there moral issues and extenuating circumstances?

Besides the drawing activity described above, this story

lends itself to performances in play form, pantomime, dance movement, shadow plays, movie boxes, animated movies or filmmaking. The story might be illustrated in a comic strip format. It might be retold, illustrated, and bound into a book for the kindergarten and first grades. It might also be retold as an allegory with Jack representing a minority group and the giant representing the sources of prejudice. If so, what do the beanstalk, Jack's mother, the giant's wife, and the various things Jack stole symbolize?

Teachers Might Like to Read:

- —Berne, Eric. *What Do You Say After You Say Hello? The Psychology of Human Destiny.*
- —Jung, Carl G. *Four Archetypes: Mother, Rebirth, Spirit, Trickster.*
- —Radin, Paul. *The Trickster, A Study of American Indian Mythology.*
- —Von Franz, Marie-Louise. *Interpretation of Fairy Tales.*

Children Might Like to Read:

- —Graham, Lorenz. *David, He No Fear* (a Liberian folktale of David and Goliath, beautifully told).
- —Grimm (Brothers). *Household Stories by the Brothers Grimm.*
- —Jacobs, Joseph. *Jack, the Giant Killer* (with historical notes).
- —Ungerer, Tomi. *Zerelda's Ogre.*
- —Vance, Eleanor. *Tall Book of Fairy Tales* (in which the giant first robs and kills Jack's father.)
- —Werth, Kurt, and Watts, Mabel. *Molly and the Giant.*

Columbus Day

One year, on Columbus Day, a substitute teacher for a second-grade class told me that she had drawn three boats, the *Santa María*, the *Niña*, and the *Pinta*, on the blackboard so the students could draw them, then asked me if that was all right. Since these three ships were actual historical objects and not a figment of the child's imagination, some bona fide visual examples should be given. I asked to see them before agreeing or disagreeing. Unfortunately, the three ships were small sailing boats, single-masted, with triangle sails. She had given them her own stereotype for boats. The example was false.

The following year I worked up an art lesson in which historical detail was consolidated with imagination. From a two-page article cut out of *Life* magazine, I pasted up a series of pictures on the reconstructed *Santa María*, and showed it to the students. We discussed the quarterdeck, the number of masts, the types of sails, and the flag insignias. We also spoke about the way the sailors felt about the sea, and the voyage—their fears and superstitions. The students were asked to draw the *Santa María*, as a caravel, in a sea drawn so as to express the types of fears which the sailors had. The result was a group of more or less historically accurate concepts of the *Santa María*, among giant waves, on plates with water flowing over the edge, of sea monsters and storms surrounding the ships, and combinations of these. Some students also drew in the *Pinta* and the *Niña*. They based their drawings on the only historical source they had. Even though they were drawing from the picture, their interpretation was their own, and the source was firsthand historical data, not someone else's pictorial concept. By dealing with sea monsters and storms,

they were extending their imaginations. It was a combination of cognitive information and imaginative expression.

Since then, I have thought it reasonable to lead up to Columbus Day by plotting the first voyage of Columbus on a map. Columbus set sail from the harbor of Palos on August 3, 1492 (almost a month before the school term starts). On the first day of school the teacher might begin where Columbus would be about September 6th, after backtracking to bring the class up to that date. On each date of a journal entry, the related passage might be read to the class. If possible, his course might be plotted on a map together with record of the birds, weather conditions, and floating logs seen along the way. It would be a fresh approach to dealing with an annual tale.

For creative writing, students might write counter-journals or prepare a play or puppet show on the *Niña* and the *Pinta*. They might make murals, or get into other activities. Sources: *The Journal of the First Voyage to America with an Introduction by Van Wyck Brooks* by Albert and Charles Boni (1924) may still be available in many public libraries. I found one in our local library. A fifth-grade teacher, not having the journal available, used Samuel Eliot Morison's, *Admiral of the Ocean Sea, A Life of Christopher Columbus* (1942) instead. The students plotted his course on a map, and made a mural of the Atlantic Ocean, with Spain, Isabella, Ferdinand and some Spanish architecture on one side, and on the opposite end of the paper they painted the shore of Santo Domingo, with Arawak Indians and their thatch houses. Between the two shores sailed the three caravels: *Santa María*, *Pinta*, and *Niña*, some birds, logs near the Western shorelines, and so on.

Students might also study the earlier explorers/discoverers of the Western Hemisphere: the Egyptians, Phoenicians, the Asian peoples (ancestors of the American Indians) through the Bering Straits, the expeditions of Hoeiskin (about 400 A.D.), the Vikings Leif and Thowald Ericson (about 1003-1007 A.D.)—even Thor Heyerdahl's modern-day *RA Expeditions*. Such a study unit might begin in September and terminate on Columbus Day, the day of discovery, as the culmination.

Teachers Might Like to Read:

- —Ashe, Geoffrey et al. *The Quest for America.*
- —Ceram, C. W. *The First American. A Story of North American Archeology.*
- —Columbus, Christopher. *The Journals of . . . .* (Liveright Company).
- —Heyerdahl, Thor. *The RA Expedition.*
- —Martinez-Hidalgo, José Mario. *Columbus' Ships.* Howard I. Chapelle, ed.
- —Morison, Samuel E. *Admiral of the Ocean Sea, A Life of Christopher Columbus.*
- —Morison, Samuel E. and Obrégon, Mauricio. *The Caribbean as Columbus Saw It.*

Children Might Like to Read:

- —Coen, Rena Neumann. *American History in Art.*
- —Gracza, Margaret. *The Ship and the Sea in Art.*
- —Martinez-Hidalgo, José Mario. *Columbus' Ships.* Howard I. Chapelle, ed.
- —Showers, Paul. *Columbus Day.*
- —Los Casas, Bartholemew. *Log of Christopher Columbus First Voyage to America in 1492* as copied out in brief by Bartholemew Los Casas.

Humanistic exemplars

Here are two types of lessons which can lead to humanistic enterprises. "The Wave and Lafcadio Hearn" uses a Japanese folktale to deal with social values not often found in Central European folktale traditions. "*Noyes Fludde* and Project CREATE" deals with a core monument as it might have been used in a Title III project, and is a summary of suggested guidelines first written for that project.

The Wave *and Lafcadio Hearn*

Lafcadio Hearn tells a short story in his book *Gleanings in the Buddha Fields* (1897) which has been retold several times since, most recently by Margaret Hodges as *The Wave* (1964). Hearn's life, if we were to study it, would probably provide an exemplar of growth in the affective domain. Identified as an American journalist and author, but born on a Greek Island (1850) of an Irish father and Greek mother, he was sent as a boy to America. He grew up here, became a journalist and in 1890 was sent to Japan on an assignment for *Harper's Weekly*. He encountered and was fascinated by the Japanese culture, wrote several books sensitively interpreting that culture, and adopted its ways. He took out Japanese citizenship and adopted the name Yakumo Koizumi after his wife Setsuko Koizumi. Although he organized his life around Japanese customs and manners, he seems not to have gone beyond a "generalized set" at the top of the affective hierarchy, since his immersion in Japanese culture did not include an ability to speak or write in Japanese. He taught English literature at the Imperial University, in Tokyo, where he died in 1904. His English versions of Japanese tales were later used in the teaching of the English language to Japanese students.

On the other hand, Ojiisan, the old grandfather in Hearn's story of the tidal wave provides an example of the type of Skinnerean hero-programmer mentioned in chapter 5. Ojiisan knew the people of the village well enough to program an event which would save their lives.

The old man lived high on a Japanese mountainside above a small village by the edge of the sea. He had rice fields which were precious to him. He worked them daily and they made him wealthy. (My first memory of this story is that there was enmity between the old man and the villagers, but in the Hodges version a very close and friendly relationship existed.) One day from his vantage point on the mountain he saw a dark line rising along the horizon of the sea. He recalled from earlier experience what it meant. He ran to his rice fields and set fire to them. The people of the village, seeing the smoke and flames, ran up to the mountain with their children to help him fight the fire. As they arrived he stopped them and let the rice fields burn. More villagers continued to climb the mountain. They were bewildered to find no one fighting the fire. And then, Ojiisan turned and pointed to the sea. The villagers saw a great tidal wave coming from far out in the sea swiftly roll up towards them, gather itself up to an enormous height, and with tremendous force plunge down upon the village below. The houses and shops were completely destroyed, but the people were not—except, of course, those who were too indifferent to Ojiisan's burning rice field to run up the mountainside to help save them.

With the exception of Jesus' parable of the Good Samaritan, I know of no tale which deals in quite these terms with the moral responsibility of human beings for each other. It deals with the type of self-sacrifice found among fire fighters, the police, and soldiers who give up their lives in battle, far different from the Western culture heroics of the dragon-slayer who fights for fair lady and fame.

Hearn's tale of the tidal wave could be read and discussed in terms of material values (one man's rice fields) as compared with the value of human lives (the villagers); of the enmity each felt for the other (if this version is used), yet who helped one another in time of need; and the fate of those who were too indifferent to Ojiisan's needs to cast their enmity aside and climb the mountain to fight the fire.

From the news, we read of incidents of rape, murder, and other crimes in our cities to which apartment dwellers close their windows and doors, or passersby cross to the other side of the street. Stories like *The Wave* might help children clarify their own values in terms of moral responsibility to others. Such values may become even more important as our cities become more overpopulated and survival becomes severely competitive.

Noyes Fludde *and Project CREATE*

With the passage of the Elementary Secondary Education Act (ESEA) in 1965, and through its Title III, Arts and Humanities phase, the Education Committee of the Connecticut Commission on the Arts, under the chairwomanship of Belle K. Ribicoff, developed a project to place the arts in the schools through the use of professional artists in a planned program. Following discussions with consultants in the State Department of Education, others also professionally involved in the arts, and school administrators, six schools were selected throughout the state. They represented rural, urban, suburban, inner-city, and industrial communities at the lower, middle, and upper-middle socioeconomic levels. It was also decided at that time to focus on the performing arts as the most expedient means for bringing unity to the program.

The first year saw an ambitious program called "Project CREATE," get under way (it gradually grew less structured during the two subsequent years). During that first year, CREATE commissioned special productions from the Paper Bag Players in New York City, the National Theater for the Deaf in Waterford, Connecticut, and the Hartford Conservatory of Music. Each production was staged in each of the six project schools. The actors, dancers, directors, art-

Figure B.1 Cardboard and papier mache rooster mask for Brittain's "Noyes Flude" in Project CREATE production. (Photo: Courtesy Connecticut Commission on Arts)

Figure B.2   Benjamin Brittain's "Noyes Fludde." Cast from Hartford Conservatory of Music, Hartford, Conn. Children and masks from a Project CREAT school. (Photo: Courtesy Connecticut Commission on the Arts)

ists, muscians met with the students and teachers in each school before and after the performances. Each school had a project consultant, an artist, crafts person, filmmaker, dancer, or the like, who influenced the direction the arts took in their particular school and coordinated professional and school population interaction.

During the second year, three more schools were added to the program. The logistics proved too great to permit continuation on the basis of the original plan, and CREATE became a visiting artists project which acted as a model for other such programs in the state. ESEA funds diminished, besides which they were drastically cut in the spring of 1970. As a result Project CREATE terminated several months before its scheduled conclusion date—the end of the school year.

Among the first year productions was Benjamin Britten's *Noyes Fludde*. This opera was originally composed with the intention of incorporating local amateur talent with a small nucleus of professional singers and musicians. The Hartford Conservatory of Music was commissioned to set the CREATE production. Designed around a medieval miracle play, and using sixteenth-century English for its libretto, it dealt with the story of Noah, his wife, the ark, the flood, and the rainbow.

Students and teachers in each school were involved in painting some parts of the scenery while the major set was part of the traveling production. They learned to play improvised musical instruments such as glasses, jars, and triangles with the orchestra. Their major participation was in the making of animal masks and costumes for the loading of the ark, and in taking part in the finale. For the masks

they used papier-mâché boxes, cardboard, cloth, and a wide variety of other materials (figs B.1, B.2).

Although not fully realized in the project schools, (which were encouraged to go in their own directions), *Noyes Fludde* does have core monument potential. As a musical production, and a work of art, it provides the stimulus for learning activities related to the many aspects of the work itself, among which are: the miracle play in theater history; the use of sixteenth-century English for the libretto and the changing quality of the English language; the structure of the opera, and Britten's objectives in composing it as he did to include both professional and amateur voices; the story of Noah's flood, and the animals.

By comparing the sixteenth-century English with current usage for similar words, the children could learn something of the flexible nature of English usage, spelling, and pronunciation. They might even supplement their learning by reading other examples of written texts, or famous documents, for what they teach about the heritage of the English language.

This might lead, through the reading of Chaucer's *Nun's Priest's Tale*, with "Chanticleer and Pertelote," to animal fables by Aesop and LaFontaine, and learn how human characteristics are given to animals for the purpose of satire and as a means of drawing morals. Further reference to medieval bestiaries, or Dürer's drawings may bring a rather unique parade of animals to the ark. There could be, along with still extant animals, such ancient ones as dinosaurs, or extinct ones such as the dodo, or such mythological ones as dragons, griffins, and unicorns. In a medieval setting they may all be appropriate (except for the dinosaur).

Figure B.3 Rehearsing the final sequence of Brittain's "Noyes Fludde" in a Project CREATE school. (Photo: Courtesy Connecticut Commission on the Arts)

The making of animal masks might lead to a study of masks in the theater, and their purposes, such as Greek masks of exaggerated character for seeing and hearing at a distance, and Japanese masks for expressing character. The symbolism and rituals of masks could also be incorporated in such a unit. The children might make their own miracle play, or present tableaux and pageants.

A study of the verbal tradition of passing down epic events from generation to generation, and how they may change slightly or vastly depending on accuracy and extent of memorization might be demonstrated through the game of "gossip." The leader whispers the description of an event in the ear of one who tells to another, and so on until all present have been told. The final person tells what he or she heard. Then indicate what could happen to a story that has been passed along for thousands of years! They might also study early forms of recorded history, such as the Babylonian tablets with the tale of Gilgamesh, which contains the Babylonian version of the flood. They could make nar-

rative sequences in visual form in drawing, painting, or bas-relief. The alphabets might be devised from pieces of wood, somewhat like cuneiform, and pressed into clay or plaster of paris vats.

The concept of Noah as a hero, who presumably spoke to God or received His instructions might lead to dealing with concepts of other religious heroes and saints who received similar direction. The aloneness of the hero as a leader, such as Noah, the Greek Deucalion, or the Babylonian Utnapishtim who oppose prevailing attitudes and follow their own direction can be portrayed in visual form, pantomime, dance, or other forms of expression.

Children might speculate about life on the ark, how the animals were fed and housed, how the passage of time inside the ark was recorded, the interior construction of the ark. How did the people who had laughed and ridiculed Noah feel when the floods came? How did they try to save themselves. If Noah could have selected only a few animals and birds, which ones should they have been? How have such symbols as the dove, raven, olive branch, and rainbow survived meaningfully within our current cultural framework?

Translating the size of the ark, as stated in cubits, to inches, feet, and metrics, and then comparing that size to the size of the classroom or school building could well become the subject matter of a mathematics lesson.

Information about archeological studies made to identify a real flood of vast proportions occurring in ancient times, investigations to give scientific proof to it, and expeditions for locating the legendary ark might provide material for extending the story into science and high adventure.

The students might also simulate coverage of the events of the flood through news media, videotaping, recording, or newsreels. But, as such tales move into interpretation through the arts, theater, ballet, music, pantomime, poetry, and fiction they go beyond just the historical event. They enter the realm of the humanistic enterprise.

Teachers Might Like to Read:

- —Frazer, Sir James. G. *Folklore in the Old Testament.*
- —Keller, Werner. *The Bible as History.*
- —Montgomery, John Warick. *The Quest for Noah's Ark.*
- —Rehwinkel, Alfred M. *The Flood in the Light of the Bible, Geology, and Archeology.*
- —Sanders, N. K. *The Epic of Gilgamesh.*
- —Velikovsky, Emmanuel. *Earth in Upheaval.*

Children Might Like to Read:

- —Bryson, Bernarda. *Gilgamesh, Man's First Story.* Upper Elementary.
- —Feagles, Anita X. *He Who Saw Everything: The Epic of Gilgamesh.* Age 9-up.
- —Fuller, Catherine Leuthold. *Beasts: An Alphabet of Fine Prints.*
- —Graham, Lorenz. *God Wash the World and Start Again.* (An ancient Liberian version of the flood.)
- —Haley, Gail E. *Noah's Ark.* A modern-day Noah gathers up the animals and takes them to a new Garden of Eden, away from air pollution and extinction.
- —Harker, Ronald. *Digging Up the Bible Lands.*
- —Turner, Philip, ed. *Brian Wildsmith's Illustrated Bible Stories.*

appendix c

Resources for elementary "core monuments" in the humanities

The following resources are principally literature rather than media resources and curriculum packages. A few selected nonverbal resources and packages are mentioned at the end. The listings are by no means comprehensive. I have, however, favored reading materials of the type that will, hopefully, encourage teachers of programs which emphasize reading skills to use those materials as parts of arts- and humanities-related study units. It is from these traditional sources for continuing humanistic concerns, myths, and beliefs that the various arts can be used for student interpretation and expression. The concepts, knowledge, and stories must be in the child's mind before they can be expressed through the arts.

These titles are grouped under the general categories of core monuments as described in chapter 6. They include background sources which may interest teachers in planning their own approaches, and titles which children may like to read for library research or for purely recreational reading. Titles listed previously as references, although recommended, have not been repeated here.

Origins of Animal Characteristics

For Children:

- Courlander, Harold. *The Hat Shaking Dance and Other Tales.* 8 yrs. and up.
- ———. *Olode the Hunter and Other Tales from Nigeria.* 8 yrs. and up.
- Haley, Gail E. *A Story A Story, How Anansi Got His Stories.*
- Harris, Joel Chandler. *The Complete Tales of Uncle Remus.*
- Hodges, Margaret. *The Fire Bringer, A Piute Indian Legend.*
- Kipling, Rudyard. *Just So Stories.* Illus. by author. Large type edition.
- Newell, Edyth W. *Rescue of the Sun and Other Tales from the Far North.*

Origins of Natural Phenomenon (Stars Constellations, Fire, Rainbows)

For Teachers:

- Campbell, Joseph. *Masks of God: Primitive Mythology.*
- ———. *Myths to Live By.*
- Clarke, Arthur C. *2001: A Space Odyssey.* (A discussion and study unit is part of the Individualized Learning Program in paperback, American Book Company).
- Ferguson, George. *Signs and Symbols in Christian Art.*
- Frazier, Sir James G. *The Golden Bough* (Macmillan Co.) One volume edition.
- Graves, Robert. *The Greek Myths.* Two volumes.

- Lévi-Strauss, Claude. *The Raw and the Cooked.*
- *Man, Myth and Magic, An Illustrated Encyclopedia of the Supernatural.* (vol. 7, Evil to Flood for "Fire," and vol. 17, Prince to Ritual for "Rainbow")
- Matthaei, Rupprecht, ed. *Goethe's Color Theory.* An excellent facsimile edition.
- Munsell, Albert H. *A Grammar of Color.*
- Ostwald, Wilhelm. *A Color Primer.*

Children Might Like to Read:

- Bierhorst, John. *The Fire Plume, Legends of the American Indian.* Ages 7-11.
- Campbell, Ann. *Lets Find Out About Color.*
- Colum, Padraic. *Legends of Hawaii.*
- Dayrell, Elphinstone. *Why the Sun and Moon Live in the Sky.* A Nigerian tale.
- Foley, Bernice W. *Star Stories.*
- Gates, Doris. *Lord of the Skies: Zeus.* Ages 8-12.
- Hillman, Hal. *Art and Science of Color.*
- Hirsh, Marilyn. *How the World Got Its Color.* Ages 4-7.
- Hodges, Margaret. *The Gorgon's Head.*
- Max, Peter. *Land of Blue, Land of Red,* and *Land of Yellow.* (3 books)
- Rockwell, Anne. *The Dancing Stars: An Iroquois Legend.*
- Wolff, Robert Jay. *Feeling Blue, Seeing Red, Hello, Yellow.* (3 books)

Myths of Creation

Teachers Might Like to Read:

- Campbell, Joseph. *Masks of God: Creative Mythology.*
- Shepard, Paul, and McKinley, Daniel. *The Subversive Science: Essays toward an Ecology of Man.*
- Stanford, Barbara. *Myths and Modern Man: A New Look at Ancient Myths.*
- Von Franz, Marie-Louise. *Patterns of Creativity Mirrored in Creation Myths.*
- von Däniken, Erich. *Chariots of the Gods.*
- Watson, James D. *The Double Helix.*

Children Might Like to Read:

- Angrist, Stanley W. *How Our World Came to Be.*
- Branley, Franklyn M. *The Beginning of the Earth.* Ages 7-8 years.
- Cooper, Margaret. *Gift From the Sun: the Mastering of Energy.* Age 12 and up.
- Courlander, Harold. *People of the Short Blue Corn.*
- Crowell, Ann. *Shadow on the Pueblo, A Yaqui Indian Legend.* Grade 4 and up.
- Gleason, Judith. *Orisha: The Gods of Yorubaland.*

—Helfman, Elizabeth S. *The Bushman and Their Stories.* Ages 8-12 years.

—Lyons, Grant. *Tales the People Tell in Mexico.* Ages 8-11.

Conflict Between Good and Evil, and Fairy Tales

Teachers Might Like to Read:

—Armour, Margaret (trans.) *The Fall of the Nibelungs.* (Everyman's Library).

—Ashe, Geoffrey, ed. *The Quest for Arthur's Britain.*

—Cocteau, Jean. *Cocteau: Three Screenplays.* Includes "The Eternal Return," and "Beauty and the Beast."

—Jung, Anna, and Von Franz, Marie-Louise. *The Grail Legend.* A Jungian analysis.

—Levy, G. R. *The Sword and the Rock, An Investigation Into the Origins of Epic Literature and the Development of the Hero.*

—McNally, Raymond, and Florescu, Rader. *In Search of Dracula.*

—Miller, Helen Hill. *The Realms of Arthur.*

—Ronay, Gabriel. *The Truth About Dracula.*

—Sexton, Anne. *Transformations.* Poems based on stories by the Brothers Grimm.

—Summers, Montague. *The Vampire, his Kith and Kin.*

—Ward, A. G., ed. *The Quest for Theseus.*

—Weston, Jessie L. *From Ritual to Romance.*

—Wolf, Leonard. *The Dream of Dracula.*

Children Might Like to Read:

—Aylesworth, Thomas G. *Werewolves and Other Monsters.* Age 11 years and up.

—Fraser, Antonia. *King Arthur and the Knights of the Round Table.* Age 11 or 12.

—Hibbert, Christopher, and Thomas, Charles. *The Search for King Arthur.*

—Hieatt, Constance. *The Sword and the Grail.*

—Lang, Andrew. *King Arthur, Tales of the Round Table.* Large type edition, complete.

—Perrault, Charles. *Fairy Tales.* Large type edition, with historical introduction.

—Reiger, Shay. *Gargoyles, Monsters and Other Beasts.*

—Stevenson, Robert L. *Strange Case of Dr. Jekyll and Mr. Hyde.* Age 12 and up.

—Williams, Diane. *Demons and Beasts in Art.*

Packaged Programs of Art and Humanities Resources Suitable for Elementary School Use, Briefly Annotated

American Book Co., 450 W. 33rd St., New York, N. Y. 10001.
Teaching through Art designed and written by Robert J. Saunders. Three sets (K-6, K-3, 4-6) of twenty Abrams art prints each; and teacher's manual, relating subjects to art to creative writing, mathematics, etc., with lessons and extensions in behavioral terms, visual perception, and special education.

Art Education, Inc., Blauvelt, New York 10913.
An art appreciation program of sixty-four full-color art reproductions, mounted and varnished. Package contains adjustable frame, teacher's commentaries and materials. Written by Olive Riley and Eileen Lomasy.

Barton Cotton, Inc., 1405 Parker Rd., Baltimore, Md. 21227.
Guidelines for Learning Through Art, edited by Clyde McGeary and William M. Dallam. A series of manuals, charts, bibliographies, and individual 6-by-9-in. prints for student use and for comparative purposes (relating to other study areas).

Benefic Press, Inc., 10300 W. Roosevelt Rd., Westchester, Ill. 60153.
Meaning, Method and Media, a series of art texts written by Guy Hubbard and Mary Rouse, with teacher edition, grades 1-6. Include activities for making art projects, using materials, tools, and looking at art.

Bowmar, Inc., P.O. Box 5225, Glendale, Calif. 91201.
Art World Series written by Dotty and Harvey Mandlin. Contains art reproductions, filmstrips, records, and audio cassettes, and teachers guide; for sets on self-awareness, visual-awareness, and expression.

CEMREL, Inc., Five Sense Store and Aesthetic Education programs published through Viking Press, Inc., 625 Madison Ave., New York, N. Y. 10022.
Each package contains ten hours of instruction in: Aesthetics and the Elements; Aesthetics and the Creative Process; and Aesthetics in the Physical World.

Center for Humanities, Inc., 2 Holland Ave., White Plains, New York 10603.
Although a secondary- and college-oriented program, it is listed here because it provides slides, recordings, and manuals for studying various aspects of art in relation to society, history, American culture, and social, moral, and aesthetic values, myths, heroes, protest, and so on.

Films, Inc., 1144 Wilmette Ave., Wilmette, Ill. 60091.
The Art of Seeing, produced by the American Federation of Arts—Rudolph Arnheim, project advisor. Deals with museum paintings and sculpture in terms of children's everyday experiences, visual observations, perception, and awareness of their environment.

Joseph W. Foraker Associates, Inc., 520 Speedwell Ave., Dayton Bldg, Suite 116, Morris Plains, N. J. 07950.
"The Mini-Museum"; consists of sculpture replicas (reductions), and full-color art reproductions of the New York Graphic Society, with teacher's manual, carrying portfolio, and a chest of drawers for sculpture.

Miller-Brody Inc., 342 Madison Ave., New York, N. Y. 10017.
"Meet the Artist" and other filmstrips and recordings of quality featuring Picasso, Van Gogh, Audubon, and others. Facilitate concentration on a single artist's work and his development.

National Gallery of Art, Extension Service, Washington, D.C. 20565.
Free loan slide programs with records and manuals on aspects of art and cultural history through art. The slides, 40-60 in a set, may be too much for elementary units, but teachers using manual can arrange their own units from the sets.

Sandak, Inc., 110 Harvard Ave., Stamford, Conn., 06902.
"Visual Sources of Learning," designed and written by Flora and Jerome Hausman, consists by ninety color slides of works by famous artists. Teacher's manual has suggestions for activities in art, music, language arts, etc.

Warren Schoat, Productions, Inc., Pleasantville, N. Y. 10470.
A wide-ranging and diverse program of slides and filmstrips on the arts and humanities, with special programs for student reading, filmstrips, slides, records, and teach-toric, primitive, Eskimo, American colonial, and UNICEF, and a series on visual perception, "The Art of Seeing" induces students to focus their attention on painting, sculpture, architecture, etc.

Scholastic Magazines, Inc., 902 Sylvan Ave., Englewood Cliffs, N. J. 07632.

"Art and Man" series, prepared in cooperation with the National Gallery of Art, consists of bimonthly magazines for student reading, filmstrips, slides, records, and teacher's manual. Humanistic themes, varying with the school year: Picasso, filmmaking, Japan, Science and Technology, the American Indian, and the American West, etc. Prepared for junior high and above, adaptable to upper elementary. Also available: the "Scholastic Black Culture Program" with slides, filmstrips, cassettes, and records.

Shorewoods Reproductions, Inc., 724 Fifth Ave., New York, N. Y., 10019.

Comprehensive program of inexpensive art reproductions with correlated study units for humanities, social studies, black studies, etc., with cross-referencing, filmstrips, display equipment. Art reproduction range includes Western European Oriental, contemporary American, and Afro-American.

References, unless quoted or commented upon in the text are indexed by author only. Authors, composers, and artists are indexed only when commented upon or when their works are resources for arts activities.